BANKING

GHANA AND BIAFRA TO BERMUDA

A DOZEN COUNTRIES
IN FIFTY YEARS

BANKING

GHANA AND BIAFRA TO BERMUDA

A DOZEN COUNTRIES IN FIFTY YEARS

Calum Johnston

Matador
9 Priory Business Park,
Wistow Road, Kibworth Beauchamp,
Leicestershire, LE8 0RX
Tel: 0116 279 2299
Email: books@troubador.co.uk
Web: www.troubador.co.uk/matador
Twitter: @matadorbooks

ISBN 978 1789017 922

British Library Cataloguing in Publication Data.
A catalogue record for this book is available from the British Library.

Typeset in 11pt Adobe Garamond Pro by Troubador Publishing Ltd, Leicester, UK

Matador is an imprint of Troubador Publishing Ltd

For Maggie and Malcolm

Contents

Introduction

The King grew vain;
Fought all his battles o'er again;
And thrice he routed all his foes,
And thrice he slew the slain.

"Alexander's Feast"
John Dryden

I have been researching my family tree and have traced as far back as Johne Duncane, who, according to the parish record, a copy of which I now have, was baptised in Errol, Perthshire, Scotland on 7th March 1554. He was my great-great-great-great-great-great-great-great-great-great-great-grandfather and his parents, Johne Duncane and Helen Hogg, were my eleven-times great-grandparents, born probably about 1530. It should not be forgotten that everyone has two grandfathers and, by the time you go back through the generations to your eleventh great-grandfather, you will find that you have 4,096 of them. It makes for a big tree. Imagine the consequences of just one of them not having lived long enough to pass on his genes. The thing that impressed me most about the research and the results is that, although I have over 5,000 names on my family tree, all with at least some of the relevant dates, and despite having two boxes full of copies of birth, marriage and death certificates, I know little or nothing about most of my ancestors or my second, third and fourth cousins. I left home and Scotland at age eighteen and so had little opportunity as an adult to make enquiries of my grandparents. As a child it never occurred to me to ask.

Ancestors older than my grandparents are little more to me than ghosts on paper. John Thomson, born in 1764, was the sixth of the ten children of my fifth great-grandfather, who was a tenant farmer in Lanarkshire, Scotland. How John became a wealthy merchant and ship-owner in England, rich enough to buy the farm for his father, is a story now lost in the mists of time; a missing tale that gave me an urge to commit to paper some of the things I did and saw in Africa and in other countries, so that, perhaps, my as yet unborn great-grandchildren may come to know something about me and the times in which I lived. I assume they will have jobs that do not now exist, if they have jobs at all, and, undoubtedly, they will live in a world I cannot imagine, just as my world will seem strange to them.

Now that I am well past the years allotted to me in Psalm 90:10 and even well beyond the extra ten years earned by reason of strength, I plan to recount a few stories from a world now gone. I was involved in things that would no longer be possible. Who now would hire a twenty-year-old with no more than a public (meaning private) school education, a few months' clerking in a bank in Scotland and a couple of years in the army, and send him to Africa to become a bank manager by age twenty-one? Who in Africa would permit such a thing? I'll tell the story and try to avoid writing a hagiography or, unlike King Alexander, attempting to slay the already slain.

Clydesdale Bank, Glasgow

Work is much more fun than fun.

Sir Noel Coward

When I was put to work, at age seventeen, in the Clydesdale & North of Scotland Bank, Paisley Road, Glasgow, I was so embarrassed that I did not want my friends to know what I was doing. I was a tough rugby and football player, I loved to go camping and sailing. I was a marksman with a .303 Lee-Enfield rifle and I boxed a little. The most satisfying remark ever made about me on a school report was "A tower of strength on the rugby field". Why was a boy like me sitting behind a desk in a bank?

For my first day at work my father drove me to Paisley Road and dropped me off at the door of the bank. As I got out of the car he said, 'Tonight, you'll get the tram into town and the blue bus home. Take note of the tram number, because I'm not driving you here again.'

I have always assumed he had taken me on that first morning because he was afraid that if he didn't I would not show up for work. I arrived early and was admitted to the bank by the only other person to be there before me, Mr. McKinley. He was the number two man in a seven-person branch and was an old, old avuncular man of about forty. After an exchange of introductions, he led me to a large freestanding safe, the main door of which he opened. Inside I could see several small compartments and I was impressed as he spun open the combination lock on one of them. He removed a small bundle of banknotes and taking a single note he handed it to me.

'Put that in your pocket.'

Glancing at it before stuffing it into my coat pocket I saw that it was a £100 note. This was something I had never seen before; indeed, I doubt I knew such a thing existed. I was astonished and wondered if I was being paid one year's wages in advance, because £100 per annum was the promised salary. The whole thing seemed extraordinary, but no sooner was the note in my pocket than Mr. McKinley asked me to return it and I watched, confused, while he restored it to the bundle, replaced the bundle in the safe and closed both doors, all the while saying not a word. When he was finished, he turned to face me.

'When you go home tonight you can tell your mother that you had £100 in your pocket and if you are going to be a banker it will be a bloody long time before that happens again.'

Mr. McKinley was a stickler for the basics although seemingly this did not extend to dual custody or he would not have had access to the £100 note. That was not something of which I was aware at the time. Mr. McKinley required everything to balance to the penny. We did not go home until it did. An incorrect number was never to be altered. It was to be crossed out with a single line through it, in such a way that it could still be read, and the correct number written above. And this was never done on anything to be handed to a customer. If a mistake was made, you started again. He did not allow me to use the hand-cranked adding machine until I could stand before him every morning for a week and correctly add in my head the columns of pounds, shillings and pence he had machined on three tapes, from which he had removed the totals. Twelve pence to a shilling, twenty shillings to a pound; it made sense only because we had grown up with it. The branch was so small I was able to see how the entries flowed from one set of books to another and how everything came together to achieve balanced books at the end of the day. To my surprise, I began to like the precision of it all.

My tasks included sweeping the floor and making the tea, mixing the powder with which I made the ink for the inkwells and keeping the pens on the counter clean without crossed nibs, a common condition few will remember today. I received a boost to my growing belief that I had the makings of a banker when a customer remarked to the manager that the pens on our counter were the only ones in any public building with which he could actually write. It doesn't take a lot to make a boy happy. In addition to my mundane tasks, I occupied much of my time counting banknotes. In 1952 there were six Scottish banks with the right to issue their own notes. Now there are only three. Each bank would accept the notes of any other bank as well as those of the Bank of England but would pay out to customers only its own notes. As a result, each day, as the two tellers in my branch received deposits, they would make bundles of 500 one-pound notes issued by all the different banks and send the bundles back to me where I sat at the spreading table, unguarded in the middle of the back office. I would then sort the notes into a pile for each bank, Bank of Scotland, Royal Bank of Scotland, British Linen Company and so on, the piles carefully arranged in order of the date each bank had been founded, starting with the Bank of Scotland in 1695. I also had to separate the notes of the Bank of England and our own bank which, in my judgement, were unfit to be re-issued because of wear and tear. The notes for each bank were made up into bundles of five hundred pounds and naturally, at the end of the day, there could be no note left over or short. I learned to be very careful to avoid the need for recounts. If I happened to be busy at some other important task at a different desk, such as recording and putting stamps on outgoing mail, anyone who had a few minutes to spare would spread the notes waiting on the spreading table. The only security was that we trusted each other. On Thursdays I was sent on the tram-car to head office in St. Vincent Place with a large suitcase containing £8,000 (the equivalent of about £230,000 today) in bundles of the notes of other banks. These then went to the note exchange, with each bank receiving all its own notes from all the other banks. After a few weeks it was deemed unsafe for me to travel alone and so Margaret, an eighteen-year-old girl, was sent with me for protection. This proved to be a distraction and I remember us walking towards the exit door of a Birrell's shop, chatting after buying sweets, before we remembered that the case was still on the floor by the counter. I think Margaret must have mentioned this incident because soon thereafter we were dispatched each Thursday with the case secured to my arm by a leather wristband and chain. I remember thinking that the chain, which was difficult to hide, was a pretty good advert I was carrying something of value.

At the Clydesdale Bank I learned the basics and to carry out each of my tasks, no matter how mundane, in the approved manner, except, perhaps, the art of concentration while carrying a case full of money. Everything had to be done in exactly the prescribed way and there could be no exceptions. I remember being told of the great fuss that occurred when one of my predecessors, long departed to the army before my arrival, was five pounds short at the end of a day on which he had been deputising for the second teller. The search and the checking and rechecking lasted long into the evening, without success, and the incident was remembered and discussed for a long time. Some years later, when I visited the branch, almost the first thing I was told was that the mystery of the five pounds had been solved. The branch had been renovated and the workmen had removed the beautiful mahogany counter-top which rose from each side in gentle curves towards the crest in the middle and so wide that an arm from either side could reach little farther than halfway. And you guessed it. Nestling underneath the base was a five-pound note. In the banking world of today, nobody would take the trouble to look too long for a loss of five pounds and they would not talk about it for years after the event. More is the pity.

During my days at the bank in Paisley Road, not far from the docks, from time to time ships of the American fleet would arrive to give their crews some rest and recreation. As a result, a few of our customers would deposit dollar notes. The exchange rate fluctuated between four shillings and two pence and four shillings and three pence for a dollar; four and tuppence and four and thruppence in the local parlance (almost five dollars to a pound). Of course our tellers always paid four and two pence and we waited until the rate in the *Glasgow Herald* newspaper was four and three pence before sending the notes to head office at that rate. The difference of a few pennies between buying and selling price was added to the biscuit money. To send the notes to head office I had to list the number of each note on a long blue form. Then I had to wet the form lightly with water, careful not to make the ink run too much, and place the damp form between the tissue paper pages of a large thick book. The book was then closed and placed in an iron press with a bar handle on top which I screwed to create pressure. In due course we ended up with a damp blue form and a back to front image in the book. Don't ask me why!

My lasting memory of Paisley Road branch is of standing each day at the side of his desk waiting for Mr. McKinley to look up over the spectacles that were far down towards the end of his nose. I waited to ask him if I could look in the general ledger, the holy of holy of all the books. This was a very large volume bound in red leather that lived during the day in a special stand next to his desk and in which he alone wrote. I needed to see the total of an account in order to fulfil one of my tasks.

'Mr. McKinley, please may I look in the general ledger?'

There was always a pause before he answered, as if he was considering whether or not he should refuse permission. He never did, but his answer was always the same, given in his slow-drawn-out Scottish accent.

'Are your hands clean?'

Oh, how banking has changed!

The Sweat Box, London

The closest to perfection a person ever comes
is when he fills out a job application.
Stanley J. Randall

In January 1955 I completed my two-year term of compulsory National Service. I had been fortunate to have been chosen to serve in The Royal Highland Regiment, The Black Watch; the senior Highland Regiment in the British Army before it was massacred by Mr. Blair in his reshuffle of the Scottish Regiments. That I was fortunate is certainly true. On the recruiting form I had completed, at the time of my initial medical some months before being called up, and on which I had been given an opportunity to fill in my three choices of regiment or branches of the armed forces in which I would like to serve, with no guarantees of course, I, with the supreme hubris of youth, had written "The Black Watch, The Black Watch, The Black Watch". Apparently, my service in the school cadet corps, where I qualified as a marksman on the open range and the winning of the shooting cup with a .303 rifle outweighed the desire of a functionary somewhere along the line to satisfy a sadistic urge by having me directed to the Pay Corps or by ensuring I became a cook.

During my several years in the Combined Cadet Force, a Ministry of Defence-sponsored youth organisation attached to my school, I had earned the imaginatively named certificates A and B. These purported to provide evidence of certain military capabilities and at the start of my recruit training I was considered to be a potential officer. About two or three weeks into the ten weeks of training several of us were told we were to meet with a visiting officer who would answer any questions we might have about officer training. We were assured he would be there as a resource to guide and assist us. I mistook this lie for a fact and as a result, instead of being gung-ho during my few minutes with the officer, I questioned him about the expense I would have to fund out of my own pocket and made it clear to him that under no circumstances would I ask for monetary assistance from home. My supposed guide was non-committal and towards the end of my service I was able to have a look at my records. The comments of the officer who had interviewed me, still there for all to see, were that I was uncertain and not sufficiently determined. As a result, I was not offered officer training. I did not worry about it. I doubted that I could have afforded from my own resources to be an officer in The Black Watch and I did not want to serve anywhere else.

I enjoyed my two years in the army. Starting as a boy, I ended it a man, almost. I was disappointed to have seen no combat. I had been too late for the Korean war but by the time my service ended I had learned never to say that I had nothing to do and that the life of a soldier, with its interminable periods of boredom interspersed with brief intervals of panic and fright, was unlikely to suit me.

Not long before the date of my demobilisation, while stationed in Norfolk, in England, a civilian employee at the army base handed me a newspaper with the words, 'Here you are, Jock. This is the very thing for you.'

'Why? What's in the paper?'

'Look at the adverts.'

I found an advert placed by the Bank of British West Africa seeking young men who desired "A place in the sun". With a palm tree and an elephant featured the prospects seemed exotic and attractive. I was keen to travel and even more keen not to go home at the end of my military service and so was quick to submit an application. Soon thereafter I was summoned by letter to appear for interview at the bank's head office at 37 Gracechurch Street, London.

In the mess I asked Sergeant Button, who almost certainly had less idea of the correct answer than I did, 'What on earth should I wear for an interview in the City of London?'

'Full dress kilt. You look good in it.' A nice compliment from an Englishman!

'I think that's a bit over the top Alf; and I can't wear my old suit. It's not smart enough. It will have to be boots and gaiters.'

I wore plain battle dress, which a civilian tailor had altered, taking out the bulge at the back of the jacket so that it fitted me perfectly. I sported highly-polished boots and freshly green-blancoed belt and gaiters. The lead weights on strings at the bottom of my trouser legs made them fold neatly and evenly over the gaiters and helped to maintain the knife-sharp crease down the front, which I tried to preserve by sitting as infrequently as possible. As a concession to my desire to be recognised as a member of the finest regiment in the British Army, I wore my blue bonnet with the distinctive Black Watch red hackle. I was a proud soldier and took schoolboyish pride in the wearing of my uniform. Incidentally, to this day I wear a red hackle in my bonnet, to the amusement of many, and I wear on my kilt a small silver Black Watch badge given to my grandmother by her brother Rob. In 1915 he had enlisted in the Canadian Black Watch and after being wounded in action and sent from France to England to recuperate he visited his sister in Glasgow. He returned to the front line and three months before the end of the war he was killed in action. He was twenty-one years old.

On arriving at the bank in London I was shown upstairs to a waiting room. In later years I came to know this spot as "the sweat box" where, having returned from the West Coast of Africa, one sat and waited to be interviewed by various head office officials, while sweating over the possibility of a new eighteen-month contract being offered or refused. In my early days with the bank, second and later contracts commenced after paid home leave of three and a half months. Those unfortunate enough not to receive another contract had their hand shaken, offered thanks and bid farewell. On the Saturday morning of my first visit there were no sunburned "coasters" in the sweat box. Seated on upright dining chairs, arrayed in neat order round the walls of the small room, sat about half a dozen young gentlemen. All were smartly dressed in dark business suits. There was little conversation, but what there was made it seem to me that the speakers were struggling with several marbles in their mouth. I was conscious not only of my distinct apparel but of my marble-lacking Glasgow accent (at that time a little more refined than the norm in Glasgow but certainly not "Kelvinside"; I am told it is now "mid-Atlantic" but still with an easily detected hint of Scotland I am glad to say). Ah well, I thought, as I reviewed the young gentlemen who were my competitors, no point in leaving. I had come this far and I might as well go through with the interview. It would be practice for my next job application.

In turn, we were questioned by bank officials and one by one the other candidates and two accompanying fathers departed. When there were only two of us remaining, a functionary told us we were to be interviewed by the general manager. Many years later, while employed by a Canadian bank, I was one of almost numberless general managers. In London in 1955 there was only one general manager of the Bank of British West Africa and by the way in which the staff spoke I gathered that to have one's existence acknowledged by him was considered a great privilege. When my turn came, I was shown into what obviously was the boardroom and told to sit on a chair almost halfway down one side of the long highly-polished table that dominated the heavily curtained room. Mr. Frank G. Wright sat at the head of the table. There was space for several people to sit on the empty chairs separating us, but, as my usher had left, Mr. Wright and I were the only ones in the room. I had never been in such a room or seated at such a table and I never did find out if this seating arrangement was meant to impress or to intimidate. At the time of my interview Mr. Wright was probably in his late fifties but, as he sat shuffling the papers in front of him, to me he looked ancient, with a lined and careworn face. Having worked in West Africa for many years he might well have served as proof of the then urban legend that one year in West Africa was equivalent to two years anywhere else in the world. His first question suggested to me that the prospect of a job with the bank had evaporated.

'Where,' he asked gruffly, 'did you win your Military Cross?'

Military Cross! I had never heard a shot fired in anger, far less been decorated for bravery. Fortunately I realised immediately the reason for the question. On my letter of application I had written my name as I had been used to do at school where surnames only were used. In my case initials were added after the surname to distinguish Johnston M.C. from Johnston T.A. (whatever happened to Thomas Alan?). In writing to the bank I had given my rank and thoughtlessly added my initials to my surname.

'M and C are my initials,' I explained.

From his hunched position Mr. Wright raised his head only very slightly and tilted it a little to one side to look at me out of the corners of his eyes. Then, after the slightest pause, he growled, with what seemed to me to be utter contempt, 'Bloody silly way to write your name.'

The rest of the interview with Mr. Wright seemed to be a charade. Inexperienced as I was, even I realised that, with impunity, you do not make a general manager feel foolish. And it seemed unwise to have made him think I was. I certainly did not mention that as a sergeant, had I been fortunate enough to be decorated for bravery, I would have been awarded a Military Medal, not a Military Cross. Seemingly, Mr. Wright did not know how to get rid of me without going through at least some of the normal routine. This he proceeded to do without looking at me and in what I decided was a distinctly disinterested, gruff and unfriendly manner. I did the best I could in the circumstances. Once back in the sweat box I waited to be dismissed and was very surprised to be told the bank would like me to be examined by a doctor in Harley Street. Could I go there now?

As I learned later, the board of directors of the bank had decided in the early 1900s to have every potential employee examined by a doctor to ensure they had a reasonable chance of withstanding the rigours of West Africa and were not likely to become an early casualty of the climate and conditions, as so many had done before. The first doctor to examine bank employees was none other than Major Sir Ronald Ross, who, in 1902, had been awarded the Nobel Prize for having identified in India the Anopheles mosquito as the carrier of malaria and for having determined the process by which the mosquito transmitted malaria from an infected to a healthy subject.

The doctor I saw, of course, was not Major Ross but he did seem elderly. As I arrived from the waiting room into his Spartan consulting room, tired aspidistra in the corner, he greeted me cheerily, 'Strip off and lie on the table.'

'Down to shorts?'

'No, no. Everything.'

I did as I was told and was soon lying naked on a green leather examination table. No protective paper or towels covered the table as one would expect, and demand, today. Under the table lay a large long-haired shaggy dog.

The doctor asked, 'How did you get these bruises on your legs?'

'I play rugby. I've played a few games for Bury St. Edmunds. It's near where I am based. They allow me to get there on an army motorbike. I'm a hooker, middle of the front row. The legs tend to get a bit of a bashing.'

In a friendly way we chatted about that for a few minutes as I lay freezing on the table, wondering whose bum previously had been where mine was now resting. The doctor then determined that my heart was beating, that my breath would fog a mirror and that, after standing up, I did not have whatever coughing and a firm grip on the nether regions proves you don't have. He then weighed me and noted my height and that concluded the examination. Why it was necessary to lie naked on the green leather table I never discovered. Perhaps it was a simple way of determining I had all the required parts.

I returned to Brandon in Norfolk on the train, which gave me plenty of time to regret I had not been awarded a Military Cross. Although I lacked that very significant honour I was encouraged that the bank had paid for a medical and I wondered if the mistake about an award for bravery had caused the bank to grant the interview in the first place.

At the station I was picked up by a colleague for the drive back to camp and was asked, 'Well, how did it go, Jock? Are you on your way to Africa?'

'Not yet, but I think it went pretty well. They sent me for a medical. It was so superficial that even if there is something wrong with me, I doubt the doctor could have found it.'

As I spoke it occurred to me in a frisson of disappointment, perhaps the examination had been so brief because it had been obvious that I did not meet the bank's requirements. What could they want that I did not have?

For the next few days at Stanford Ranges, West Tofts Camp, near Mundford, I went about the daily routine of my military duties, distracted by thoughts of palm trees and elephants. One minute I was sure I would be offered a job and the next equally sure it was all too good to be true. Fortunately I did not have long to wait to be relieved of my agony. Within a week of returning from London I received a letter offering me a job starting in February 1955, a couple of weeks after my army service would come to an end. I was to train in London at least until I was twenty-one and then, if I proved suitable, I would be posted to one of the bank's branches in Nigeria, the Gold Coast, Sierra Leone, or the Gambia. At this time, in addition to the head office in London, the bank also had branches in Duala, Hamburg, Liverpool, Manchester, and Tangier. At some time since its founding in 1893 there had been offices or agencies in Abidjan, Alexandria, Cairo, Casablanca, Fernando Po, Fez, Gibraltar, Grand Lahou, Las Palmas, Lomé, Madeira, Marrakech, Matadi, Mazagan, Mogador, Monrovia, New York, Saffi, and Tenerife. I had been invited to join the staff of a bank clearly more adventurous and exotic, if less certain about its focus, than Clydesdale & North of Scotland Bank Limited. I was offered the princely salary of £680 per annum with a 10% annual bonus, paid quarterly. I did not need to go back to the Clydesdale Bank where I had started at age seventeen at £100 per annum. On my return there I would have been paid about £140 per annum and forced to live with my parents, who would have no option but to clothe and feed me. Hurrah for a place in the sun. Of course, I had no knowledge of the cost of living in West Africa.

Two weeks after completing my army service I reported in February 1955 for work in the City of London with the Bank of British West Africa (BBWA). I was twenty years old and thrilled to be in London again. When I was fourteen I had persuaded my parents to allow me to attend the 1948 Olympic Games, which were held in a London still showing the enormous scars of war-time bombing. Now in 1955, in London for what promised to be a longer stay, I arranged to rent a room in a club for serving and former non-commissioned officers of the British Army. The club was in a pleasant square with a garden in the middle not far from Baker Street and the fictional abode of Sherlock Holmes. The rooms were very small and furnished only with a single bed, a chair and table and a cupboard. A shilling in the meter fuelled an electric fire. Meals were available and costs were reasonable. They had to be because as I remember it I was paid a good deal less than the salary promised for service on the West Coast of Africa. I usually had money for a seat high in the gods at the theatre but on the days before payday often I was forced to live only on a cheap lunch. This I could obtain on weekdays with an inexpensive ticket bought from the bank and which provided a subsidised meal at a shabby canteen nearby.

The work at the bank was routine and monotonous. I sat on a high stool at a sloping wooden desk like a Dickens character. I was insulted when asked if I knew how to calculate interest. Of course I knew and they put me to work calculating. Surely, I thought, they are not going to send me to Africa to calculate interest. Next to me sat Dennis, a man in his thirties with a wooden leg. He usually lunched with Pat, who worked in the bills and letters of credit department. They were kind enough to allow me to tag along at lunchtime and when I asked them why they were not on the list to go to West Africa they just laughed and said, 'No bloody fear, laddie.'

I gathered they knew too much about West Africa to want to go there. My friend Eric Anderson told me that during his so-called training in London he was working at a desk sitting between Pat and another man. His job was to receive a bundle of documents, separate them, staple the now separated bundles and pass them to his neighbour. After a few days of this he was standing at a urinal in the office basement complaining to another trainee about the stupidity of it all when a toilet flushed, a cubicle door opened and out stepped the office manager. The following

Monday Eric was on his way home to Ayr in the West of Scotland for a week's holiday and with a ticket for Accra in his hand. All this was a couple of years after my own experience in London, so not much had changed in the training routine.

Frustrated by the boredom of the very commonplace work I was being asked to do I approached a senior man at the bank.

'Mr. Paterson,' I asked, 'when do you think I will be sent out to the Coast?'

'Well,' he replied, hesitating, 'if I remember correctly you are only twenty years old. We certainly will not send you out until you are twenty-one because, if you steal any money, as a minor we would not be able to prosecute you.' He seemed to be serious.

Nevertheless, in May 1955, after close to four months' "training" which did little or nothing to prepare me for what lay ahead, and still a couple of months short of twenty-one, I was told to go home to Glasgow for a week and then get myself to Accra, capital of the Gold Coast. Remembering the comment about stealing, I wondered if the bank had decided I was a bit slow and that it would take me a few months to figure out how to steal money. I did not remind anyone that I was not yet twenty-one and have always assumed this fact had been overlooked. I was equipped with an air ticket for Accra, a voucher for £100 and a list of clothing I should buy before my departure. After the celebration with the other trainees waiting for their own assignment, all of them several years older than I, part of the one-hundred-pound allowance had been spent on liquids not on the list of essential purchases. Perhaps that was just as well, because if I had had more money I might have been tempted to buy a pith helmet, mosquito boots and spine pads to prevent the sun melting the marrow in my bones. These exotic items were not on the list I had been given but frequently were recommended by the old West Africa hands working in the head office of the bank. They had been out on the West Coast in the 1920s and 1930s when, apparently, such things were standard attire. I have never been sure if they were serious in their recommendations or if they were having a joke at the expense of a neophyte. Certainly, it was not until the arrival on the West Coast of Africa in the 1940s of American soldiers who walked out in the midday sun hatless and shirtless, that it became obvious such behaviour did not cause instant sunstroke. Until then, Englishmen, like mad dogs, may have gone out in the midday sun, as in Noel Coward's song, but if they did, they went out fully protected.

After a series of injections, said to be defence against smallpox, yellow fever, tetanus, cholera, typhoid and paratyphoid, and having started my daily dose of Paludrine to prevent malaria, I felt invulnerable, despite a painful arm. As a result, I was disconcerted when, on arriving home and announcing to my family that I was soon to be bound for the Gold Coast, my dear old grandmother, Mama McPherson, shed a quiet tear and moaned, 'Oh son, the white mans' grave.'

In a letter to a friend in 1872, Sir John Pope-Hennessy, Governor in Chief of the West African Settlements, maintained that, "In no part of Her Majesty's Empire is one brought so constantly face to face with death as on the West Coast of Africa."

And that was the reputation West Africa still had at the turn of the century and perhaps into the 1930s and even the 1940s, but things were much changed by the 1950s. There is an interesting story about the development of Paludrine, the anti-malarial drug. Despite having been stripped of its foreign colonies during the First World War, Germany was still the source of anti-malaria drugs. In 1938, in anticipation of war, the Emergency Drug Committee of the Association of British Chemical Manufacturers drew up a list of essential synthetic drugs that Britain imported from Germany. Five of the Association members were asked to work out the constituents of these drugs and the methods by which they could be manufactured. ICI was assigned two German anti-malaria synthetic drugs and by 1939 had developed and tested the process by which Mepacrine and Plasmoquine could be manufactured. Subsequently, Mepacrine was used by Allied troops but it soon became apparent there were problems. The drug coloured the skin yellow and it was toxic. About a third of those who used it suffered gastrointestinal distress and many became anaemic. In 1942 a decision was made to try to find an alternative and ICI developed Paludrine, which, for the next forty years, proved to be the most effective anti-malaria drug available. However, just as becoming sunburned was considered by the army to be a self-inflicted wound, being diagnosed with malaria originally was similarly regarded. If you had malaria, you had not been taking your Paludrine tablets; that is until it was realised and eventually admitted that Paludrine was not 100% effective, as I was soon to learn.

Flight to the Gold Coast

Travel in the younger sort is a part of education.

Francis Bacon

The flight that began to shape my life as a banker and in many other ways was listed as BA257. It helped to extend an unremarkable few months as a bank clerk into a career that lasted for more than fifty years.

In May 1955 BA257 set out from a large wooden hut which was the only terminal building at London Airport, now called Heathrow. The hut was a temporary building, replacing the group of surplus army khaki tents erected in 1946 as the very first terminal at London Airport.

My early arrival at the airport gave me time to observe the other passengers as they turned up to check in. One by one single men presented themselves at the check-in counter. They were all much older than I and to me they looked confident, tanned and experienced. A very few were accompanied by a lady I presumed to be their wife. All were Europeans except for two very distinguished-looking Africans. Nobody but I was dressed in a thick dark wool suit. I had bought the only suit I owned in January that year and it was designed to cope with a London winter. The tropical gear

I had been advised to purchase, lightweight suit, several pairs of slacks, linen jacket and evening dress complete with dress shirt, bow tie and cummerbund, were all carefully packed in my checked luggage. Most of the others turning up for the long trip to Accra seemed to be wearing the kind of clothing I had packed, and their suits did not appear to be designed to keep them warm.

I was in no hurry to board. Sitting in what passed for a lounge, with a ticket for Accra in my hand and at my feet the small carry-on case then issued by British Overseas Airways Corporation to First Class passengers was, to me, as much a part of my exciting new world as the journey and the destination to come. Such experiences, I felt, were to be part of my life in future and in spite of my suit, I was enjoying just being there. I would have been content to sit all day, happily trying to suppress the involuntary grin on my face, but eventually it was time to board the BOAC Argonaut that was really an upgraded Canadair DC-4. The Argonaut carried about forty passengers. Six or eight of us filled all the available seats in First Class, ranged singly on each side of a centre aisle. I was in A3. As I discovered later, the seats could be reclined to a horizontal position and a footrest extended to create a bed. A quilt and pillow were supplied. At that time the bank allowed even its most junior employees to travel in First Class. This privilege was lost to us five or six years later, at least until we became senior officers. This happened when the bank discovered that some took advantage of the possibility to forgo First Class travel in order to add a trip to New York, for example, to the journey home to the United Kingdom, flying tourist class for about the same price as the First Class ticket. I was disappointed because I had never traded in my First Class ticket and I did not see New York until I worked on Wall Street many years later.

On the plane I was glad to be isolated in my single seat because this avoided the need for me to speak and to confess that all this was new to me. Thinking back, my very youthful looks (you should see my passport photograph) to say nothing of my suit, must have made it obvious to the seasoned hands round about that this was to be my first tour. Not long after I had fastened my seat belt the four Rolls Royce Merlin supercharged engines, propellers spinning into invisibility, lifted us into the air smoothly but very noisily. My long journey to a new life had begun. I did not know then that this phase was to last for over fourteen years and would end during a violent civil war. On this particular journey refuelling stops were made at Rome, Tripoli, and Kano before arrival in Accra. At each stop we spent about an hour. I remember being surprised by the sophistication of the airport in Rome and the fashionable apparel and accoutrements beautifully displayed for sale on marble counters and in vitrines. Were not the Italians so thoroughly beaten during the war that their king rid the country of Mussolini, changed sides, and declared war on Germany on 13 October 1943? Why, I wondered, do they have an airport like this when we have a wooden hut?

Idris Airport in Tripoli was different. The hangers surrounding the terminal were made mostly of corrugated iron and were riddled with bullet holes, a reminder of the destruction of much of the airport during the Second World War. The shabby terminal building was oppressive, with a dry heat. The indolently revolving ceiling fans, the first I had ever seen except on a cinema screen, seemed to have minimum effect on the temperature but maximised my sense of adventure. This was further enhanced by a local gentleman dressed in an ankle-length white djellaba and a tarbush. As I stood at a urinal taking care of bodily needs he startled me by attempting to polish my shoes. I did not buy any of the postcards he later offered to sell me.

The next leg of the long journey involved a bumpy night flight over the Sahara Desert, the largest hot desert in the world and almost as large as America. I was too excited to sleep, despite the comfortable bed-seat. From time to time, far below, I was surprised to see scattered pinpricks of light piercing the vast areas of darkness, giving evidence of human habitation in the most remote areas. As we arrived at Kano in the north of Nigeria in the early morning light I saw for the first time the famous silver dome on the building of the Bank of British West Africa. Traditionally until 1974, when the building was replaced, the dome was used by pilots as a guide to the airport. On landing we were greeted, as was every plane until the 1980s, by a trumpeter seated high on a large camel. This really was West Africa. Next stop Accra, where I would find out if I was to be one of the young men who would adapt to life and work in the tropics or one of those who succumbed to the heat, humidity and the pressures of a life so different from anything they had known before and who, after a few months, were glad to go, or be sent, home. My thoughts turned more and more to Accra, where I was determined to make a success of my new life. The entire trip from London took eighteen hours, compared to the non-stop six hours of today. I had not been apprehensive about flying, or in the least frightened during the long trip, but it was fortunate I could not know that a few months later, on 21st September 1955, a BOAC Argonaut would crash on its fourth attempt to land at Tripoli, killing two crew members and thirteen of the forty passengers, or that on 24th June 1956, just over a year after my own visit, yet another BOAC Argonaut would crash immediately after take-off from Kano, killing three of the seven crew and twenty-nine of the thirty-eight passengers. I believe in that accident the Bank of British West Africa lost two members of staff. The thought of those untimely deaths reminds me of the bank's code book which contained many pages of five-letter code words, each representing a phrase to be used in telegrams between branches and cables to head office in London. The code words were intended to make the contents of messages secure but also, when security was not required, to reduce the number of words, thus lowering the cost. One phrase, represented by five letters, was "We regret to advise you of the death of" and the very next phrase was "We deeply regret to advise you of the death of". I never learned who among us would merit the use of the more compassionate code word.

I arrived at Accra Airport on Sunday morning May 29th, 1955. After we landed it took some time for the stairs to be manoeuvred into position. When the door of the plane was opened a uniformed lady came striding down the aisle spraying a smelly insecticide in the air over the heads of passengers. In later years, once I was familiar with all the things that could bite me in West Africa, it amused me that the locals might not want an insect from somewhere else invading their territory. Soon we were permitted to disembark. I remember so well the rush of almost scalding air that surged up the leg of my thick London trousers as soon as I put my first foot onto the tarmac to be followed, one step later, by a matching whoosh up the other leg. It was hot, really hot! The temperature was about ninety degrees but a great deal more in the heat reflected by the tarmac. The humidity of about 80% made the walk to the terminal sticky. The not unfriendly immigration officer examined the documentation I presented and stamped my passport "Form A issued. 2 years". Customs gave me no trouble. After I said I had no alcohol and nothing to declare, my unopened trunk was marked with chalk and I was on my way. Sturdy young men wanted to assist me with my luggage.

'Master, master, I help you,' and, with more determination, 'Master, give me your trunk.'

Not knowing how I should compensate them for their help I refused the offers and struggled out of the terminal building into the blinding sunshine. The sun had me scrabbling in my pocket to find the sunglasses that clipped onto my own heavy prescription spectacles. I had been persuaded to buy the clip-on in London by the old West Africa hands who said I would certainly need it. In those days there were no transition spectacles that darken automatically as the light becomes stronger.

Once outside I saw that the terminal was opposite the Lisbon Hotel, with which I was soon to become familiar as a Saturday watering hole and dance spot. I went there with my colleagues, most of us hoping to make the acquaintance of air hostesses; without much luck I should add. I think the beautiful and charming young ladies were looking for more mature companions. As I hesitated on the threshold I surveyed the assembled crowd waiting to meet the arriving passengers. Before I had time to worry about what I had let myself in for, Bob Andrews and Arthur Ball approached me.

'Are you Johnston?'

They seemed to have had no difficulty in picking me out from the throng of more suitably dressed older gentlemen. Bob and Arthur were young Englishmen, two or three years older than I, who had arrived in Accra for the first time a few months earlier. My inconvenient trunk, too big for the boot, was loaded into the back seat of Arthur's Morris Minor motor car. With me perched doubled up in the back we set off for the bank flats about ten or fifteen miles away at Tesano, on the outskirts of Accra. We drove along a country road with cows in pastures on either side. These were strange-looking cows with horns, but cows nevertheless, as I discovered a few months later when Dave Hywel Bevan smashed his Jowett Javelin motor car into a herd of them with me in the back seat. When it was discovered, to my surprise, that he had no driving licence, I was persuaded to tell the authorities that I had been teaching him how to drive. In truth, I had been telling him to brake! The trip to Tesano was through rural areas with hardly a house in sight and during the entire twenty-five minutes of the journey Bob and Arthur discussed letters of credit and bills for collection, ignoring me in the back of the car. Letters of credit and bills for collection are relatively simple bank instruments relating to the export and importation of goods and with which I was soon to become very familiar; indeed, I would end up considering myself an expert. At that time in the car, however, I had had no experience of either type of document, despite my London "training". I was somewhat intimidated, which, much later, I realised had been Arthur and Bob's clear intent. Then I did wonder what I had let myself in for. On arrival at a very new block of six two-bedroom apartments, I was told that two were empty and had never been occupied. I could have my choice. Until I bought bedding and other essentials for living I was to stay with Jim Wright, middle left apartment. Jim, a Londoner, was older than the rest of us. As a teenager he had been captured in 1940 and remained a prisoner for the rest of the war in Stalag VIIIB, later renumbered 344, at Lamsdorf in Poland, after which he had worked in the bank's London office for some years before volunteering for service in West Africa. He had arrived in Accra for his first tour of duty only a few months prior to my own arrival but was already supremely organised for living in the Gold Coast. Possibly because of his experience as a prisoner of war Jim already had a cupboard full of shoe boxes in which he stored bits of string, elastic bands, wrapping paper, empty tins and jars, pins, needles and thread and all manner of useful things not readily available in a block of bachelor apartments. I learned my lesson from him and soon started my own collection which became doubly valuable when I was transferred "up-country". This is the origin of the habit of a lifetime, which makes it difficult for me to throw away anything that might possibly be of use sometime in the future. As a friend told me, the quickest way to make something useful is to have discarded it a few days earlier. However, I have two sisters who say they suffer from the same hoarding problem, so it may be in the genes.

It did not take long for four or five young men to gather in Jim's flat to look over the new man. They were all smartly dressed in white shorts and white open-neck shirts. Some wore long white stockings and slip-on shoes and others were more casual in sandals without socks. There was no air-conditioning. The windows were open and it was HOT.

'Take off your jacket. Have a beer.'

I was tired after a sleepless eighteen-hour flight and was so warm in my London suit that I could feel the sweat trickling slowly down my spine.

'No, I'm fine thanks.'

I declined the invitation to remove my jacket because in those days I believed a gentleman did not show the braces that held up his trousers; unlike in later years on Wall Street when my braces, by then called suspenders, became a fashion statement and I needed a different set for each day of the week.

'Well, have a beer.'

'No. I'm all right, thanks.'

I was told, scornfully, 'You'll never last out here unless you drink plenty beer. Just wait until you get your knees brown.'

In the next fourteen years I heard the brown knees expression regularly. Usually it was addressed to someone with a few weeks' or months' service in Africa by a colleague who had been there a little longer.

'Have a beer,' someone insisted once again.

'No thanks. I don't drink,' I announced, becoming a teetotaller in that instant. No alcohol of any kind passed my lips for the next seven years, until I was married; but that is another story. To this day I have no idea why I said I did not drink alcohol. I drank in the army, but very moderately. I had learned soon enough that in a sergeants' mess where I was the only teenager in a bunch of regular soldiers, none of whom was much under forty years of age, I could not hope to keep pace with the others and so had limited my consumption to a small fraction of that of my colleagues. Nevertheless, I had not been a teetotaller. Perhaps my reaction to "you will never last" came from sheer cussedness, of which, over the years, I have been accused of having more than my fair share. Or perhaps it was out of a desire to do nothing that might cause problems with my work or might hamper the success I was so determined to achieve. It might also have had something to do with the fact that my childhood had been negatively affected by my father who had an unhealthy fondness for a drink. I think he was frustrated by a medical condition which not only reduced his tolerance for alcohol but prevented him from being permitted to serve in the armed forces. I never heard if he had been given a white feather, but it must not have been pleasant for him to be one of a very few men of his age not in uniform. In fairness to him I am pleased to say that after a short sharp shock over the Christmas when I was seventeen he never drank again, except, I was told, for a few beers with the lads in Nigeria at my wedding reception, which lasted long into the night after I had left with my bride. Whatever the reason, I became a teetotaller, which saved me no money at all because I always had a fridge well stocked with beer, of which some of my colleagues took advantage from time to time; some more often than others. When at a hotel or club, I always paid my rounds in my turn, drinking orange juice while my friends drank litre bottles of Heineken beer.

Big Jim Gilbert, former military policeman, joined the Sunday morning crowd and asked my name. When I said, 'Calum,' he responded, in a Scots accent very like my own, 'I can't call you that. I'll call you Jock.'

Thus, I became Jock to all and sundry for the next seven years. I was not sorry about this. Indeed, I was proud of the nickname as I had recently been a Jock, as soldiers in the Highland Regiments were known. The irony of my re-naming by Jim did not become apparent for a few years, when I happened to be going home on leave at the same time as Jim. Each of us would be staying with our respective parents in Glasgow so we arranged to be in touch.

One morning, once home, I telephoned Jim and the phone was answered by a lady I assumed to be his mother.

'Good morning, may I please speak to Jim?'

'Jim,' the lady responded in a very questioning voice. 'Jim, oh, do you mean Hamish?'

Hamish is the Gaelic for James, just as Calum is the Gaelic for Malcolm, but only if spelled with one l. Spelling it Callum is like naming somebody Robbert.

In due course most of the crowd left and Jim Wright showed me the small bedroom that was to be mine for the next few days. I noted that there was no shower in the bathroom. Jim said there were no showers in any of the apartments and I asked if I could have a bath.

'Certainly. Felix will run a bath for you.'

'I can do that myself,' I protested.

'Felix is my cook/steward,' said Jim, 'and he will be upset if you do his work for him.'

I was learning the ways of my new life. After my bath and feeling almost human again I was glad to be able to unpack some of my gear and change into more sensible clothing.

Diamonds

I was anxious to see what lay beyond the isolation of the bank
apartments, but I had arrived in Accra on a Sunday. The next day
was the Spring Bank Holiday in the United Kingdom. Although it
was hardly spring in Accra, I presume that the colonial masters had
ordained that in this, as in many other things, we would follow the
British custom. Frustratingly, the banks in the Gold Coast were
closed. I had to content myself with walks in the extensive, but
largely unplanted, fenced-in grounds of the new apartment block.
In front of the entrance to the flats there was a gravelled circle
with a few exotic but sad-looking plants languishing untended in
the tropical sun. Later I learned to drive round this circle with
a squeal of brakes to announce my presence, until the arrival of
one or two wives began to civilise the apartment block. In front
of the circle there was a large area, in which, in the months to
come, Jim Wright and I planted a variety of citrus trees purchased
inexpensively, but with our own money, from the Government
Agricultural Department. Some years later, when overnighting in

an apartment whilst in transit, I was picking a grapefruit when I heard a shout in a shrill strangulated upper-class English voice. A lady, leaning out of a window, called to me, 'I say, I pick the fruit, you know, and share it fairly among all the flats.'

'Madam,' I replied in an equally unfriendly but less shrill voice, 'I planted this bloody tree and I am having one grapefruit with my breakfast.'

'Oh, I suppose that's all right then.'

Six garages were at the rear of the apartment block and beyond those, as far back as the extensive grounds would permit, was a row of six single rooms in which the servants lived; one room for each apartment. A common bathroom served them all.

On the Tuesday following my arrival Jim Wright drove me to the bank, leaving at seven, in time for the work of the day to start at seven-thirty. The main office at High Street, Accra, was housed in a bifurcated building, one part obviously much older than the other, but neither particularly modern. The whole thing was replaced in the 1960s. When I arrived in Accra the staff numbered about 120, and the eight or ten most senior men were European expatriates. I was directed to the office of the manager, to whom I was told to introduce myself. W. John Haymes, former naval officer, probably in his forties, was formal, almost severe in his welcome, which he ended by saying, 'This morning you will go to Swedru to collect the diamonds.'

Not wishing to show any lack of confidence, I replied, 'Yes, sir. Thank you, sir,' and left.

Where the hell was Swedru? Was I going on a journey of an hour, or a week? And how was I to get there? And if and when I arrived, how was I to tell a diamond from a piece of glass? This could be a disaster. Perhaps it was a joke. Surely it was a joke. They would never trust me with diamonds on my first day. But John Haymes did not look like the kind of person who would play jokes on unsuspecting new arrivals. He had been formal and correct and acted like the very senior person he was. And yet… Oh lord, on my very first day! What had I let myself in for?

I approached an expatriate, to whom I had been introduced the day before.

'Mr. Haymes says I have to go to Swedru to collect some diamonds,' I said casually, hoping to disguise my unease. 'How do I get there?'

'Oh, the Land Rover will be waiting for you now, outside. Kofi, the driver, will take you.'

Sure enough, in the small entranceway between the two halves of the building, Kofi and the functional all-grey metal Land Rover waited for me in the early morning sunlight. Seated in the back was a police constable wearing boots, puttees, long blue stockings, black shorts and a blue woollen sweater with leather shoulder patches. By his side rested what I recognised instantly as a .303 Lee-Enfield rifle. It looked as if this Swedru thing was real and not a joke.

'I'm Johnston,' I said to Kofi, as I climbed in and sat on the baking leather of the front seat. 'We're to go to Swedru.'

'Yes, sah,' said Kofi, confidently. 'I goes every week.'

'Good, how far is it?'

'Not too far, sah.'

'Oh, eh… how long will it take us?'

'Not long, sah.'

'You got a map I can look at?'

'Oh no, sah, I knows the way.'

Swedru, more formally Agona-Swedru, proved to be about forty miles from Accra. The road, a two-lane, adequately surfaced, busy thoroughfare, was crowded with mammy wagons coming and going, with passengers on benches packed inside the wooden structure behind the metal cab. Intriguing and sometimes insightful slogans were painted on the front and rear of every multi-coloured vehicle; "Direct line to God", "Slow but Sure",

"No Condition is Permanent", "They Speak What They Do Not Know", "Forward Ever, Backward Never" on the front and on the rear "We'll be Back Tomorrow". The journey took us over two hours. I suppose it would take a good deal less on the roads of today. Long stretches of scrub land separated the villages and as Kofi drove I sat entranced by the early morning sights, sounds and smells of the Gold Coast. We were often stopped behind a mammy wagon in a village as stout ladies in voluminous apparel debarked or embarked with much cheerful laughing and shouting. I watched as the driver's assistant climbed high to unload or secure bundles on the roof of the wagon and I could observe the goings-on in the village. Children were walking to school, barefooted but in immaculate uniforms, starched and pressed. The boys, in khaki shirts and shorts, were moving in groups, often kicking a ball. One boy, never to be forgotten, taller than the rest, had a pen stuck though his curly black hair and, centred on the top of his head, effortlessly balanced as he ran, a bottle of Parker ink. The girls, in white blouses and tartan skirts, were demure, walking in small groups, laughing and giggling and I thought of Logan Pearsall Smith (1865 – 1946) who is remembered for his essays and his autobiography, *Unforgotten Years*, and who said, 'What music is more enchanting than the voices of young people, when you can't hear what they say?'

Looking at the simple village houses with their mud brick walls and corrugated iron roofs, bare red laterite earth in front swept smooth and clean, I wondered how the mothers produced such perfect uniforms for their children. Ah, but yesterday had been a holiday. Today was the first school day of the week. That explained it. But it did not. As I learned in due course, on every school day throughout the week the uniforms looked perfect, at least in the mornings.

As we passed each village I marvelled at the women, straight-backed and dignified, large enamel basin or bucket of water carried regally on the head or sitting at a small fire, cooking, or bathing naked infants in tubs of soapy water. Men, standing in small groups, kente cloths artfully draped over one shoulder, hitched up every now and then with a one-armed shrug, the other shoulder bare to the early morning sun, discussing – discussing what? I could only guess. I knew nothing of these people. Everything was new to me, but I had never wanted anything more than to fit in, to do my job well and to contribute to this country and its people, now heading towards independence. It was all marvellous. I was really here in the Gold Coast and as long as we were on the road, on this my first day at work, I could put out of my mind, for minutes at a time, the inevitable and dreaded moment when I would have to examine and count and take responsibility for a consignment of diamonds.

On arrival at the bank branch at Swedru I presented myself to the manager, George Ellis, a thin well-groomed Englishman, perhaps thirty years old, debonair and impeccably dressed in the standard attire of casual slip-on shoes, slacks, long sleeved white shirt and a tie. As I learned later, on Saturday mornings in the bank, for the slacks we were allowed to substitute neatly tailored white shorts and long white stockings folded over once just below the knee. The incongruity of wearing a tie with shorts did not strike me at the time and I thought nothing of it, which no doubt helped me to adjust rapidly to the local dress when I arrived in Bermuda some forty-two years later. In Swedru George gave me a friendly welcome.

'Good to meet you. If you go upstairs my cook will have some tea and sandwiches prepared for you. Come down when you are ready.'

Upstairs, in the cool and airy sitting room of the manager's residence, comfortably furnished and with traffic noises from the street below coming in faintly through the open wooden louvred windows, I lingered under the slowly revolving ceiling fan as long as seemed reasonably acceptable, and perhaps longer. I was dallying over the lettuce and cucumber sandwiches, elegant with crusts removed and served on fine china, but tasting faintly of Milton, the antiseptic in which, as I learned later, we believed lettuce and the like had to be washed to make it safe to eat. Eventually I felt I could delay no longer and I returned to the manager's office. George left, saying, 'I'll get the diamonds.'

From beyond the office I could hear keys rattling as a strong room gate was opened, and as I sat trembling at the thought of diamonds needing to be examined there came from George a loud shout, 'Johnson!'

Good lord! He seemed such a pleasant chap, and even if it is my first day… I was halfway out of my chair when I heard an answering shout. A very small man in the khaki uniform of a bank messenger, obviously named Johnson, trotted past the open door of the manager's office.

George returned and Johnson laid at my feet a metal box, about eighteen by twelve inches and about nine inches deep. A lid overlapped the box on all four sides. A metal bar ran through slits in the lid and in the box. At one end the bar was larger than the slits and at the other a padlock prevented the bar from being removed and thus secured the lid on the box. George explained that Accra branch had a carefully guarded key that would open the padlock and he laid a receipt on the desk.

'You have to sign this.'

To my great relief I signed for one locked box said to contain diamonds. Much to the consternation of the police constable, who insisted it was his duty to guard it in the back of the Land Rover, the box returned to Accra in the front of the vehicle. My feet never lost contact with it.

Diamonds in the Gold Coast in those days were dug from the ground by individuals using the very basic method of digging a hole and sifting the earth. There were stories of fatalities when the walls collapsed. I heard also of diamonds being found glinting from mud walls after rain had exposed them. I was told that only small industrial diamonds were ever found, but in later years, when the Government took more control of the industry, about 10-15% of production proved to be in the form of gems which could be cut and polished for use in jewellery. It seems likely that in the early days the gem stones followed a different path from the industrial diamonds. The latter were brought by the diamond winners to the bank's branch at Tarkwa, some hundred miles west of Swedru. The business of making loans against diamonds had been introduced to the bank in 1935 by C. J. Green, who had joined the bank at age twenty-four in 1911 and became manager at Tarkwa in 1933, which position he held until he retired in 1948. In my day, the branch manager at Tarkwa, with no training whatsoever, except that proffered by his predecessor, would examine the small chips brought in by the diamond winners, clean them, peer at them through a magnifying glass and weigh them on a very delicate scale, after which he would make a loan amounting to whatever he thought was a safe percentage of the value, usually not more than 60 or 65%. Once a week he took the diamonds to Swedru, from where they were picked up and taken to Accra. There they were boxed and shipped by air to London. In due course the manager at Tarkwa branch would receive a cable stating, 'Lot ABC and lot XYZ, we have credited your account with…', whatever the values of the particular lots might be, whereupon the manager would breathe a sigh of relief.

Not long after my trip to Swedru the government took more control of the industry and the involvement of the bank ceased. Indeed, the official history of the bank, *Bankers in West Africa* by Richard Fry, incorrectly suggests that the bank was no longer involved in the trade after about 1953, whereas I collected diamonds in 1955. I was never again sent to Swedru and do not recall anyone else having to go, so perhaps my trip was the last one.

Mr. Bikhazi, Angustus and the Chicken

Business: The art of extracting money from another man's pocket without resorting to violence.

Max Amsterdam

Within a few of days of my arrival in Accra I was comfortably installed in my own flat at Tesano. Each unit had a combined sitting and dining room, a large bedroom with huge built-in wardrobes, a kitchen, laundry room with a large tub, a storeroom and a bathroom. There was a second small bedroom which, peculiarly, could be accessed only through the main bedroom and the bathroom or from the sitting room via an outside veranda, which I soon learned to call a stoep. On writing home, and spelling it stoop, I later received a rebuke and the correct spelling in a letter from my mother.

Basic furniture was provided but no carpets or curtains. The floor was tiled in cork except in the kitchen area, where it was plain concrete enhanced by red Cardinal polish which the stewards brought to a high shine with a bumper, a heavy cloth-covered weight with a long handle. There was no air-conditioning.

Allowed to select my apartment, I chose the ground floor right to save the walk up to the third storey, which was the alternative. This was a mistake resulting from my inexperience. Apart from the fact that there was less breeze reaching the bedroom, the watchnight – why we called them watchnights and not watchmen, I never found out – the watchnight sat outside my open window. A Muslim, dressed in a long white gown, armed with a bow and arrow, a spear and a kettle of water for his evening ablutions, he prayed long and loudly each night. I was never able to decide if this was real devotion or just his way of letting the occupants of the building know he was awake and guarding us well. The mosquito net under which I slept seemed to provide an impenetrable barrier to any slight breeze that might venture through the open windows but provided no protection at all from the incessant rhythm of the watchnight's prayers. Nervous of making a religious blunder, it took me several weeks to decide that without causing offence I could ask him to move.

Soon after my arrival I was instructed by my new colleagues that one of the first things I must do was to visit the British High Commission to sign the book.

'What book?'

'At the front gate there is a large book and you need to sign it and write your name and address. You can leave your business card in the tray.'

'What business card and what for?'

'Well, even if you don't have a card you can leave your name and address to let them know you are here. If there is an emergency we might need to be evacuated and if you are lucky you will be invited to a garden party.'

And indeed I was. Had I been more senior I would have been invited to dinner, as happened many years later when I signed a similar book on the remote South Atlantic island of St. Helena. In due course I signed books and left my cards at embassies, high commissions, deputy high commissions, consular offices, the governor's office and district commissioner's offices in more places than I care to try to remember. While in many instances it seemed a futile and outdated ritual I took pride in knowing the correct form for a man of the empire, even when the empire no longer existed.

Another ritual was my first Saturday curry lunch. This was hosted at his home, Milner House, by the district manager, who had invited the bachelors on the bank staff. A British West African curry lunch is a wonderful institution, not to be missed. It consisted in my day of a large pot of beef, chicken or lamb curry and a mountain of white rice, surrounded by as many different side plates as the cook could muster. Essentials included a red powder, roasted ground nuts (peanuts), chopped bananas and pineapples fresh and fried, orange liths, fried plantain, raisins, tomatoes, onions, grated coconut, boiled eggs, and probably many more I have forgotten. A kind colleague insisted on showing me the ropes.

'You take your soup plate and start with a sprinkling of this red stuff. No, a bit more! Now some rice and a ladle of curry. Now you go round all the side plates taking a spoonful from each and dumping it on top. Yes, like that. OK, now mix it up like a dog's breakfast.'

It tasted a lot better than it looked until I discovered that the 'red stuff' was cayenne and the hottest thing ever to touch my lips. Clearly I had been induced to be more generous with it than was sensible but I struggled through and, like Frank Sinatra, I ate it up but, unlike Frank, I did not spit it out, although I was severely tempted. I think that was the only time a large bottle of Heineken beer looked inviting. I stuck to my orange juice.

So keen was I to be independent and to have my own transport to take me to and from work each day, I overpaid John Gait £100 for a beaten-up beetle-back Standard Vanguard car. Previously it had been abandoned, late one evening, engine stalled, on the nearby railway crossing by, I assume, its inebriated driver, whom, I must say before being sued by John, was likely to have been an even earlier owner. The cars of bank employees tended to make the rounds as people were transferred or went home on leave. The Vanguard, subsequently reclaimed after having been struck a glancing blow by a train, forevermore sported a battered left front wing. I had borrowed £200 from the bank to finance the purchase and, against all the rules, the remaining £100 enabled me to buy locally-tailored shorts, cutlery, crockery, pots and pans, bed linen, and, extravagantly, cheap curtains and a blue carpet to make my quarters look less Spartan. I also had the £100 I had borrowed from my father before leaving home and which I repaid, without interest, on my first leave.

The word had gone out that there was a new man at the bank flats. Within hours of my arrival several applicants appeared, all keen to serve the recently arrived "master". Largely based on his confident recounting of his many skills, which subsequent events proved to have been grossly exaggerated, I hired Augustus to be my cook/steward. He was a thin young man in his mid twenties with a cheerful demeanour and whose frequent smiles revealed a prominent gap in his large white front teeth. He bore cicatricial scars on both cheeks. So, there I was, twenty years of age, with my own rent-free two-bedroom apartment, a cook/steward, a car and a job I thought I could handle. How could life have been any better?

After engaging Augustus the next task was to provide him with the wherewithal to prepare the sumptuous meals he had promised. I was sent by my colleagues to Gabriel Bikhazi's grocery store near the old Kingsway Store, not far from the lighthouse in James Town. Mr. Bikhazi was Lebanese. Many years later, when cutting the ribbon at the opening of a branch bank in Beirut, Lebanon, I told the assembled businessmen the story of my relationship with

Mr. Bikhazi. On arrival at his store I told him who I was and that I worked for BBWA. Without being obsequious, Mr. Bikhazi, a short, rather rotund gentleman, treated me most deferentially. 'Sit down here, Mr. Johnston. Have a cold drink of Fanta,' said the middle-aged Bikhazi to the very young banker while proffering a cigarette from a round tin of fifty Player's Navy Cut. At first I thought Mr. Bikhazi had mistaken my identity. Confusion was possible because at the time, working at the bank was a more senior man, Charles Patrick Johnston, known as Johnny, with whom I was later frequently and embarrassingly confused. But of course Mr. Bikhazi knew who I was and exactly how much, or to be more precise, how little, I earned, as the most junior and most recently-arrived bank employee. Nevertheless, he gave me a small double-leaved book and a sheet of carbon paper. I was instructed to write in it from time to time whatever supplies I needed. My steward (Mr. Bikhazi knew I would have a cook/steward and not a cook and a steward, but subtle flattery was part of his stock in trade), my steward would bring the book and collect the order. At the end of each month I would receive a bill, delivered to me directly at the bank. As a result of this generous treatment, and as he knew he would, Mr. Bikhazi received the major part of my income for the next ten months, until I moved north to Kumasi, at which time my quarterly bonus was just sufficient to clear the outstanding amount my salary had not covered. The Lebanese are great businessmen.

Prior to his first trip to Mr. Bikhazi, Augustus presented me with a long list of his requirements which included, in addition to the basics, exotic spices and ingredients. I was impressed and cannot honestly say I was suspicious, even though, on most other subjects, Augustus appeared to have a rather limited range of experience and knowledge. On my return from work on the evening of Augustus's first visit to Mr. Bikhazi, I inspected the store cupboard and was a little disappointed to find that although there was an impressive array of supplies, they had not been arranged in any order I could perceive. Small bottles were scattered among bags of potatoes and flour and a round tin of Australian butter, the only kind of butter available in those days, was on the floor next to a bag of sugar. Nevertheless, I awaited my dinner with expectation. The first course turned out to be mulligatawny soup which came from a tin, but nevertheless a new and enjoyable experience. The soup was followed by a somewhat misshapen omelette containing barely warm and practically raw green peas. No dessert. Trying not to upset Augustus, I complimented him but suggested that a different dinner tomorrow would be appreciated. On the following two evenings I was presented with different dinners, but the only difference was that the soup came from different tins and I was introduced to jungle juice, a refreshing dessert made of chopped up oranges, bananas, pineapple and any other fruit that came to hand. The omelette with the raw green peas turned out to be the only entrée Augustus had mastered and even that not well. After a lengthy interrogation, he finally admitted that his list of requirements had been copied from the shelves in the kitchen of a house occupied by an expatriate senior enough to be accompanied by his wife and with whose cook Augustus was friendly. He had no idea how to make use of many of the things he had copied onto his list and he admitted that before I employed him he had been a steward in a household which employed a cook.

In those days nearly all house servants were men and every expatriate was expected to hire one or more. The titles, equating roughly to job descriptions, ranged from small-boy through cook/steward and steward, to cook. A wife with a child might employ a girl as a nanny and somebody to take care of the laundry. A small-boy, usually in his mid-teens, did little but fetch and carry and might learn to do basic housework and would be found only in grander establishments with other servants. A steward would wait on table and do housework and a cook would do little but cook. A cook/steward would do everything. Young expatriates usually employed a cook/steward and in Accra in 1955 would pay them an absolute minimum of £8 a month to start, although an experienced cook/steward could command a pound or two more. I soon learned not to be surprised by how quickly some middle-class young men from the United Kingdom adopted a very decided *de haut en bas* attitude. Servants addressed their employers as master and madam, the latter with the emphasis on the last three letters. When I hired Augustus, who, after all, was older than I, I did suggest to him that master was not appropriate and that sir or Mr. Johnston would be fine. Augustus responded deferentially, 'Yes, master.'

After a couple of days I gave up. Despite his execrable cooking, which improved little, even with help from me, who could not cook at all, Augustus lasted several weeks. The last straw was the chicken.

It was not unusual for businessmen to bring gifts to bank officers; the more senior the officer, the better the gift. I had been given a live, scrawny chicken, which placed me firmly at the bottom of the pecking order, along with the chicken. Among my duties in the bank was the selling of travellers' cheques. In those days, the regulations required me to stamp on the back of each cheque that was to be cashed outside the Sterling Area "This cheque may be cashed only in…" and to write by hand the name of the appropriate country or countries. Nobody ever explained to me why this was necessary or what it accomplished. One morning I was nearing the end of writing on the back of fifty two-pound cheques for a very attractive young lady, barely out of her teens I assumed, very neatly dressed and wearing, unusually, a cloche hat, who had said she was going to France. I asked her, for the sake of making conversation, why she was going to France.

'Because the church is sending me for training,' she replied.

'You must be excited. Where in France are you going?'

'Rome,' she answered.

'Oh, I had better write Italy on the back of these,' I said, as I started over.

Covering her mouth with the tips of the fingers of both hands in the most charming and attractive gesture, which made me wish she wasn't going to Italy, or France, she whispered, 'I'm sorry, I made a mistake.'

The result was that the next morning a middle-aged man, dressed very simply in shorts, string vest and flip-flops with the soles made from old car tyres, and not at all like the businessmen who usually brought gifts, appeared at my desk and presented me with a live chicken "for being kind to my daughter".

I was embarrassed by the sight of a live chicken tied by the string on its leg to the leg of my desk in the cavernous open banking hall, until a bank messenger took pity on me, or on the chicken, and removed it to a more suitable place to await the end of the working day. Despite the embarrassment there was no way I could have refused the gift. In any case, I was pleased to have received my first dash; ('dash' – the word used in British West Africa meaning anything from a large gift to a small tip. The boy who said that, unasked, he had looked after your car while you were in the cinema would plead, 'Dash me, master').

On arriving home with the chicken under my arm, I asked Augustus, 'Do you know how to cook a chicken?'

'Yes, master.' 'Oh, never mind. I will ask somebody and will help you.'

'Do you know how to prepare a chicken?'

'Yes, master.'

'Good, you go and prepare it.'

Prepare was a euphemism for kill, which I did not want to witness. A few minutes later, from the kitchen, came the noise of running water and tremendous clucking, splashing and beating of wings. This went on for a good five minutes until a bedraggled

Augustus appeared in the doorway, holding by the neck a very live, very wet and loudly protesting chicken. He announced, 'Master, this chicken no fit drown.'

He had been holding the chicken's head under the running tap.

Augustus and I parted company on reasonably friendly terms, aided no doubt by the one-month notice pay I felt obliged to give him. He told me he would look for employment as a steward in a house with a madam and a cook, because, he confessed, he still had a few things to learn about cooking.

After a rather more careful search than the one that had produced Augustus, I hired Jackson. He was a short man, impeccably dressed in a white uniform provided by his previous employer. This was a mistake on his part, he later admitted, because it obviated the need for me to buy a uniform for him, at least for a couple of months until, remarkably, the uniform disappeared and was reported to have "spoiled". Jackson also wore a very smart black Anthony Eden hat and I rarely saw him out of doors without it. He produced a very good letter of reference from his previous employer, who had recently left the country. Jackson was in his mid-thirties and had a wife, whom, he said, would give no trouble if allowed to live with him in the servants' quarters in the grounds of the apartment block. She never did cause any trouble and I saw little of her. Nevertheless, I believe it was she, rather than Jackson, who wished me a safe return to Africa, judging by the writing on the note which accompanied a small parcel of groundnuts that arrived at my parents' house in Glasgow during my first home leave.

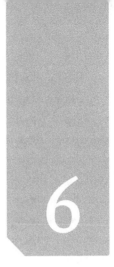

Learning my Trade

Tell me and I forget.
Teach me and I remember.
Involve me and I learn.
Benjamin Franklin

As the result of having learned the basics at Clydesdale Bank, I had little difficulty in coping with my responsibilities when, a couple of months after arriving in Accra, I was placed in charge of the Journal Department. Accra branch had no mechanisation whatsoever. Everything was done by hand in pen and ink. The working day began at 7.30am, when the call-over started. Each officer, other than the most senior two or three, was assigned responsibility for one or more large bound ledgers containing the record of customer accounts. A clerk would call to the officer the name and amount on each deposit slip, cheque or internal debit or credit voucher entered in the ledger the day before, so that the officer could tick the entry as correct. After the call-over the officer would examine the vouchers and cheques, looking for anything that seemed to him suspicious or out of order. The call-over was a wonderful procedure but quite impossible now because of the volume of entries processed each day by computer, and already under strain in my time in Accra.

The Journal Department was housed in a large room upstairs, well away from the customer counter, and it had the reputation of being a bad place to work because going home time was rarely before 6pm even though the bank closed to customers at 1pm. The ten or twelve young men who comprised the staff sat at tables round the perimeter of the room and each was responsible for one or more large bound journals. While Journal Department staff members were expected to arrive ready for work at 7.30am there was little for them to do after they had fulfilled any responsibilities they had at call-over and they would sit around and laugh and joke for a good deal of the morning until the vouchers and cheques started to trickle in. I gained some credibility by harrying the tellers and ledger keepers to let us have the cheques and vouchers as quickly as possible and insisting that the journal keepers started their hand posting as soon as they had something to work with. In this effort I remember receiving help from Mr. Tetteh, the senior local officer, and the result was an improvement in going home time. Usually we left at about 5pm and everyone liked that.

Mr. Tetteh had worked for the bank for many years and was certainly as old as or older than my father. If ever he resented my youth, or my lack of experience, or the fact that I was paid more than I presume he was, he never let me see a hint of it. He helped me whenever he could. He wrote a note to the examining officer that gained me a driving licence after a test that lasted all of five minutes. The local staff of the bank in Accra was made up of a large number of young men and a very few older men, even fewer of whom were junior officers. This mix was probably due to the rapid expansion of the bank after the war, when the additional hires were mainly school leavers. Young ladies started to be employed only towards the end of the 1950s. At the founding of The Bank of The Gold Coast in 1953 the managing director, Alfred Eggleston, an experienced Scottish banker on secondment from the Imperial Bank of India, said he was able to recruit whomever he wanted from BBWA because that bank had a firm policy of not promoting locals. It is difficult to deny that such a policy existed when the bank, quite obviously, favoured inexperienced young expatriates over much more experienced locals, even though the expatriates were more expensive. Part of the problem, I think, was that when an expatriate got himself or the bank into trouble, and some did, one going to prison during my time in Accra, it was considered to be the result of a character flaw of the individual. If a local made a mistake there seemed to be a tendency for the bank to regard it as a national failing. However, in the hubris of youth I gave none of this much thought. I was not clever enough or sufficiently perceptive to stand against the crowd. As did the majority of people of all ages in all times I conformed to what those around me considered the norm but I did believe that in doing my job to the best of my ability I was contributing to the well-being of the bank and the steady march of the Gold Coast towards independence.

In July 1955 I celebrated my twenty-first birthday, but I celebrated quietly and alone, not wishing to remind anyone I was younger than all the expatriates and most of the locals with whom I worked. My birthday fell on a Sunday, and as we often did, a small group of us went to the cinema in the evening. We sat on metal chairs on the sloping concrete floor of the open-air cinema. The locals were enthusiastic participants, particularly in films that included fist fights, and with every blow they would shout out in unison a lusty and well timed, 'Oosah.' What they thought of us, decked out as we were in dinner jackets, black tie and cummerbunds, I never knew. We usually dressed like this to go the cinema, which startled me at first until I was told we would be going to the club after the show, and on weekends at the club, black tie was obligatory.

Later in the year I was promoted to the Bills and Credits Department which dealt with goods being imported. One of the things that made this job interesting was that Accra had no harbour.

Ships would anchor off-shore and all goods would be transported to the beach on large canoes manned by eight or ten sturdy young men. These lads propelled their canoes with paddles that ended in five fingers and flashed in the sun in perfect time to a chant. It was thrilling to watch the empty boats struggling over the surf to get to the steamers. Even more exciting was to see the canoes, loaded to the gunnels with bales and boxes, speeding in on the crest of a wave to slide gently onto the sand. Once beached, the boatmen would jump out and heave the cargo onto shoulders and heads and struggle over the sand to dump their loads on the concrete floor of the huge number one shed. A consignment of ten or twelve bales or boxes could easily be brought to shore on several different canoes and end up scattered all over the shed. This could become a problem if the customer did not come to the bank to pay or sign a promissory note after I had notified him of the arrival of the ship. I would then have to follow the instructions of the shipper to 'protect the goods'. This meant that I had to find them and have them moved to the security of the bank store. In all this Harris Aquaye, in charge of the store and a contemporary of Mr. Tetteh, was a great help. He knew everybody and everything and kept me out of trouble. Early in my assignment I told Mr. Aquaye, 'I have a real problem. I need to clear to store ten bales of cloth consigned to a Syrian trader, but I can find only nine bales. I've searched the shed again and again.'

'Well, it's possible that one bale went into the sea. Did you know that there are cars and a lot of other stuff at the bottom, just off-shore? But I think we would have heard if a bale of cloth had fallen over recently. I'll come along and have a look for you. I know a couple of places it might be hidden.'

'Oh, thank you,' I said, 'but if we can't find it, eventually it will be sold at auction by the port authorities. Can I just go along to the auction and buy it?'

Mr. Aquaye laughed, and still chuckling as he spoke he said, 'A young expat at the auction, ha, ha, ha! Have you seen the size of the mammies who go to the auctions? They would never let you get close enough to bid. They know exactly what is to be sold and probably have agreed which of them is to buy each consignment and at what price. No, we had better find your bale.'

Fortunately, we found it tucked away in an unlikely corner.

The Miscellaneous Bills desk was the largest I had ever seen. It was at that desk, facing the assembled throng of bills clerks, that I experienced my first Harmattan. Wind storms to the north raise large amounts of dust into the atmosphere and the wind that blows south over the Sahara to the Gulf of Guinea between the end of November and mid-March carries so much dust that for a few days each year the sun can be blocked out. Humidity can be reduced to a low of 15%, causing spontaneous nosebleeds in any susceptible to the extreme dryness. The effect is usually felt in Accra in January and cracked lips and dry skin are the norm at that time of the year. The Harmattan of 1955/6 was severe and I remember my surprise when the papers on my desk curled up into tubes, the paint on the wall behind me began to fall off in strips and wooden furniture cracked, often with a loud report. Interestingly, the word Harmattan is one of only two words of the Ashanti language, Twi, to have entered the English language. The other word is ackee, a fruit well-known as part of the dish of ackee and salt fish which I came to like very much during the time I lived and worked in Jamaica.

In March 1956, less than a year after my arrival, I was told I was to proceed to Kumasi, the capital of the Ashanti Kingdom, to relieve the manager of Kejetia branch during the three and a half months of his home leave. I was advised not to get a swollen head. I was going not because I was so smart but because nobody else was available. So it was that early one morning Jackson and I, with all our worldly possessions on the back seat, set out in the Standard Vanguard, the car with the crumpled wing, to drive about 150 miles north to Kumasi.

Kumasi, Tepa and Yendi

Responsibility educates.

Peter Drucker

As are most countries in Africa, the Gold Coast, which became Ghana in 1957, is a creation of Western Colonial Imperialism, with the lines on the map drawn to suit the exigencies of the times, the needs of foreigners working on trading relationships with locals, empire building and historical accident. This has led to many problems all over Africa as peoples of different ethnic origins, religious beliefs and speaking different languages struggle to live together peacefully under a single flag. Ghana has been more successful at this than most other countries.

Ghana can be described very roughly as the coast, the tropical forests of Ashanti, the dry lands of the Northern Territories and in the east the former British Togoland. The German Protectorate of Togoland was divided between France and Britain in 1916. British Togoland, as the result of a vote by its citizens, became part of the Gold Coast in 1956, leaving the thin strip of the French half with a coastline of only thirty-five miles eventually to become Togo. The whole of Ghana is about the size of the United Kingdom or Michigan in America. Although many languages are spoken

English is the official language of government and the language used for business and educational instruction. An English-speaking visitor is likely to be understood everywhere in the country. If you want to go to Africa, go to Ghana first! It is almost certainly the best place for English speakers looking for their first experience of Africa and for a warm and friendly reception.

On arrival in Kumasi in March 1956, unable to find the small branch that was to be my responsibility, Jackson and I made our way to the easily located main Kumasi office. Outside the branch we were greeted by the manager, Roddy Hughes, together with armed policemen and assorted local and European staff who were supervising the loading of a truck with a consignment of Ashanti Goldfield Corporation's gold to be dispatched to the airport and flown to Accra, from where it would be sent on to London. Mr. Hughes, probably in his early fifties, and very senior in the bank hierarchy, had been on the Coast since long before the Second World War. He took a look at my battered old car and asked, 'Did you come from Accra in that?'

I was afraid he was about to say that with its crumpled wing it was not a fit mode of transport for a bank official, but, having no option, I replied meekly, 'Yes, sir.'

Pointing to a motorised bicycle belonging to one of the staff Mr. Hughes said, 'That would be more suitable for a young man like you. When I came to Kumasi for the first time I walked all the way from Accra.'

As Winston Churchill said, 'Life is fraught with opportunities to keep your mouth shut.' But, then as now, often too quick with my mouth, I did not have the wit to leave well enough alone and started off on the wrong foot with Hughes by saying that Jackson and I with our possessions would have had a difficult time coming from Accra on a bicycle.

Aided by the directions given, we found Kejetia branch close to Kejetia Circle and the lorry park. Within the hour, despite blackened hands from having changed a punctured tyre, I had counted the cash, accepted the keys and taken responsibility for the five-man branch. My predecessor left and that was the total of the introduction to my managerial responsibilities. I did find a manual that purported to provide guidelines for any eventuality. Each manager was required to read the thick book and sign on the flyleaf as certification that he had done so. The copy at Kejetia presumably had been dug out of storage for the opening of the branch a year or so earlier and I found it of very limited help. The last manager to have signed was none other than Frank G. Wright, the current general manager who had interviewed me in London, and he had dated his signature in the book sometime in the 1930s. There had been no amendments or updates since then.

The next morning four or five potential and existing customers were lined up, keen to see what they could pry out of the new callow acting manager. As I recall, the customers waiting for me that first morning were all easily spotted as being unworthy of receiving whatever it was they were seeking but later I did fall for the oldest trick in the book, a spurious deadline to encourage the inexperienced into undue haste. A Lebanese car dealer, a customer of Barclays Bank, called on me to say that he had fallen out with the Barclays manager and he wished to move his account to my branch. Of course, he salted this brief explanation with all the great things he had heard about me and my abilities, which I would have liked to believe despite his considerable over-egging of the pudding. However, he would move his account only if I would grant him an overdraft there and then, to enable him to go to Barclays that day with a bank cheque to close his account and, I presumed, give the Barclays manager a two-finger salute. The overdraft required was far in excess of the small amounts I was authorised to lend without approval from Accra but that did not deter me from attempting to acquire what I thought to be a most desirable account. I went to the car dealer's showroom where I examined his books and counted and valued the vehicles for sale, checked the papers that proved his ownership and, having decided they provided adequate security, took hypothecations over the vehicles and granted the requested overdraft. I filled in the usual forms and sent them to the district manager's office in Accra. This informed him exactly what I had done. I based my actions on the presumption that it would be better to beg forgiveness than to have asked permission, which certainly would not have arrived in time to meet the dealer's time limit, which, in retrospect, was probably not genuine. Over the next week or two I waited nervously for the inevitable reprimand. Unaccountably, it never arrived. I can assume only that somebody had taken pity on me and filed the report away without drawing the attention of the district manager to my breach of regulations or, perhaps because I had filled in all the right forms, it had not been noticed that the overdraft I had granted was far in excess of my small limit. Fortunately, and probably surprisingly, the account proved to be good and did not give any problems during my brief sojourn in Kumasi. If it had done so later I am sure it would have been brought to my attention.

A problem I first encountered at Kejetia and then at every branch at which I worked was running out of the forms we used on a daily, weekly or monthly basis. All forms were ordered from London and the shipments took at least six months to arrive. At the time this seemed to me to be an indictment of senior management, who could not be bothered to organise local printing. However, they may just have been playing the traditional role of making sure a colony bought as much as possible from the mother country.

Kejetia branch had been opened in the premises of a large trading company and my predecessor, who was in charge at the opening, always insists that the trading company had an account at the new branch. I am not sure about that, but I am sure that if there was an account the company did not use it. I remember very clearly sitting at the desk of the CEO asking him to use the branch which was right on his doorstep, indeed, on his own premises.

'But,' he said, 'the main branch tells me immediately if a cheque I have deposited bounces.'

'I can do that, and I am right on your doorstep.'

'The main branch delivers statements of my account by hand each week.'

'I can do that.'

'I get a lot of coins from the main branch.'

'I can provide coins.'

And so on it went until I wore him down, with the result that I gained a large important account and incurred the wrath of Mr. Hughes, who lost one of his most profitable customers. I was not politically attuned in those days. Many will say I never improved. My relationship with Mr. Hughes was not enhanced when I found him one day in my branch leafing through a customer ledger and told him that I thought he should have poked his head through my office door to let me know he was there.

While in Kumasi I shared a bank-owned two-storey, two-bedroom house which stood in its own garden. My co-tenant was Roger Piggott, an Englishman who worked at the main branch. We passed some of our spare time playing badminton in the garden until Mrs. Hughes, unasked, uninvited and for no apparent reason other than that she felt authorised to inspect the bachelor quarters while we were at work, arranged to have the hedge that protected the court from the wind cut to a level that made play impossible. My complaint to Mr. Hughes was received unsympathetically. After Roger had introduced me to opera we spent many an evening stretched flat out on the floor listening to Roger's extensive collection of recordings of complete operas, played on his prized possession, a Black Box record player. Roger left the bank after only one tour and some years later I met him and his beautiful French wife Greta in London. But, like so many others, I lost touch with them as I and they moved round the world. Losing touch with so many people is one of the saddest parts of the expatriate life.

I remember well two trips Roger and I made at weekends. The first was to Tepa, some seventy miles away. We made the trip reluctantly because the tyres on my car were bald and unreliable. The manager of the Tepa branch of the bank had brought his car to Kumasi for servicing and it was to be kept in the garage. Although we were not particularly friendly with him, indeed I rather disliked him, and he could have taken a taxi home, he called on us and begged a lift to Tepa. We obliged. On our way back to Kumasi and not yet out of Tepa, in the rain, and travelling at not more than twenty miles an hour, my car skidded and we found ourselves sliding down the smooth tarmac road backwards. I had time to do little more than to warn Roger to take off his spectacles because I felt sure we would end up in the large grassy drainage ditch at the side of the road. We did. With the car leaning against the side of the sloping ditch we clambered out into the rain. We were not properly out before we were offered hospitality at a nearby house. We declined and explained that we would walk the few yards to the house of the bank manager, the only white man in town, whom we had left only a few minutes before. He would be sure to look after us. The manager, a fellow Scot I am ashamed to say, responding to our knock, stuck his head round the door and on hearing that we had had an accident and without asking if either of us was injured, politely told us where we would find a taxi to take us home. He then closed the door.

The following weekend was a quarter-end and I could not get away from my office as early as Roger could leave the main branch, so he agreed to take a taxi back to Tepa on the Saturday afternoon to have my car pulled from the ditch and brought home. Having finished all the quarterly returns in the bank I hurried home by taxi in the late afternoon, hoping to see my car sitting in the drive. No such luck. I asked Roger, 'Where is my car?'

'I sold it.'

'You did what?'

'I sold it. Where is as is. I got £50 cash and a promise of twenty more to come at £10 a month.'

'Well, Roger, … I suppose that is not a bad deal considering it cost me £100 a year ago, but I doubt I will ever see the extra twenty.'

To my surprise the first instalment of £10 was paid but that was the last I heard. I did not have the heart to chase for the final instalment. To my certain knowledge the car was pulled from the ditch and parked in front of the house of the buyer in Tepa, at the side of the main road. Years later when I passed I could see it being used as a chicken coop.

Another memorable trip, made over the long Easter weekend, was to Yendi to visit my good friend Joe Ryan. On the previous Christmas Eve Joe had been summoned by the district manager and told to leave the next day, yes, Christmas Day, and to get himself to Yendi, well over 400 miles away and a place of which none of us had heard. He was to be there for about two weeks, so said the district manager. It turned out to be eleven months. At that time the rivalry between our bank and Barclays Bank was intense, with both banks anxious to open branches, mainly to gather deposits for use in financing the import trade of the large firms headquartered in Accra but also in the case of BBWA, in anticipation of independence when, it was assumed, the valuable government business would be lost to a new local bank. John Brand, our manager at Tamale, 370 miles north of Accra, had reported seeing a Barclays Bank lorry heading out of Tamale with the only possible destination being Yendi and the only possible purpose being the opening of a branch. Incredible as it may seem, particularly if you could have seen Yendi in 1955, the district manager, in his very questionable wisdom, decided that we too would open a branch in this small village. As an example of the remoteness of Yendi and as I later discovered, petrol at the filling station was supplied from large drums by means of a hand pump.

On Christmas Day, with a few belongings in a suitcase, Joe left Accra in his new Baby Austin car with its 948 cc engine, acceptable perhaps for the roads of Accra but ridiculous for a trip to Yendi. He was followed by a lorry with a box of supplies and a cashier. John Brand, Joe was told, would have made all the arrangements to rent a building in Yendi and, as a bonus, it had been agreed that Joe could live in an unused bungalow belonging to the Assembly of God mission. However, on Christmas Day, Brand was in hospital suffering from malaria and nothing had been arranged. Joe left Tamale with a long wooden signboard painted "Bank of British West Africa" strapped to the roof of his tiny car. On arrival in Yendi, sixty miles away, he rented a mud brick house on the main road and had the sign attached to the corrugated iron roof. He then called on the Ya Na, the chief of the Dagomba, and asked him to open the bank the next day. The chief was willing but said he had already agreed to open Barclays Bank a few yards down the road. As a result, he performed the two ceremonies on the same day. But he opened his personal account at BBWA with £5 provided by Joe.

The following Easter, after the long drive from Kumasi in a car borrowed from a customer and having crossed the Volta River on a pontoon, Roger and I arrived at Yendi. We found Joe's bungalow without difficulty. All the locals knew where we should go when we made it clear which bank manager we wanted. In a village where there were no other Europeans except a missionary or two our question was easy to answer. Joe's Assembly of God mission "bungalow" turned out to be a round house with a thatched roof and no windows or doors. It had been standing empty and unused except by bats for seven years before Joe arrived. Joe told us about waking one night terrified because a lion was licking his face. Fortunately, the lion turned out to be a cow. At first Joe was envious of the luxurious accommodation provided by Barclays Bank for their young manager and he took us to see it. For some months the Barclays man had been obliged to travel daily back and forth from Tamale, on an unpaved road and over several narrow wooden bridges. Eventually Barclays sent him a very small building made entirely of corrugated iron. It was just about big enough to lie down in. One could have baked bread in it without an oven at any time during daylight hours. Sometime after our visit and to the great relief of the Barclays man the roof blew off and landed in the desert scrubland at the bottom of the nearby 100ft almost vertical escarpment. He then moved into the round house with Joe.

One of the highlights of work at Kejetia branch involved a weekly trip to move my excess cash to the main branch. This was done by loading one or more locked specie boxes (you might remember them from the diamond story) into the boot of a taxi cab parked on the busy main road while I stood guard with a revolver. It was impossible to hire a policeman because of the political unrest caused by the impending election. The revolver, apparently a substitute for a policeman, was required by bank regulations which stipulated that it was to be unloaded with the bullets carried in a small canvas bag. Since my standard attire of slacks and a shirt provided no place to hide the large unwieldy handgun, rather than being a deterrent it immediately attracted a crowd to watch the loading of the boxes. Fortunately, people were good-natured and probably did not know that if I was attacked I would have to ask for time out until I loaded my revolver. I made my weekly trips without incident.

On the return of the Kejetia manager from his home leave I was delighted to be sent to Sunyani to take over from Sandy McLean to perform yet another relief, although my own home leave was due within a few months. My leave might or might not be authorised on time. One never knew.

Sunyani

He that planteth a tree is a servant of God,
he provideth a kindness for many generations,
and faces that he hath not seen shall bless him.

Henry Van Dyke

The day I arrived in Sunyani for the first time I fell in love with the Flame of the Forest trees that lined both sides of one of the main streets. They were in glorious full bloom with bright red flowers forming a canopy spanning the road. I later learned that the correct name of the tree is Delonix regia, but it is often called Flamboyant or Royal Poinciana after Philippe de Longvilliers de Poincy, the seventeenth-century Governor of St. Kitts, who is credited with introducing the tree to the Americas. He planted specimens at the fabulous residence, Chateau de Montagne, he started building in St. Kitts in 1642. I visited the ruins in 2007. The blossom of Delonix regia is the national flower of St. Kitts and Nevis and the tree is native to Madagascar but from whence Longvilliers de Poincy introduced it I have been unable to discover. Many years later than my arrival in Sunyani I read in the diary of T.E. Fell, provincial commissioner in Sunyani from 1907 to 1916, that on 24th April 1914 he supervised schoolchildren planting twenty trees and I have wondered ever since if the trees they planted were the Delonix regia that so impressed me. Why Sunyani became so special to me I have never known but when I think of Sunyani I think of those trees. However, looking closely at a Google map on my computer I can see no trace of trees forming a canopy over any Sunyani road. The little town I knew has grown into a city of 250,000 people.

Sunyani, about seventy-five miles west of Kumasi, is the capital of the Brong Ahafo region and although on my arrival it was a small town, it lay in the heart of the cocoa and kola nut-producing area and thus was a busy and prosperous place. I was to manage the small bank, with a staff of seven or eight, and have a supervisory role over the only other bank in the region, another BBWA branch in Berekum, twenty miles away. That branch was managed by Mr. Karikari, the only local bank manager in the country and so far as I know the first ever.

Sunyani branch was situated in a two-storey building set back from the main Kumasi-Sunyani road, with the branch on the ground floor and my quarters above. The living area was reached by a long staircase at the rear of the building. On the occasions of the visits of a travelling cinema the staircase served as a viewing stand for an assembled throng who preferred to see the film backwards rather than pay a few pence to view it correctly projected on a large sheet stretched out in the yard of the Palm Hotel next door, owned by Moses Adu, who soon became my friend. The staircase gave entry to the main living and dining room. A bathroom and a kitchen were situated at one end of the main room and at the other end two bedrooms. There was no running water or electricity and the bathroom sported a "thunder box" that was removed nightly.

From the handbasin and bath the water ran into channels in the concrete floor and then through a short pipe stuck horizontally through the wall so that the water cascaded one storey down to the path below. I soon learned, after hearing a startled shout, that by straining a little I could keep my big toe on the hole for the bath plug and have my head out of the window so that I could time the release of water to avoid soaking anyone passing below.

Unless rain from the roof had filled the water tank at the back of the building, water for the bath and for drinking came from the Tano River and was rolled most of the way in a forty-four imperial gallon drum. Drinking water, of course, had to be boiled and poured into a two-part canister and filtered from the top canister to the one below through stone candles. Jackson had to learn to press my shirts with a large iron, the top of which opened to receive glowing charcoal. In the kitchen there was a kerosene-fuelled refrigerator, which, unless carefully tended, spewed black smoke that stained the ceiling. Lighting was provided by paraffin lamps with mantles that also needed to be looked after with care. Many an evening the lamp hissing on a six-foot stand behind my chair would lull me to sleep over my books, of which I had a wonderful supply. Before leaving Kumasi, for a £1 annual fee, I had collected from the library a large wooden box containing fifty books of my selection. At intervals I would receive a postcard giving notice of the impending visit of the library van and asking me to advise the librarian of any book, author or subject in which I was interested so that she could try to provide an appropriate selection. When the van arrived I was able to exchange some or all of my fifty books. What a wonderful service it was.

The bank below the living quarters was very simple and consisted of a large space divided into customer and staff areas and at one end a manager's office. At the other end there was a stationery store with most of the stationery in a large heap in the middle of the floor. In my spare time I built wooden shelves. Ranged around the walls of the staff area behind the counter, in the absence of a strongroom, stood five large Chatwood Milner safes, each about five feet high, in which the books and the cash were kept. When it came time to hand over to my successor I told him, 'I have five different combinations. But it was a pain at the beginning to remember which one went with which safe. I think it would be okay to have one or at most two combinations.'

'That is not necessary,' he replied. 'I have a system. Recurring decimals. So five will be fine.'

I had no idea what that meant and thought no more of it until several years later I met his successor and happened to mention the recurring decimals, to which the response was, 'The idiot had every safe set on ten, twenty, ten, twenty.'

On the first morning I occupied my new office the local Catholic priest, Father Pete Loosen, came to see me to ask if I played bridge. When I said I did we agreed that he would pick me up that evening. Later in the morning a young Dutchman arrived to make the same enquiry and when I said I played but that I had a game with Father Loosen, the Dutchman was delighted. He and his wife and the priest were the only three bridge players in Sunyani and they were desperate for a fourth. Father Loosen was a brilliant bridge player, the best I ever met, but the young Dutch couple fought with each other after every hand. It was a nightmare and they wanted to play several evenings a week which is why, after Sunyani, I never again admitted to being able to play bridge. In any case I have long forgotten all that Pete Loosen taught me.

Sunyani branch usually paid out more cash than was deposited. In the cocoa season the growers withdrew and took to Kumasi or Accra the money for their crop that had been credited to their accounts by wire transfer. As a result, I was obliged to go to Kumasi at least once or twice each month to replenish my supply of cash. This involved hiring a lorry and arranging for a policeman to accompany me. I would ensure the cashier had balanced and would lock up the cash and books as quickly as I could after closing time at 1pm and set off for Kumasi with the policeman in the lorry. The roads were not what they probably are now and I would be lucky if I could get to Kumasi branch much before 5pm.

The bank staff there would get everything ready while I rushed to the nearby Kingsway Stores, round which I scampered trying to fill a trolley with whatever food and supplies I thought I would need for the next several weeks.

Arriving back in Sunyani in the dark, tired and hungry, I would have to get from the bank the key for the specie boxes, unlock the chain that held the boxes together, move them into the bank and open each one and pack the contents into the safes, all by the light of a couple of kerosene lamps. While I was doing this I was trying not to offend the policeman, the watchnight and any who happened to be passing, all of whom wanted to assist. I was never happy until at first light the next morning, with nobody looking on, I opened the safes one by one and counted everything, usually about £150,000. Although there is a variety of ways to calculate today's value of a 1956 pound, an approximate estimate of the current value of my cash would be well over £3 million. That was a lot of money for a twenty-one year old to be looking after under his sole custody.

In Sunyani, sitting on a low stool in the yard behind the bank, I learned to play a game called Wari (also spelled in different ways, such as Oware and Owari) which is one of many ancient games in the Mancala family. Wari is played on a wooden board with two rows of six holes containing beans or seeds. The objective is to capture seeds from the opponent's side of the board. In Sunyani the game was played at high speed and was not a game of chance. The more skilful player who could make the mathematical calculations swiftly in his head usually won. In February 1980 I was in Antigua at the airport, waiting on a plane. A young lady was selling caps, trinkets and Wari boards. I said to her, 'Come on. I'll play you.'

We played. She was slow and not very good, but at the end of the game she said, 'So, you live in Antigua.'

'No, I don't, and this is my very first visit to the island.'

'Then how come you play so well? Antigua is the only place this game is played.'

It astonished the young lady to know that I had learned in Africa to play what is almost a national sport in Antigua.

Another experience of the yard behind the bank in Sunyani was a test I felt obliged to pass. After rain a particularly large sausage fly would appear in droves. A large enamel basin would be filled with water and a kerosene lamp with a mantle placed carefully in the middle. The sausage flies, attracted by the light, flew into the lamp and dropped into the water. The wings having fallen off, the bodies would be scooped out and set briefly on a pan over a hot fire. The roasted and now crisp morsels would be declared 'fine chop' and offered to a young European to see what kind of man he was. He passed the test, but do not ask him about the taste. The 'fine chop' was swallowed too quickly to notice. I have recently seen articles suggesting that the nutritional value of food of this kind is sufficient to warrant a concerted effort to promote such dining.

There was one other young bachelor in Sunyani, Peter Wells, an English engineer a few years older than I who was in charge of the roads in the district. Recognising that we would probably drive each other crazy if we were together too often, we usually met one evening each week and on Saturdays for curry lunch; one week at my place and the next at his. The challenge became to see which of our cooks could make the hottest curry and which of us would give in first. Both being equally competitive I think it ended in a draw, with us both stripped to the waist, dripping sweat, with Peter drinking Heineken beer and I downing copious amounts of orange juice.

My twenty-second birthday was celebrated in Sunyani, quietly and by myself. Despite my age, or perhaps because of it, I took my role of bank manager very seriously and I remember an incident that made me proud and which convinced me that I really was what I thought I should be – a resource for and at the service of the community. Hasn't banking changed? Early one Sunday morning a young man appeared at my door, at the top of the long steps. I had not met him before and after inviting him in and supplying him with a bottle of Heineken beer I asked what I could do for him. He explained that he was to be the best man at a wedding the following weekend and had to make a speech.

'Yes,' said I, hesitating, 'and…'

'Well, Bank Manager, I have come to ask you to write the speech for me.'

And together we wrote it. And after he left I never saw him again. I was delighted to think that the locals might view me as somebody who was there to lend a helping hand with whatever modest skills I had.

There were about ten European households in Sunyani and the reader may have detected that I was probably over-serious about my role as bank manager. As a result, when a middle-aged Scottish couple came to the bank, by appointment, to ask my advice, I was not surprised. Nor did it seem to me in any way strange that a middle-aged couple would ask for advice from a twenty-two year old. After all, I was a bank manager. Where else would they go for advice? They had a good-looking teenage daughter, visiting from Scotland, and they explained that they were worried that she was seeing too much of a fortyish single Englishman; well, single as far as anybody knew. He worked for the Public Works Department and owned a red Karmann Ghia sports car, the Porsche of the poor man. What should they do to distract their daughter from this unsuitable association? I don't remember what advice I gave, but I gave it seriously, as a good bank manager should. It was several years before it occurred to me in a flash of inspiration that they had not wanted advice. They had wanted me to court their daughter. But at least they could have invited me to dinner.

Not long after my twenty-second birthday I suffered greatly from an attack of dengue fever, also known as break bone fever, which is caused by one of four different but related viruses spread by the bite of mosquitoes, most commonly the female Aedes aegypti, distinguished by its markings of alternate black and white horizontal stripes; not that you are likely to see the stripes as you take a swipe at the thing biting your leg, far less be able to detect the parts that might tell if it is male or female. If something is biting don't hesitate; swipe, even though probably it is now too late. Of course I slept under a mosquito net, but in those days we did not have insecticide-treated nets, which are estimated to be twice as effective as untreated nets. Most evenings I sat reading by the light of a kerosene lamp, from time to time squirting Flit from a small tin barrel-like contraption with a long handle containing a pump. In the market or in the houses of other people it was not always easy to avoid mosquitoes. Doug and Lorna at the Forestry School on occasion hosted elegant dinner parties. One arrived neatly attired and bearing a pillowcase into which, under the dinner table, one's legs were inserted to protect vulnerable ankles from the mosquitoes.

The dengue started with a high fever and a couple of days later a red rash appeared over most of my body. The symptoms I remember most were the severe headaches and waking in the middle of the night to the sound of loud yells, only to discover that it was I who was making the noise. The Anglo-Indian doctor at Sunyani Government Hospital told me that there was no specific treatment for dengue and gave me painkillers and put me on a nightly regimen of Horlicks, a malted milk drink. I was very weak for a few days and had to be helped down to the bank in my dressing gown by Jackson and the bank messenger so that I could open the safes for business, after which, for at least a couple of days, I sat in the office half-asleep and hoping that nobody would report my illness to the district manager in Accra. It was easier to carry on than to contemplate trying to hand over to a replacement. Fortunately, dengue is not life-threatening, unless one catches dengue haemorrhagic fever, which is a separate disease caused by the same type of virus but which has much more severe symptoms. My ailment passed in a week or ten days but I lost some weight and I lost a good deal more during a severe bout of malaria not long before I went on home leave. Once again the mosquito was to blame, but this time the Anopheles was the culprit and again only the female, which feeds on blood and becomes a transmitter of malaria some days after biting an infected subject. The much nicer male feeds on plant nectar. Malaria symptoms occur anything from eight to twenty-five days after becoming infected and perhaps even longer if anti-malarial drugs have been taken, as I had been doing faithfully and without missing a day. I experienced classic bouts of coldness followed by high fever, shivering and sweating together with quite severe joint pain. The doctor decided I should change from a daily dose of Paludrine to a daily dose of Mepacrine. As I have explained previously, Mepacrine colours the skin yellow and, although I did not suffer gastrointestinal discomfort, I did look rather unusual, a couple of stones or so lighter, with my yellow skin and long hair as the result of the barber who cut European hair being unavailable in Sunyani because he had gone to his cocoa farm.

For the election that was the last hurdle before independence I was honoured to be asked to assist with the counting of votes. I sat at a long table and with many others I examined the ballot papers and counted and bundled them. I can report that everything in Sunyani was done in a most carefully supervised and correct way.

I had been appointed a member of the committee charged with organising a dance which was to take place at the Palm Hotel, next door to the bank. I must have neglected to tell Jackson, my cook/steward, because, clearly, he did not expect me to attend the function. As a result, presumably he was very surprised, although he showed no sign of it, when I spotted him on the dance floor, partnered by a young lady. Jackson was elegantly attired in his Anthony Eden hat and my thick London suit with the trouser legs neatly folded up at the bottom to more suitably accommodate his shorter stature. I nodded to him as we passed and without a word we shuffled on to the beat of The Highlife. The next day I dashed the suit to Jackson, in truth glad to be rid of it.

Time passed and I was told I was to proceed on leave in November 1956 at the end of my first eighteen-month tour. This worried me a little because on 29th October 1956 Britain, France and Israel had attacked Egypt in response to Gamel Abdul Nasser's nationalisation of the Suez Canal in July 1956. I wondered if on landing in the UK I might be recalled to the army. After my two years' full-time service I was required to spend seven years in the part-time reserve. I had been assigned to the Paratroop Regiment in Glasgow and although I had reported there I had never served because I had left for London a couple of weeks later. I was relieved when, under intense American and international pressure, the British prime minister, Sir Anthony Eden, declared a ceasefire on 6th November 1956 and then resigned. Britain had been humiliated and I was very sorry for that but glad that my banking career was not to be interrupted.

In preparing for my departure from Sunyani I wondered what a good bank manager should do before going on leave. I borrowed Moses Adu's ancient green Rover car and toured the district. I interviewed chiefs and clerks of town councils, Lebanese store owners and anyone who could provide reliable information. I submitted a long report to the district manager in which I provided statistics on all the small towns in the area and then happily went on leave. I never received a reply or acknowledgement of my report.

Home Leave and Denmark

> There is nothing like returning to a place
> that remains unchanged to find the ways
> in which you yourself have altered.
>
> **Nelson Mandela**

At the end of my first tour I flew to London, where I was supposed to report to head office. But I landed on a bitterly cold day and was so inexperienced that I was off the plane, out of the airport and on a bus headed for central London before I realised that any slightly warmer clothing I had was still packed in a suitcase stowed in the bowels of the single-deck bus. I sat in the front seat facing a round heater but this and the newspapers stuffed inside my thin jacket were no protection against the draft howling through a door that did not close properly. When we came to the Knightsbridge terminal I got off, fished some additional clothing out of my suitcase and boarded another bus to take me back to the airport. From there I flew home to Glasgow, my parents and a warm bed. To hell with head office!

My mother was distraught when she saw how thin and yellow I was and shed a tear at the first sight of me. She was most surprised when, a few days later, I mentioned my return to West Africa. Of course I was going back. I was a Coaster and I loved Africa and everything about my life and work there.

It was during the first few days of that leave that I acquired a habit not to be broken for the next twenty-four years. The family was at breakfast and the letterbox rattled as the postman deposited some mail. Nobody moved and my mother remarked, 'That's funny. When you are not here,' she said, looking at me rather pointedly, 'when the postman comes we all rush to the door to see if there is a letter from you.'

I recalled receiving letters saying things like, 'We are so worried that we have not heard from you for so long,' and once even, 'If we do not hear from you soon I am going to telephone the bank in London to ask if they have news of you.'

I cringed and resolved to write home every week, which I did until my mother died in 1980. She replied weekly although, because of mail delays, she was often responding to letters I had written two or three weeks earlier. We used folding blue airmail forms which, in my case, had the advantage of having a predetermined amount of space and thus providing an acceptable excuse for brevity. Nowadays, of course, we would be in contact by email and Skype, but in fourteen years in Africa I never telephoned home and the only call I received from the United Kingdom was when I was in Nigeria just after the birth of my daughter in Glasgow. The line was so bad I was left wondering if I had one daughter or two. This was not resolved, in my mind at least, until the next day when I went to the Post Office and had them dig out the telegram waiting there for me.

After a couple of weeks at home, during which I purchased suitable clothing, I reported to head office in London. As I had confidently expected I was offered another eighteen-month contract and it was confirmed I would receive my full pay during my three and one half month leave. I then flew to Copenhagen to be greeted at the airport by a girl whom I had met when, at age sixteen, I had visited Copenhagen with a group from the Boys' Brigade. I had been matched with the girl's brother but because the family had three children there was no room for me to be billeted with them. I had been based with a widow at a house across the street. To the amusement of my parents, quite innocently I sent home a postcard telling them that although I was supposed to have been billeted with the Ls I was sleeping with Mrs. M.

At sixteen I fell in love with Denmark, the Danes, Copenhagen, the weather, breakfast in the garden every morning and tea without milk and sugar, as I have enjoyed it ever since. And of course I fell in love with the girl. We had corresponded for years and now here she was at the airport presenting me, to my embarrassment, with a large bunch of flowers; a Danish custom I believe. Despite my falling ill and spending several days in bed, the bed of the brother, now grown and departed from the family home, we had an enjoyable two weeks in Copenhagen with visits to Tivoli Gardens and a nightclub called the Giraffe where, because they insisted I order an alcoholic drink, I assembled a row of untouched small cocktails. From Copenhagen we left for London where we spent a few days seeing the usual sights and going to the theatre in the evenings. Then home to Glasgow to my parents and Christmas. She was a beautiful girl. I have her photograph still carefully preserved, but somehow things just did not click and although we met again for a week in London on my next leave I think we both knew the relationship was not going to work. And it did not. We never saw each other again after that second leave.

One very noticeable change in Glasgow in late 1956 and early 1957 was television. Although BBC Scotland commenced television broadcasts in June 1952 I do not think I saw a television set in Glasgow before I left to join The Black Watch in January 1953. On my return to Glasgow at the end of 1956 every house sported a television set, often with a screen only about twelve inches square, but nonetheless commanding the rapt attention of the family. I remember calling on friends to be welcomed with, 'Are you home? It's great to see you. Come away in. Sit here. This will be over soon.'

And then I sat watching through the next two hours of television with hardly a comment from families for which, only a few years before, conversation and sometimes music had been the usual evening entertainment. Perhaps it was just as well because I learned soon enough that I could not talk about my life in West Africa or about most of my experiences without raising doubts about some things and perhaps everything I said. The doubts were usually unspoken but subtly expressed nonetheless; 'Oh aye, is that a fact? Imagine that! Can you believe that Jimmy?'

In Accra at the beginning of my first tour, in common with all my colleagues, I had often dressed up in my dinner jacket and black tie in order to be correctly attired when visiting the Accra Club. Like most of the others I wore a standard black dinner jacket but I had been most impressed by Arthur Ball's white dinner jacket. I am not sure now if it conformed to what was considered acceptable and proper but I thought it looked smart. So, when in London, I ordered a made-to-measure white sharkskin dinner jacket. I picked it up from the tailor on the way back from Copenhagen and was very disappointed to note that it had finger marks and looked grubby. I complained but as I was leaving for Glasgow the next day there wasn't much that could be done about it. Once in Glasgow I dropped it off at the dry cleaners. When I handed in my ticket to collect what I thought was to become my treasured sharkskin dinner jacket I was astonished to hear the young lady behind the counter say, in broad Glaswegian of course, as she handed me a small square brown paper parcel tied with string, 'Here's yer painter's jaicket.'

My sharkskin dinner jacket was ruined and I never wore it. If you do not believe the small print on the back of the ticket the dry cleaner gives you, try arguing from West Africa with a dry cleaner in Glasgow.

Ghana,
Second and Third Tours

The Moving Finger writes and, having writ,
Moves on: nor all they Piety nor Wit
Shall lure it back to cancel half a Line,
Nor all thy Tears wash out a word of it.

Omar Khayyám

I arrived in what was now Ghana on 10th March 1957, having just missed the great excitement of Independence Day on the 6th. People were singing, 'Ghana, you've got your freedom.' It might have been worth going back early to take part in the celebrations. I was lucky to have arrived safely. At Tripoli the plane had made several attempts to land, coming in as usual but then suddenly climbing and circling before making another attempt. Eventually we dumped fuel in the sea before approaching the runway once again and this time making what seemed like a normal landing. If we were told what the problem had been I now forget but I know I thought of the crash at Tripoli less than two years earlier which resulted in the death of fifteen people.

Although I continued to enjoy my life and work, my second and third tours turned out to be disappointing in some ways. I was shuffled around a number of jobs in various places, filling in and relieving people here and there. No doubt I was very quickly gathering a great deal of exposure in many different situations, some more senior than my experience warranted.

In Kumasi for a few months, I was responsible for the operations of the large main branch while the regular accountant concentrated on changing the routine from hand-written bound ledgers to loose-leaf ledgers posted on NCR machines. I remember my Luddite argument that we would never be able to balance anything because the loose leaves would be misplaced and lost. So far as I know that never happened but I did love the security of the large bound ledgers. Mark Kurlansky, in his book *Paper* said, 'There is always some loss associated with a new technology'.

On 14th July 1958 Ghana issued its own currency to replace the notes and coins of the West African Currency Board. There was a long period in which both the old and new would be valid but an exchange of currency was a novel experience and people were anxious to get their hands on the new notes and coins featuring Dr. Nkrumah. Unknown to most was the huge panic there had been when, a few days before the scheduled release of the new notes, spelling errors had been discovered. The entire issue had to be destroyed, a new lot printed and a plane chartered to get the notes from the English printers to Accra in time. On the day they were released to the public I received a call for help from the manager of an Accra branch which was being overwhelmed by customers demanding to exchange old currency for new. I rushed over to lend a hand and found the tellers fully occupied dealing with throngs of people. The only thing I could do to help, I decided, was to exchange coins so that the tellers could handle only notes. I armed myself with bags of each denomination and a large basket. I told the customers to put stacks of coins each of a single denomination in front of them on the long counter. I matched each stack of old coins with a stack of new and swept the old into my basket. This really sped things up but there was a never-ending stream of customers with a crowd still inside the bank when the doors were closed at one o'clock. Once everyone had been served I turned my hand to sorting the huge piles of coins of various denominations all mixed together in several baskets. I used a coin-counting machine, foot peddled like Granny Johnston's sewing machine. At the end I wasn't too far out.

For several months I served as the accountant of the main Accra branch. This post was usually occupied by a much more senior officer who certainly was paid a great deal more than I was earning, on top of which he was in receipt of a special allowance because he was married. I have always felt that having to pay a special allowance to anyone who is married is a clear admission that the salary of single men is barely enough to live on and certainly not enough to support two people. When I suggested I might be given an allowance for taking on this new responsibility so early in my career I was told to consider myself lucky to have been given the opportunity to learn so much.

One afternoon I was passing through the mail department, upstairs, exercising my "management by walking about" philosophy. I could not help but notice the most recent expatriate to have arrived, a small pipe-smoking former short service army officer. He was on his hands and knees stabbing at the dusty wooden plank floor with what appeared to be an empty round pipe tobacco tin.

'What on earth are you doing?' I asked him.

'I am trying to catch a cockroach.'

'For God's sake, just put your foot on it.'

'Oh no! I want it alive.'

'Why?'

'I am going to put it in the head office envelope to give these bastards in London a fright and let them see what we have to put up with out here.'

'And if it eats half the mail before it gets to London?'

'Oh, I never thought of that.'

It was the same young chap who forgot, or omitted, to show up in court to answer a charge related to his erratic driving. Sometime later two very large policemen arrived and marched him unceremoniously out of the bank. Mr. Haymes, still the manager, said I had better go and see what the problem was and what had to be done, since we had not been told why our diminutive colleague had been arrested. I went along to the police station and when I returned I reported to Mr. Haymes, 'It was all about a ticket he received. Something he did when driving that little red M.G. of his. He didn't show up for the court case.'

'Good Lord. Is he still in custody?'

'Oh no, sir. I got him out. I signed an assurance that he would show up on time for the next hearing.'

'Well,' said Mr. Haymes, 'I would never have taken on that responsibility. I would have let him rot in gaol.'

'Ah, sir, I did not take on any responsibility. I signed on behalf of the bank and if he does not show up next time I assume it will be the bank manager who will be in trouble.'

Mr. Haymes laughed and asked me to ensure that for his sake there were no further problems. I attended to his request with care.

One memorable incident started in March 1960 at the very end of my third tour of duty. The accountant of a branch in Accra fell sick, or so he said. I was sent to fill in for him. This was a branch with about fifty on the staff with a European manager and a European accountant. The term "accountant" did not mean that the incumbent possessed any formal accounting qualifications. The position involved responsibility for the day to day operations of the branch and this encompassed nearly everything except control of the cash strongroom and the granting and supervising of loans and overdrafts. Of course, the manager had overall responsibility.

On arrival at the branch I discovered that my predecessor had done little or nothing to ready the branch for the annual balance, a work-intensive exercise a couple of days away at the end of the month. I made a quick start on the preparations. At the end of a very long first day, after seven o'clock in the evening, I started what I intended to be my final task before locking up and going home. I was looking through the outgoing clearings. These were bundles of cheques paid into accounts with us during the day and drawn on accounts at other branches or banks. These were to be mailed to the appropriate up-country branches and the cheques drawn on Barclays Bank were to be presented to their Accra branch the next day. I was looking to make sure everything had been correctly addressed, listed on the right forms and, importantly, for anything that looked unusual. And I found something unusual. Three large cheques drawn on the same account with Barclays Bank in Accra had been paid in to the same account in our books. The cheques were for a total of over £160,000. In 1960 £160,000 was a very large amount and probably the equivalent of well over £3 million today. So I found the appropriate ledger in the book safe and looked up the account. There in the credit column, correctly recorded, was the deposit of the three cheques. To my horror, the balance of the account was less than £5,000. This meant we had already given credit for the three cheques although we would not know if they were good until Barclays Bank honoured them the next day. As I felt certain I would, I found as I looked back in time at the daily entries on the account, large cheques had been drawn out of the account each day and covered on the same day by equally large cheques deposited to the account. This was a classic case of kiting, which had been going on for several weeks. We were on the wrong end of it and the customer had our £160,000.

That night I drafted a memorandum for the tellers and the ledger keepers instructing that deposit slips and ledgers should be appropriately marked to indicate when cheques credited to accounts in our books had not yet cleared. This, of course, was the standard procedure that should have been followed. First thing the next morning I had my memorandum typed and a copy given to each teller and ledger keeper and a copy placed in the appropriate branch file. When the manager arrived I presented my findings to him. To this day I do not know if he knew before I told him what had happened on his watch but his complacence and unworried response suggested to me that he had known for some time but did not know what to do about it. Receiving no guidance from the manager I suggested that I would arrange to have the Barclays cheques presented specially to see if we could get Barclays to honour them before we had to honour the cheques drawn on the account in our books that doubtless had been paid in to Barclays. I did that, but Barclays were not to be caught and returned the cheques with the notation "Refer to Drawer". If confirmation had been needed that we were in trouble, this was it. I suggested that the manager report the affair to the district manager immediately. This he promised to do and a few days later I was content to hand the reins back to my now recovered colleague. I heard no more about the matter until my return from leave to start my fourth tour.

I had decided to buy a new car on home delivery. This arrangement would enable me to buy a car in the UK or Europe duty free, provided I brought it back to Ghana where I would have to pay import duty calculated on a used car. This meant I would have a car for my three months' home leave but would have to come back to Ghana by sea. In order to raise part of the purchase price I had to sell my trusty Ford Zephyr in which I had competed in several rallies. I did no more than put a notice on the car and was pleased when a couple of days later a Russian gentleman, an employee of the Russian Embassy he said, came along to the bank, looked at the car parked outside and bought it. I begged him to take it for a test drive but he said it was not necessary. Very strange, but he paid me there and then on the street in crisp new Bank of England £5 notes which was even more strange. I signed the required document, gave him the keys and went back to work. Two weeks later he was at my desk in the bank.

'There is something wrong with the transmission,' he said.

'There was nothing wrong with it when you bought the car,' I told him.

'I have to get my money back or I will be in a lot of trouble with my boss.'

'Well, I am really sorry about that but even if I wanted to give you your money back I cannot do it. The money is now in Germany; part of the purchase price for an Opel Rekord.'

I never saw him or heard from him again. I hope he is not still in a gulag somewhere.

I arrived in Frankfurt about 4am on Tuesday 19th April, 1960 and made my way to the Opel factory. I sat outside waiting patiently and trying not to fall asleep. When the factory door was rolled back I could see my car standing there in all its glory ready to be delivered. And delivered it was with German efficiency and a minimum of fuss. I set off, driving north and feeling very pleased with myself, although deadly tired. On the previous Saturday I had been driving all night in the 24-hour Rally of Ghana as a member of the Ford team in a Ford supplied car. I had spent most of Sunday night discussing with my team every move we had made or should have made to improve our fourth-place finish, which, with two Ford cars behind us, was enough to win the team prize for Ford. On Monday night I had been on the plane chatting and sleeping little.

I drove steadily north from Frankfurt all day until about seven in the evening. Exhausted and too tired to be hungry, I stopped in a small town at what appeared to be a pub with a *zimmer frei* sign. The landlady questioned me several times about whether or not I was alone. I did not understand much of her German or why my being alone seemed to bother her. I thought it might be because I had not brought any luggage from the car when I went to enquire about a room. She still seemed sceptical when I told her, 'Mein koffer… is in… mein auto.'

All became clear when I was directed upstairs into a dingy room with a rumpled bed that turned out to be still warm from previous occupants. I was too tired to care and slept soundly. In the morning I drove north through Holland in order to cross the Afsluitdijk, the marvellous twenty-mile-long causeway that dams the fresh water Zuiderzee from the North Sea on the other side. The road on top of the causeway is now a four-lane highway but in 1960 it was a two-lane road and crossing involved driving about twenty-five feet above the water with an ocean on either side.

After the thrill of the Afsluitdijk I was keen to get home to Glasgow. I came down through Holland and Belgium and crossed into France where the first channel port was Dunkirk. There were still signs of the war and the town looked uninviting. I was soon on the ferry and on the road home, to be welcomed once more by my parents and sisters.

On 18th May 1960 the final of the European Cup was held at Hampden Park stadium in Glasgow where Real Madrid played Eintracht Frankfurt. I decided to attend and take my father and his older brother, Uncle Willie. Driving to Hampden in the Opel Rekord with the German number plates, by sheer chance, we found ourselves behind the German bus conveying the Eintracht team to the match. As we neared Hampden other cars were being diverted by policemen to remote parking areas but we were waved on behind the bus. Presumably we were mistaken for part of the German entourage and we ended up inside the stadium grounds. A large policeman leaned in the front passenger window and, apparently not noticing that the steering wheel was on the wrong side for a German car, asked in broad Glaswegian if the driver could speak English. Uncle Willie, always quick, said that he would translate. We were told we could park 'right over there'. Over there was next to the team entrance. We duly parked and waited until the helpful policeman was otherwise engaged. Having found an alternative entrance, we arrived at our seats without being arrested for trespassing.

The 1960 final, widely regarded as one of the greatest games of football ever played, was watched by a crowd of 127,621. The match was initially in doubt because the German Football Association had banned their clubs from taking part in matches with any team of which Ferenc Puskas was a member. Puskas had accused the West German team of using drugs in 1954 and he had been obliged to make a written apology so that the match could go ahead. Presumably Puskas was pleased that his team, Real Madrid, won by seven goals to three and doubly pleased to have scored four of the seven goals. The 1960 match was a marvellous football spectacle and the Scottish crowd was appreciative of the skill displayed by the players on both teams, which did not prevent some of those sitting near us having a bit of fun at the expense of the Eintracht player Dieter Stinka.

When Great-aunt Annie, the widowed sister of my grandmother, was sixty-eight she remarried and she and her husband came from America to Scotland for their honeymoon. I took them on a tour of Scotland in the Opel Rekord. Among the places we visited were Loch Lomond (of course), Gleneagles, Oban, Iona and Fingal's Cave and I remember the spry sixty-eight-year-old Annie refusing to be intimidated by the leap from the steamer to the tender which was to take us ashore. She and her husband were very proud of their Scottish heritage, frequently reminding me that they were really "Scatch". After their return to America they wrote to thank me for the tour in my "wee car". I have just looked up the Opel Rekord in Wikipedia where it is described as a large family car.

Although I had enjoyed my leave, I was not sorry when the

time came to drive to Liverpool and watch the Opel being loaded onto the *MV Accra*, the Elder Dempster ship that was to take us both back to Takoradi, at that time Ghana's major port. Many of my colleagues enjoyed travelling by boat because the three and a half months' leave started on arrival in the UK and ended on departure from the UK. Since the trip between Liverpool and Takoradi took twelve days, going both ways by sea could add more than three weeks to the leave. However, I made the trip back to Africa by sea only twice in fourteen years. I was always keen to get back to work.

Sunyani Again
and Ivory Coast

Serious illness does not bother me for long
because I am too inhospitable a host.
Albert Schweitzer

My trip on the *MV Accra*, my first sea voyage other than a short crossing of the North Sea to Denmark when I was sixteen, was a great experience. I still have the telegram from my parents, which was delivered to me on board, wishing me a great trip and "a happy tour". Even they were becoming familiar with the lingo of the expatriate. The *MV Accra*, 11,643 gross tons, carried 283 passengers in single and two-berth roomy cabins but without air-conditioning until 1961. She had a swimming pool, a sports deck and spacious public rooms as well as a bar that was listed as opening for fifteen minutes at an unearthly hour in the very early morning. I determined to be there at least once to see who it was that could not survive without alcoholic sustenance until 11am, but I never wakened in time.

We set sail on 21st July 1960. On board were Jim (Hamish) Gilbert and Doug Edwards, both of whom I knew well as colleagues, and another bank employee and his wife bound for Freetown.

Naturally the men made up a foursome for cards, deck games and for late night drinking, but with me still on orange juice. Our married Freetown colleague was somewhat handicapped in the late night drinking department. As we sailed south we were glad to note the weather getting better and we began to enjoy the pool and deck sports as well as gambling on the ship's daily run. The extent of the previous day's run was announced each morning and whoever had guessed closest to the actual number of miles sailed picked up most of the wagers, which could be quite substantial. I don't remember if any of us ever won but I still have a small shaving mirror with which I was presented for picking up the largest number of pennies from the bottom of the pool. I had nearly drowned in my determination to win. The food on board was excellent and it was on the Accra that I first heard of and learned to enjoy kedgeree, European-style with fish. Not being senior enough to be seated with any of the officers we young bankers were pleased to be left to linger over long meals at our own table. After 1,656 miles from Liverpool we tied up at the dock in Las Palmas in the Canary Islands where we were able to spend some hours ashore. The five of us visited the fertile volcanic crater and some enjoyed a drink at the luxurious Santa Catalina Hotel. Another 1,345 miles brought us to Freetown, the capital of Sierra Leone, where we amused ourselves by throwing coins over the railing and watching the nimble youngsters diving from canoes to catch them. Sometimes they would snare a coin under water and then they would break the surface, wet face and white teeth glistening in the sun. With a triumphant smile they would wave the coin high for all to see. Too quickly we covered the next 856 miles and arrived at Takoradi on 2nd August 1960. My heart was in my mouth as I watched the Opel being strapped in a sling, raised from the hold and lowered slowly to the wharf by a crane, fortunately without incident. On the drive to Accra I rejoiced at being back in Ghana and looked forward to learning of my new assignment.

In Accra I reported to John Haymes, now with the title of acting executive director in place of the district manager, who had recently been re-titled and who was then on leave. To my surprise I was asked about the kiting incident. The branch manager had failed to report the matter as he had faithfully promised me he would do and the loss, for loss it was, came to light only when he handed over to his successor. I was challenged about my own failure to report the matter. I explained that the manual stated that the duty of the accountant was to support the manager. I felt I had done this by finding the problem on my very first day at the branch, by promulgating clear instructions dated the next day, by bringing the matter to the attention of the manager and by obtaining his promise, more than once, to report what had happened. I said also that I had expected that my refusal to sign the monthly overdraft report would cause questions to be asked by the executive director's staff and I concluded by saying that if I had felt that the funds could have been recovered I would certainly have done more. But, as I had been certain that this was not going to happen, I left it to the manager to make his report rather than snitching on him. Mr. Haymes appeared to accept my reasoning and I was very relieved that he had been the one to question me. Nothing more was said except that I was told to get myself to Sunyani to take over as area manager. I was absolutely delighted to know I was to be based there once again and this time to be responsible for banks in Sunyani, Berekum, Wenchi, Dormaa Ahenkro and Tepa as well as a one-day-a-week sub-branch in Techiman. A brand new bank and a stand-alone two-bedroom house had been built in Sunyani and I was to have a driver and a bank Land Rover in which to tour my area. Perhaps the report I had submitted at the end of my first tour had been useful and had resulted in the branches in Wenchi, Dormaa Ahenkro and Techiman being opened, but no-one ever said so.

The work in the Sunyani area was greatly to my liking and I was comfortable in my new house with running water pumped from a cistern fed from the roof and electricity provided by a generator. Jackson had decided that he could not leave his wife in Accra and so in Sunyani I was looked after by Yama and his young wife. The badminton court in the garden of the bank house was used by several of the local expatriates and I was able to play any day I was back in time from my travels. This did not happen often. My routine consisted of leaving home at about seven each morning and travelling to one or more of the branches to count the cash, authorise the loans and advise on any problems that might have arisen since my last visit. As I passed villages along the way children would wave and shout, 'Bank obroni' (bank white man). Often I was not back in Sunyani until 4 or 5pm, and after a shower to rid myself of the red laterite dust from the unpaved roads and a quick bite to eat for a late lunch I would go to my office in Sunyani branch. There I dealt with the mail and any messages that might have come in from Accra or London or the branches I supervised. The days were long and the travelling uncomfortable but I loved the work. All the branches in my area, including Sunyani branch, were managed by Ghanaians and I was happy to feel that I was helping them to handle their new and unaccustomed responsibilities.

At a branch I was presented with an application for a small loan.

'What do you think?' I asked the manager.

'We could try him.'

'Well, I think we need a bit more analysis than that,' I replied.

I needed a way to encourage the branch managers not to put the entire onus on me and to take some personal responsibility. I wrote to each one giving them a personal lending limit of £50 and I advised the executive director, copy to London as usual, giving the reason for what I had done but saying clearly that I would take responsibility for all the decisions the managers made. By return I received a rocket from the executive director using words like "shirking my responsibilities". Did anyone ever read what I had written? Which assistant in his office was drafting such nonsense for his signature? And why was he signing it? A couple of weeks later a letter from head office in London commended me and increased the manager's limit to £100 and stated that their decisions would not be my responsibility. Soon thereafter the executive director instructed that all mail for London was to be routed through his office in Accra.

The Brong Ahafo region is in a forested area and some of the roads I travelled were largely narrow cuts through the trees. In the rainy season it was not unusual to find the road blocked by a tree, the shallow roots of which had given way to a downpour of tropical rain. The Land Rover was equipped with a winch, chains and a large axe. If the downed tree was small it was sometimes possible to cut through or haul the tree partially out of the way. On my trips I was often carrying cash, taking it to a branch that paid out more cash than it took in or bringing cash back from a branch holding a surplus. Sometimes a tree blocking the road could not be cut or moved and traffic would have to wait for the Public Works Department to come along with the proper equipment to clear the way. On one occasion on the way back to Sunyani I found a solution to avoid being stuck until late at night or even all night. I exchanged vehicles with somebody stuck on the other side and who agreed to meet back at the same spot the next day once the road had been cleared. This meant moving the boxes of cash from the Land Rover over the fallen tree to the replacement vehicle. Volunteers from among those stranded were quick to assist and although I was aware that everyone knew who I was and probably had guessed the contents of the boxes I did not worry or feel in any danger. I wonder if things are the same today.

Notwithstanding the fact that I never felt threatened when travelling with cash, the chief at Wenchi seemed to think I needed a little protection. He organised a ceremony at which I was presented with a special stick about two feet long, partially covered with leather and nicely adorned with raffia, strips of fur and small pockets of red cloth. The cap of an aspirin bottle as a ferrule at the end of the stick detracted somewhat from the other handiwork. I was told that the pockets of cloth contained special medicine. The stick, if I looked after it properly, would ensure that no bullet would ever penetrate my body. That stick has worked perfectly as promised for over sixty years and still has a place of honour in my home. Fortunately I had left it in Glasgow together with some other Ghana memorabilia when I moved to Nigeria, so it was not lost in Biafra with nearly everything else we owned.

A Sunday trip I made with friends on a couple of occasions during my time at Sunyani was to a town called Agnibilékrou in Ivory Coast. It was about seventy miles from Sunyani, passing Berekum and Dormaa Ahenkro on the way. The roads were good as far as Dormaa Ahenkro but soon after passing through the border control we were in no man's land and on a single track through the forest between the two borders. If a vehicle came in the opposite direction both stopped to decide how and where we would pass and on which side, because in Ghana, in those days, since changed, we drove on the left while in Ivory Coast driving was on the right. There was at least one crossing of a stream bridged by small logs, but the logs were laid the long way over the stream and one had to drive carefully along their length guided by disembarked passengers. The attraction that caused us to make this hazardous trip was a small restaurant, circular with a thatched roof so low that one had to stoop to pass under. The establishment was run by a French lady. Her shy teenage daughter would serve us. That was attraction enough but added to that was the food. In Agnibilékrou we could observe the difference between the French colonial system and the British. We Brits were all on short-term contracts and went home on leave regularly at the expense of our employers. It was extremely unusual for a Brit to be allowed to buy land or to settle in Ghana, although my Dutch brother-in-law and his Ghanaian wife were able to do so. The lady who owned the restaurant in Agnibilékrou lived there with her daughter and her husband, who ran a small garage, and they were saving up for a trip to France that they might make once in ten years. Côte d'Ivoire was their home.

One Saturday, just after lunch in Sunyani, I received a telephone call from the manager of Tepa branch, some forty miles away. He was in the process of handing over to an incoming manager and they were having trouble with the Chatwood-Milner five-foot-high cash safe. It was open but locked with the locking bars extended and they could not unlock it in order to close the door. I advised them to take the books out of the book safe and lock the cash in it; I would be with them in not more than a couple of hours. I had to retrieve from the Sunyani branch strongroom the sealed envelope in which the manager of Tepa had written the combinations for his safes when he had taken responsibility for the branch. When I arrived at Tepa I was told that the incoming manager had been about to practise before attempting to set a new combination and he had spun the combination dial, fortunately with the door open. Had the door been closed there would have been no way to open it except to try every possible combination, which might have taken years. The alternative would have been to drill the safe but it was unlikely that could have been done in Ghana.

After many attempts neither the outgoing nor the incoming manager could break the combination. Considering myself an old hand with safes I had no doubt that I would be able to open the door.

'What are the numbers?'

I made two attempts and proved to my satisfaction that the numbers I had been given did not work. On the envelope I had brought from Sunyani I broke the ubiquitous red sealing wax seal with the bank's official imprint applied with a brass stamp. We used that imprint on everything that needed sealing. The numbers in the envelope were the same as I had been given by the manager.

'You must have used the change key and changed the numbers,' I insisted.

They both swore they had not done so and that the change key had never been inserted. Eventually the outgoing manager confessed that he was in fear of the whole process and that in the two years he had been in Tepa he had never broken the combination after it had been set for him by his predecessor. The safe had been secured only by the two keys.

'Now we have a problem,' I told the two rather despondent managers.

'Clearly the numbers we have are not the numbers of the combination, but don't worry. I'll take the back off the door and if the worst comes to the worst I'll remove the tumblers, unlock them and set a new combination.'

It sounded simple but, disaster! The back of the door was so rusted that after sending for tools and spending an hour trying to turn the screws I admitted that there was no way I could open it. The unfortunate outgoing manager was in a sweat. He could see himself being dismissed and I confess I was a bit hard on him, mentioning the cost of shipping the safe or at least the door to England to have it opened. I sat down and thought for a few minutes. The numbers in the envelope were a basic progression, something like fifteen, twenty-five, thirty-five, forty-five; a dreadfully weak combination. The numbers for the book safe were a similar progression, and also had not been used during his tenure. But I proved that they at least did work. Unfortunately they did not work on the cash safe when I tried them. I figured that if I could find one number of the combination of the locked safe possibly I could guess the rest. I fiddled blindly with the change key through the small port in the back of the rusted door and eventually felt it slip home into one tumbler. This revealed a number on the dial on the front of the door. I tried for more numbers but could not get the change key to engage another tumbler. So after withdrawing the change key without turning it I took a guess at the remaining three numbers. I hit a home run on the very first try. The lock opened to relief all round, tinged almost with unbelief on the part of the two managers. As I had been his supervisor and had failed to discover the manager's problem I felt a little responsible. I promised no further mention of the matter provided they each took from me a half hour instruction on combinations. They were pleased to do so and I learned to be on the spot in future before anyone attempted to change a combination.

Father Loosen, the Catholic priest, my bridge partner on my first sojourn in Sunyani, was still at his post and his sister worked in a mission hospital at Hwidiem, then about sixty miles away on paved roads. My modern map suggests that many of the laterite roads of my day have now been paved and made into secondary roads. These would make the journey from Sunyani to Hwidiem a good deal shorter. One evening, when I was hosting a dinner in the bank house for all the expatriate bachelors in town and the four of us, including Father Loosen, had retired to the sitting room for coffee, two young ladies arrived in a Volkswagen Beetle looking for the priest. At his residence they had been told he was at my house. One of the ladies was his sister, Mimi, who had recently returned from leave in Holland and had gifts from home for her brother. Mimi had brought with her for company on the journey a Dutch colleague who worked in the pharmacy in the mission hospital. The colleague was Ans, who impressed me with her flaming red hair and by the fact that she was the only person I ever saw in Africa wearing stylish elbow-length gloves. She had been in Ghana for a few months. Soon after, when my young American friends the Reeves, a married couple with three children, were throwing a small party I asked that Ans be invited and, of course, collected her and took her home. Ans became a frequent weekend visitor to the Reeves, which enabled us to get to know each other and to develop a relationship. I have always been sorry that the Reeves never knew that their kindness to me and to Ans eventually resulted in our marriage.

On my first tour in Sunyani I had heard of Jo Mattens. She was a tall strong Dutch woman who had trained as a midwife in Holland but had worked for the Catholic Mission in Gold Coast/Ghana for some years. Most of her time was spent as the only European in small clinics in very small towns in the Brong Ahafo region. During my second spell in Sunyani Jo was for a time stationed at the same hospital as Ans, so I got to know and admire this great lady. Some years later, when we were on leave in Holland, we met Jo. After fifteen or more years the mission had told her she was not suitable to work in Africa! You should understand that Jo knew her job and, by all accounts, did it extremely well. Probably she had told some young Dutch doctor, recently qualified and in Africa to practise on the locals, that he did not know what he was doing. Jo was frustrated. She disliked working in Holland and was considering an offer to go to East Africa with yet another mission. They were to pay her a few pounds a month and provide her with a place to stay. I remonstrated with her, telling her that she needed to earn enough to save for her old age. There was no way she could rely on any mission to look after her. Jo produced the papers for emigration to Australia, which she had considered, but she said there was no way she could fill them in. Jo's English had been learned in the bush from people who themselves did not have the best grasp of the language. Jo's famous evening shout to the watchnight instructing him to turn off the generator that provided the hospital's electricity was, 'Watchnight, quench the fowl.'

It was no use correcting her. She was Jo Mattens and she was Dutch, with all that that implies. The watchman knew what she meant. So I filled in all the papers in my best English and in due course Jo was on a ship bound for Australia and a government job at a salary she could not comprehend. We received an exultant letter posted from the ship at some point along the way. Jo had been asked to assist in the nursery and they were paying her more money than she had ever earned and for doing something she would have been glad to do for nothing. On arrival in Australia I guess it was soon discovered that Jo's English did not quite match the forms and the application letter she had submitted. So they sent her post-haste to New Guinea to run bush clinics, which was exactly what she could do incomparably well. Later she was the only white in an Aboriginal town in Northern Australia where, if I know Jo, she was not only running the medical clinic but acting as unofficial magistrate, counsellor, mentor and friend to all. Last heard of, somewhere north of Perth, she had retired to her own home with a small garden in which she grew fruit and vegetables.

Ans contracted typhoid fever and was sent to the hospital in Berekum which was run by American nuns, who were considered to be better able to look after her than the doctor and nurses at the hospital at which she worked in Hwidiem. The bank at Berekum was one of my regular stops and I had to pass through that town to get to Dormaa Ahenkro, so I was a frequent visitor at the hospital over the next month. The manager at the bank's Berekum branch began to feel over-supervised. When she recovered Ans was shipped home to Holland to recuperate but not before finding out that the Dutch bishop, van den Bronk, had refused to pay her while she was in hospital on the grounds that he did not pay people who were not working. He saved her wage of £15 a month.

Some months later I had been feeling unwell for a few days but had carried on with my usual routine. On a Sunday afternoon I collapsed on the floor of my bedroom. I have no idea how long

I lay there but I remember hearing the sound of a car engine I recognised. When it stopped at my front door I called out to the driver, my friend Peter. My next memory is of waking up on the back seat of Peter's car and of asking him where we were going.

'To Berekum hospital.'

I woke up again to find myself on a bed surrounded by several nuns with my head covered with ice in cloth bags. I learned later that the nuns had toured Berekum gathering ice from home refrigerators. I had typhoid fever and it was necessary to try to keep my high temperature from scrambling my brains. I have heard it suggested they were not entirely successful.

The nuns looked after me with care and I am eternally grateful to them. There was never any explanation as to the source of the typhoid. I was in hospital for just over two weeks, during which time I was hoping to be able to continue with my normal routine when I was released. However, the executive director had been alerted to my illness and had been told that I would need a long period to recover. He sent Taff Williams to relieve me. I was bitterly disappointed even though I was told to stay in Sunyani and take as much time as I needed to recover. A week later the executive director told me to get myself to Accra the next day. Exchange Control had been introduced by the government, naturally with no warning. No funds could be remitted out of the country without the permission of the Bank of Ghana. For our bank I was the man to take charge of the confusion. Before I left Sunyani I again thanked Peter for finding and rescuing me from the bedroom floor on that Sunday evening. I remarked that it was lucky for me that he had heard me calling to him. He laughed and said that when he arrived at my house he knew something was wrong because although it was dark the front door was open, my Land Rover was in the drive and the house lights were not on. He took a torch from his car and came looking through the house. When he found me my lips were moving but I was not making a sound.

Resignation

Because I had the use of the bank Land Rover my Opel had been sitting in the garage, from where it moved only once a week or so when I took it for a spin. After a few months I sold it; another poor decision on my part, one of many in my lifetime. Even though I was not out of pocket on the transaction I was very sorry when I learned I was leaving Sunyani and had to get myself to Accra. This I did by agreeing a price with a local taxi driver to take me all the way, stopping off in Kumasi to return my books to the library. In Accra I bought a station wagon, sight unseen, from a colleague who was going on leave. There are not many people I would have trusted enough to do that.

The first morning in my new office in Accra I soon discovered a small throng of people outside my door. Their complaints were not of a lack of money but of the seeming impossibility of sending some of it out of the country. The banks had been instructed that no outward remittances could be made without express permission from the Bank of Ghana. No exceptions. How was he to pay for his son's school fees, asked one man? A representative from a large European trading company wanted to know how they could stay in business if they could not pay their head office for the goods they had already imported and sold. What about alimony that had to be sent in order to avoid serious consequences in England? How about a subscription to a magazine? The problems, which were legion, ranged from the most serious to the outright trivial but each was important to the person involved. In BWA (we had dropped the British from the name at the time of independence) I was the sole source of help both for customers in Accra and for the branches up-country. Until some additional guidelines were issued, giving the banks some authority in well-defined cases, approval from the Bank of Ghana had to be secured for each individual transfer and each request had to be supported by the correct paperwork. I quickly got to know the responsible officials at the Bank of Ghana. When I learned that the Bank of England was to send out an advisor I persuaded one of the officials to give me his name and flight details. I was the only one to take the trouble to meet him at the airport. As a result, although I never received any significant favours from Mr. Rose or anyone else at Bank of Ghana, I could always ask for a little priority when needed. I got into the habit of walking applications over to the Bank of Ghana personally and waiting until the approval stamp had been applied. This enabled me to secure a lot of valuable remittance business from the large trading companies because often I was able to obtain approval in a single day for their applications, each of which amounted to tens of millions of pounds Sterling. The bank charged a healthy 1% on every remittance and I rejoiced in taking business from Barclays Bank. Over the years I usually had a Barclays Bank pencil on my desk and many a customer has fallen for my ruse. They would point to it and laugh about the fact that I used a Barclays pencil. I would pick it up and, showing the broken point, I would tell them that it didn't work. I know, I know. It was a pointless joke.

Within a couple of months what had been a challenge became routine. Additional guidelines were issued by Bank of Ghana and things became easier. I began to chafe at the monotony and was relieved when I was asked to hand over to a more junior expatriate and to assume the management of Adabraka branch. This was a relatively new branch in a custom-built building on Kwame Nkrumah Avenue, Accra. I believe it was the first steel-framed building erected in Ghana. It was a show branch and my friend Joe Ryan's pride and joy. Joe and Brenda were going on leave and when he returned in three or four months I would be due for my own leave. While they were away Joe and Brenda wanted me to move into their apartment at Tesano. I obliged them, reluctantly although I didn't say so, because for some months I had enjoyed my comfortable air-conditioned quarters above Adabraka branch. Fortunately, the bedrooms of the apartments at Tesano were now air-conditioned. Mr. and Mrs. Parry had arrived from up country some time before, bearing their self-purchased air-conditioner and their African grey parrot, which used to confuse me by sounding at the wrong times the BBC pips it had learned from the radio. Apparently the non-air-conditioned residents, spurred by the now obvious fact that it was a simple matter to cool the bedrooms, had shamed the bank into providing air-conditioners for all.

Not long before my arrival at Adabraka branch there had been a break-in. Nothing had been stolen but it was obvious that tools had been used on the combination dial on the vault door. The dial, while still operating perfectly well, was marked and the knob slightly twisted. My concern was that perhaps the burglars had somehow possessed keys and the only thing that prevented their access to the vault had been the combination held by Joe. But why was the knob on the combination twisted? If the combination had been broken the knob would have turned easily. Compromised keys were a real worry and in due course, in response to my request, new locks arrived from London, together with a diagram of the workings of the vault door. There was no suggestion that there was a professional in Accra who could change the locks. I decided the safest thing was to do the job myself. On a Saturday afternoon, once the staff had left, I made sure that the bank was well locked up. Previously I had withdrawn from the main Accra branch the duplicate keys for the strongroom so that the holders of the two originals did not know what I was about to do. I had assembled as large a variety of tools as I could lay hands on. Fortunately, when I opened the door, unlike the safe at Tepa, I was able to access the workings easily. I compared the locks and mechanics of the door with the diagram that had been sent by the manufacturer. They were quite different. However, it looked to me as if unscrewing two locks and screwing two new identical locks in their place would be a simple matter. So I started on the task of removing the existing locks, being careful not to disturb the string that was supposed to drop a weight into the door frame to secure the door in the event of blasting. Everything took a lot longer than I had anticipated and by the time I had the new locks in place it was growing dark outside. The moment came to use the new keys and test my craftsmanship. Nothing worked! It took another hour of fiddling with the locks and adjusting them so that they meshed precisely with the bars and levers connected to them. At last everything worked smoothly. After many, many successful tests of locking and unlocking the door while it was open I closed and locked it. Now came the real test. I held my breath, almost to the point of asphyxiation, while I broke the combination and used the keys. Everything worked perfectly. As I was about to leave for home I realised that I held the combination and all the keys to the vault. What if word somehow had leaked as to what was going on and people were waiting outside to grab me? My fertile imagination was at work. I locked the original and duplicate keys for one lock in the safe in my office, hid the keys for the other lock in the main office where I was sure they would never be found and substituted them in my pocket with the old keys; then went home to dinner, safely. On Monday I wrote to the manufacturer to let them know the job had been completed successfully 'despite the unhelpful diagrams'. In due course I received an apology and congratulations on having carried out a difficult task.

The customers at Adabraka branch were a bit more cosmopolitan than my Brong Ahafo friends, whom I missed. No cocoa farmers here. But I settled into the routine of big city banking. I remember one well-known building contractor, an Armenian, who came to ask me if it was correct that CFA francs, the currency of neighbouring Ivory Coast and of many French African colonies, could legally be imported and exported. I confirmed that this was the case. I had suggested that the bank engage in this profitable trade. How this strange situation came to exist in concert with the then current strict exchange control of the Ghana pound is interesting. Dr. Nkrumah had long been an advocate of a united Africa and in furtherance of his views he was instrumental in bringing into being the Union of African States, a very loose union of Ghana, Guinea and Mali which lasted from 1958 until 1963. Nothing much came of the union and no other countries joined but in Ghana it was legal to buy and export CFA francs. My customer told me he intended to buy as many as he could get his hands on and send them with a friend to Switzerland. I warned him against this course for a variety of reasons, not least of which was that I did not know his friend. Nevertheless he proceeded on his course and in due time came to tell me that his "friend" had disappeared and had reappeared in Accra a few days later with the story that he had been arrested at the airport on his way out of Ghana and thrown in jail. He had been obliged to bribe the officials with all the CFA francs in order to escape a long prison sentence. We both doubted the story and I reconfirmed that the export was legal. The thing that makes all this interesting is that my customer went to Switzerland, somehow traced the bank in which the money had been deposited – so much for the vaunted Swiss secrecy – and secured an agreement from his friend to repay him over a number of years. Well, that was the story he told me.

One of my customers was the owner of a popular nightclub. He was well known to many of the European bank employees who would occasionally spend an evening at his club which from time to time featured a singer or magic act. It was there I was taught to do the twist by an Egyptian belly dancer. One day a cheque was presented that overdrew the owner's account by a few pounds. An overdraft of this size was well within my authority to approve. I looked in the file and saw that small overdrafts had been granted by my predecessor from time to time and in some cases, but not all, the normal reports had been sent to the executive director's office. All overdrafts, whether reported or not, had been repaid within a few days by normal deposits to the account. I had no hesitation in authorising an overdraft to cover the cheque and the correct report was submitted to the executive director's office. A few days later, and after the overdraft had been repaid, I was astonished to receive a letter signed by the executive director instructing me to seek his permission before granting overdrafts "to your friends". I laid the letter aside for a few days before telephoning the executive director to ask him the meaning of his comment about my friends. I made the mistake of saying that I was upset.

'You are what?'

'Sir, why did you feel it necessary to write to me like this?'

'What did you say you were?'

'Sir, surely I am entitled to know the meaning of your letter.'

'You're what?'

'Have I not always been absolutely forthright with you in everything I have done?'

'What did you say you were?'

'All right sir, since you will not give me an explanation, and obviously you think I am not to be trusted to perform the bank's business in a proper manner, you will have my resignation on your desk first thing tomorrow morning.'

And he did have my resignation the next morning with my letter giving detailed reasoning for it and with his copy clearly marked to show that the original had been sent to head office in London. Neither letter was ever acknowledged.

Time passed and the date for my leave came and went. Joe Ryan was ill and had not returned, so I soldiered on without complaining. I refused to be the first to raise the issue of my leave. The weeks passed and nothing was said until six months after my normal departure date. After a tour of two years I was instructed by letter to proceed on leave. There was no mention of my resignation. I arranged to go home by sea so that I could take all my personal effects. On the dock at Takoradi I bought a small, heavy, coffee table, the thick wooden top of which is held up by two well-carved elephants. After persuading the purser to stow my impetuous purchase with the "not required on voyage" luggage I sailed for Liverpool on the *MV Accra* on 26th July 1962. I was close to tears about leaving Africa, even although I had become so disillusioned by the bank, Nkrumah and Ghana in general. As prime minister the Osagyefo had accomplished much and I had rejoiced at what was happening in the country. Nkrumah had overseen enormous infrastructure improvements including the construction of Tema harbour and the Akosombo dam, which created the largest man-made lake in the world measured by surface area. Many roads had been properly surfaced, medical services and access to education had been greatly improved. Unfortunately, the reduction in world cocoa prices, excessive spending, poor planning and mismanagement had depleted foreign exchange and reserves. Food prices were rising, as was unemployment. In the midst of the suffering of the ordinary people Nkrumah seemed to be encouraging a cult with himself at the centre. At the time of my departure I was told that school children sang every morning,

'Kwame Nkrumah is our saviour. Kwame Nkrumah will never die.'

In 1964 Nkrumah was declared President for Life with an implausible 99.9% of the vote. The detention without trial of enemies, real or imagined, accelerated. In February 1966 while he was out of the country Nkrumah was overthrown by a military coup. He never returned to Ghana and for years he was reviled there and elsewhere. However, as time passed a reassessment of his legacy gained increasing acceptance. It is now acknowledged by many that in leading the first black sub-Saharan country to independence (Liberia is rarely mentioned) Nkrumah became an inspiration for Africans everywhere. His accomplishments were legion and his failures not all of his own making. In 1972 he died in Conakry, Guinea, where President Sekou Toure had made him Joint President. His legacy is now celebrated in Ghana and his birthday is a statutory holiday.

After a couple of weeks at home I called on head office and asked for the release of my provident fund, money put aside for me by the bank in lieu of a pension. Mr. Kewley was surprised and it was as if my resignation had never been submitted. He said I had six months' leave due to me because of the extended tour and I would feel differently at the end of that time. However, I insisted that my resignation be accepted and the provident funds were released. My salary for the six months' leave was duly paid each month.

At home with my parents, with little to do, I applied for a job selling investments in pigs. I was offered the job, but once I saw all the material it looked to me like a pyramid scheme and I refused the offer, somewhat to the chagrin of the company, which did not like my assessment of their business. I went to see a hotel that was for sale on the main road about ten miles south of Perth. I examined the books carefully and it looked like a good business. I called on the bank in Edinburgh which held the mortgage and had an enjoyable conversation with the assistant general manager, who appeared to be interested in my stories of West Africa. While nothing was approved there and then, it seemed the bank was favourably inclined to grant me the loan I needed. However, after much thought and consultation with my parents I decided against it. This was fortunate because many years later I stayed at the hotel, now very run down and turned into not much more than the local pub. A new highway had been built bypassing the village and the locals had petitioned against an off-ramp leading directly to the village. To get there now one has to go several miles past on the new main road before finding a way back on a minor local road. This is a good reminder of the real estate mantra of location, location, location with the caveat that locations can change.

I wrote to Barclays Bank in London and during an interview I was offered a position in the Caribbean. However, the terms and conditions seemed less favourable than I was used to. I would have to find my own accommodation and I was told it would be easy to become a boarder in a nice house. A boarder! I asked for time to think. I said I would let them know that afternoon. I called at my old head office to take my friend Jim Wright to lunch. He was now working in London again. I was spotted by Mr. Kewley.

'I knew you'd be back,' he said.

'Oh no, sir. I am here only to take Jim Wright to lunch. In fact, I have a job offer from Barclays.'

'Barclays! Good lord! Better the devil you know than the one you don't. You know Ghana so well. We have a job for you.'

'I'll never work again for Mr. X.'

'Now, now, you cannot dictate your terms.'

Things were left like that but I did tell Barclays I was not interested in their offer. And you guessed it, I ended up working once again for the Bank of West Africa but this time in Nigeria. I jumped at the opportunity to go back to Africa to a lifestyle I loved and work that suited me and which I thought I did well.

Onitsha, Nigeria

*Failure is the opportunity to begin again
more intelligently.*

Henry Ford

On Saturday afternoon, 16th February 1963, after a bitterly cold winter in Scotland, I arrived at Enugu Airport in Eastern Nigeria. I was to be met by somebody from the Enugu branch of the bank and driven the sixty-odd miles to Onitsha. I waited patiently for half an hour, relishing the warmth, but nobody showed up. So I hired a taxi and agreed a price for the trip to Onitsha but asked to be taken first to the Enugu branch, where, as I suspected I might, I found some young Europeans living above the bank. They had forgotten all about me but now wanted to drive me to Onitsha. No doubt the petrol allowance they would receive for the trip would be welcome. However, I had made a deal with the taxi driver and I stuck to it, having confirmed with the bank staff that the agreed price was fair. On arrival in Onitsha we found the bank but there were no quarters above it. On an inspiration I asked the taxi driver to take me to the club. There, at the Onitsha Sports Club, among the assembled throng of expatriates and a few locals enjoying their Saturday afternoon, I found three or four young European bank employees. They were easy to spot because of the bank's red-covered code book sitting beside them on the bar! When they finished their beers I was conveyed to my quarters.

That night I rejoiced quietly and alone at being back in Africa. I had landed in a country I knew little about. I had been abandoned at the airport, driven sixty miles in a taxi over a strange road to a strange town without a definite destination in mind and I relished the fact I had not experienced the smallest frisson of worry. I had felt quite at home and in command of the situation at all times. I knew I was about to start a new phase of my life and I was supremely confident I would enjoy it and that I would be able to handle whatever was to come. I did not wonder what I had let myself in for.

River crossings and ports have been the genesis of towns, and eventually cities, the world over. Onitsha is no exception. Situated on the east bank of the River Niger, Onitsha is the northern terminus of the part of the river navigable by anything more than small craft. On the opposite side of the river, nearly a mile away, is Asaba. A bridge now spans the river but in 1963 the crossing was facilitated by a car ferry and all manner of smaller craft. Important since at least the seventeenth century and perhaps before, and the site of a British trading post since 1857, Onitsha is now a city of over half a million people. In 2012 a United Nations Settlement Programme Report described Onitsha as *The Gateway to Eastern Nigeria and economic nerve centre of Nigeria*. A 1960 census put the population at only 76,000. I have no idea if that total included or excluded the non-resident overnight visitors who had come to buy goods at what was reputed to be the largest market in West Africa, if not in all of Africa. As I learned later through my work, such visitors were legion. One of the most surprising things about the Onitsha market was that in my day many of the goods sold there were imported through Port Harcourt over one hundred miles away and brought to Onitsha by road. Why was the market not in Port Harcourt? Dare I suggest it was in Onitsha because of the skills of the Onitsha traders?

The trading system, with which I was to become so familiar over the next five years, was very special. Most of the hundreds of traders in the main market had small stalls, not much bigger than an executive desk, although the business of many had grown over the years and not a few also owned warehouses in the vicinity of the market. From the stall they traded retail and from the warehouse they could supply on a wholesale basis. Traders came to Onitsha from towns and villages hundreds of miles away; from the north and west of Nigeria and from neighbouring Cameroon they arrived to replenish their stocks which, once purchased, were loaded onto a lorry for the trip home. An Onitsha trader who had anything more than a very modest business would be assisted by an apprentice, or perhaps several at various stages of their apprenticeship. A young apprentice would start out in his early teens and, in the beginning, would be paid little more than food, a place to sleep and an occasional shirt and short pants. As time passed the apprentice would become familiar with the range of goods in which his employer specialised. This might be almost anything, because in the Onitsha market it was said you could buy everything from a needle to an anchor and things unimaginable in between. Once he was able to accumulate a shilling or two of his own the apprentice would be allowed a small corner of the stall on which he might display, for example, his own two tins of Andrews Liver Salts and a couple of tubes of toothpaste. At the end of his apprenticeship, often four or five years, and depending on how well his employer's business had fared, he would be given a small sum of money and perhaps permitted a modest line of credit. These he would use to buy from his former employer a range of the goods about which he had learned over the years. Then he would go off to wherever he had decided to start his own small store, which might be almost anywhere but often would be in a village or small town where a relative was already established. He would come back to Onitsha regularly, usually monthly, to replenish his stock and thus contribute to the ever-growing prosperity of Onitsha.

Above the traders in the hierarchy were the merchants, who owned one or more very large stores from which they traded in general merchandise or hardware or motor tyres or almost anything you can name. Christopher Uba, Stephen Okonkwo and Mr. Ugochuckwu spring to mind even after the passing of the years and, of course, Chief Isaac Mbanefo MBE, highly respected businessman and trader in palm oil, brother of Sir Louis, who was a judge at the International Court of Justice in the Hague. In Onitsha several prominent families produced and still produce formidable businessmen, doctors, lawyers and diplomats.

At the bank, the manager, Englishman Geoff Higgins, an aggressive marketer, brought me up to date on the state of play. Business had boomed over the last few years with an increasing number of borrowing customers. Although he had five or six European assistants and two or three senior Nigerians, including dear old Pa Williams, among the staff of about sixty, he had little or no help with the administration of the lending portfolio. The correspondence and follow-up were badly in arrears and as his assistant manager he wanted me to sort it out. A great number of borrowers worked on monthly overdraft limits secured by a hypothecation over goods in store. When a trader first applied for an overdraft his current account over the last year or so was scrutinised in order to assess his average turnover. He was then granted an overdraft limited to an amount he was thought to be able to repay comfortably from normal sales within one month. Usually the overdraft was fully drawn immediately and the funds used to supplement the borrower's own cash to buy goods. He was then expected to pay his daily takings into his account and to bring the account into credit within one month. After maintaining a credit balance for a few days he would visit the bank where Higgins, if he was satisfied with the performance over the last month, would authorise a new overdraft, perhaps eventually in an increased amount. There were several hundred customers borrowing on this basis as well as twenty or more larger traders, each of whom had a long-term loan or loans. Also there were many customers with mortgages on their house or business premises. An advice of each loan or monthly overdraft was sent to the executive office in Lagos and this created a lot of work and provided opportunities for things to fall through the cracks.

My routine became to work through the customer files in sequence, looking for any that were not fully up to date, where an advice had been omitted, a repayment not made on time, a lawyer had not responded in connection with security being taken, an enquiry from the executive director's office not dealt with and a dozen other matters that might need attention. Next morning when my secretary, Liz Tranter, arrived I would dictate twenty or more letters for her to type and which I would sign that afternoon. I created a carefully maintained diary system so that nothing would be overlooked. We soon had things up to date and under control and I had time to remove my tie two afternoons a week and march down New Market Road and along Bright Street to the great market. There I would wander round trying to identify our customers, chatting with those I knew, asking about business and trying to learn as much as I could from each one about his particular trade and the problems inherent in it. I always asked our customers if they were giving credit to their customers and I would have a look at the records. Initially I was amazed by the level of trust displayed and I remember asking one trader about an entry in his books. It said simply "Red Man, Kano" opposite which was recorded the amount of credit given. Kano is 520 miles from Onitsha by road.

'Who is Red Man,' I asked, 'and why is there no address for him?'

'Oh,' said the trader, 'I know his brother well. Same father same mother. Red Man has been buying from me for years. He would never let me down.'

This was a fundamental lesson for me. Not only were we lending to the trader but we were lending, indirectly, to Red Man in Kano. I never forgot this, even many years later when I was authorising loans to internationally known, publicly traded companies. When visiting Onitsha market I always asked to be introduced to the neighbours and was happy if they were customers; if they were not I became a salesman. I remember persuading Mr. Ugochuckwu to open his first bank account and authorising an overdraft for him. He operated out of a large store on New Market Road in which he had a huge stock of car and lorry tyres. For two or three months thereafter I called on him, at the end of the month as I had promised, to help him to reconcile his cheque book with the statement of his account until he was comfortable doing it himself.

Many of the larger traders and merchants imported goods directly from the Far East and/or Europe and most, not having lines of credit from their suppliers, were required to open letters of credit. An irrevocable letter of credit, an l/c, is a document issued by a bank that guarantees payment by the issuing bank if the exporter provides documents that prove the ordered goods have been loaded onto a vessel and consigned to the buyer and that the goods have been insured for the journey, unless insurance had been arranged by the buyer, as occasionally it was in Onitsha. The exporter's bank would send the documents to us through our London office with a request for payment, which we could not refuse if the documents conformed to what had been required by the l/c. Note that the l/c did not guarantee the quality of the goods or even that the customer would receive them. Our customer was obligated to pay us the full value of the l/c when we handed to him the documents that gave him title to his goods. It was essential therefore that the buyer trust his supplier. I spent a lot of time trying to make sure our customers understood all the implications, particularly those customers who for the first time were asking us to issue an l/c. During my years in Onitsha we issued over 3,000 letters of credit every year and I approved the issuance and put the second signature on most of them. Many customers needed to obtain approval on an individual basis for each l/c. I would consider the nature of the goods being ordered. If they were readily saleable, non-perishable and standard in their category I would ask our customer for a small cash deposit, say 10% of the total amount of the l/c. If the goods were high-fashion Italian shoes, for example, or goods which were perishable or subject to the vagaries of the market I would require a larger deposit, sometimes as much as 50% of the cost. This ensured that if the customer did not pay on arrival of the documents I would be able to sell them to a competitor at a discount which would make the goods attractive. It happened perhaps once or twice a year at most that I had to find an alternative buyer and the bank never lost a penny.

One case, amusing only in retrospect, reinforced the need for the buyer to know and trust the seller. About a year into my sojourn in Onitsha, by which time I knew the customers and they knew me, a rather frenzied dealer in shoes demanded that I come to his store to see the goods he had received. I reminded him of my oft-quoted mantra "the bank deals in documents not goods". Nevertheless he was insistent and, after all, he was a customer, so I went along. There in his store was a large crate. Inside was a consignment of shoes which, after careful inspection, appeared to match the requirements of the l/c covering their importation. However, they were doll's shoes marked with sizes that conformed to normal shoe sizes. Our customer wanted his money back from the bank but that could not be done. I satisfied myself that the brochure from which the shoes had been ordered made no mention of dolls or very tiny people and in what I was sure would be a useless exercise I agreed to write to the supplier. Not unexpectedly there was no answer. Over the next few months I wrote to every organisation that just might intervene, including the police and the Hong Kong Chamber of Commerce. Incredibly, after almost two years our customer received a refund of all or nearly all his money.

When I first arrived in Onitsha the accountant of the main branch, an Englishman, in my opinion was not much good at his job. I was outraged when he wanted me to authorise reimbursement by the bank for the petrol he said he used visiting his daughter in hospital. Being the pain that I am, once my own work was in order I started to take a more active part in the daily routine of the branch, looking after things the accountant should have been doing. By the time we acquired a more competent accountant, another Englishman, it was taken for granted, I suppose, that I was heavily involved in the routine of the branch. One thing in which I took great pleasure was organising holiday schedules which enabled me to provide cross-training for promising young staff members. Providing relief staff for the other branches in town grew naturally into persuading the executive director in Lagos to authorise me to be the source of relief for several small branches in the east of Nigeria. This allowed me to recruit two additional young men and to provide even more training by sending a junior clerk on a tour round three or four small branches. On top of that, our business was growing and because of turnover of staff we regularly hired new employees. For a young man or woman in Onitsha a job in the bank could be an attractive proposition and not a few sought employment with the intention of working for two or three years to save money before going off to university. This caused regular turnover and I remember a bank inspector challenging me.

'There seems to be something wrong here. There is excessive turnover of staff. Look at the numbers you have recruited recently.'

'Well, the business is growing and we have no more staff than we need. We are recruiting the best and the brightest and not a few leave after a couple of years to go to university or are hired by other businesses in town. We have the reputation of having excellent staff. I am glad to see so many move on because we cannot promote them all, but we have bright young people on entry-level jobs for as long as they stay. Those who do not leave can move up the ladder. It makes for a contented staff.'

I ensured that I was recruiting promising candidates by arranging regular written tests which applicants sat in batches from time to time in the bank staff room. There were excellent schools in Onitsha. Dennis Memorial Grammar, an Anglican school founded in 1925 and Christ the King College, CKC, a Catholic school founded in 1933 and several other schools turned out very capable youngsters. CKC was named the best high school in Nigeria in 2014. Most who sat my tests did well but there was sufficient difficulty to cause a range of results. After I was married my wife and I marked the papers at home in the evening and I made a pile of the marked tests, best results on top. When we needed to employ somebody I interviewed the first few from the top of the heap until I found a candidate with a personality I thought would fit. The result after four or five years was the best staff I ever worked with anywhere in the world. Of course, not all members of the excellent staff had been hired by me. Many years later the annual report of the huge First Bank of Nigeria, successor to Standard Bank of West Africa, and with over 700 branches all over Nigeria, displayed the pictures of its twelve most senior officers. Three of them had worked with me in Onitsha. I was thrilled when I heard from a man I had hired as a youngster just out of school that he had taken over as chief executive of First Bank of Nigeria in March 1998.

I became friendly with Armando Rogero, who was Italian but was the boss in Onitsha of Compagnie française de l'Afrique occidentale (CFAO). The company sold cars and trucks out of a well-equipped garage and workshop. I bought my Morris 1100 from Armando and we got to talking about the financing of Morris Minor cars which were used locally as taxis. We came to an arrangement. Armando would sell the cars and I would grant loans for most of the purchase price on the understanding that if a loan fell into arrears Armando's people would repossess the car, refurbish and resell it so that the bank was unlikely to lose on the deal. This is a standard arrangement except that it is usually the bank that repossesses the cars, but Armando and I thought we invented the whole process! In any event over the years Armando sold and I financed hundreds of cars. I do not remember any losses. We later expanded the deal into the financing of lorries. In one case where a loan for a large lorry was in arrears and the lorry could not be found Armando put his best man on the job. He disappeared for over a week. When he returned with the lorry it had some damage at the front and Armando's man apologised. He had found the lorry in Cameroon and not having any papers for it to get back to Nigeria he crashed through a customs barrier in the middle of the night. Or so he said.

Within a couple of months of my arrival in Onitsha I was disappointed when Higgins was transferred and I was not appointed manager in his place. I accepted that I was still an unknown quantity to the executive director in Lagos but I was confident my time would come. The small disappointment was made much easier by the fact that I felt I was on top of my job and that I was happy in my comfortable two-bedroom semi-detached house set in a large garden opposite the Onitsha Sports Club. Ron Deeley was the replacement for Higgins. He was as laid back as Higgins had been aggressive and he gave me a larger role to play in all aspects of the branch and the two other branches in town that formed part of his remit. Specifically, he liked to go home for an early lunch with his wife and left me to handle the borrowing customers who arrived after he had left and so gradually I became more involved and more borrowing customers came later.

I had been corresponding with Ans, yes, she of Sunyani and the typhoid fever. She was in Dublin studying midwifery. I had asked her to marry me and she had said that her studies were not complete. I told her I wanted a wife not a midwife and the wedding was set for September 1963.

A couple of stories about the marriage, the first of which illustrates how the relationship between employer and employee has changed over the years. The bank required Ans to be interviewed in London to make sure she was suitable to be the bride of "one of our promising young men". I am not sure what the bank would have done if I had refused to countenance any such interview or if Ans had been deemed unsuitable. Thinking of some of the wives I met in West Africa, I cannot imagine what unsuitable could have been. I am sure the bank would never have declared any wife unsuitable but the husband might well have found himself posted to a branch in the back of beyond and left there for years wondering why he could never get a promotion to civilisation. In any event I was sure that any woman who was brave enough to go alone to Scotland to meet my parents for the first time could handle anything the bank would be likely to throw at her. And she did. When the new general manager, John Reed, asked my Dutch bride where she had learned her English she told me she replied, 'In Ghana, so you can stop telling me all these stories about how wonderful West Africa is.'

Refusing the advice of the bank to set sail from Liverpool, Ans sailed from Rotterdam on a cargo boat. It sounded like a good idea to avoid the extra journey from her home in the south of Holland to Liverpool, but it began to turn sour when the ship was diverted to pick up additional cargo and it looked as if Ans would be late for her own wedding. With great good luck, with which my life has so often been blessed, on the ship with Ans was an employee of the Bank of West Africa; this with a passenger contingent of not more than half a dozen. We had never met or even heard of each other, but this kind soul arranged for Ans to disembark at Freetown and took her to the BWA branch, where the manager looked after her and arranged for her to fly to Accra. There she met her brother, then a phlegmatic Catholic priest in Winneba who expressed no surprise when she turned up. He and Ans flew to Lagos and then Enugu where Armando and I met them. I put the brother in Armando's car and Ans and I drove to Onitsha.

To my surprise and great pleasure my parents had announced that they and my younger sister Lorna would attend the wedding in Onitsha. Most unfortunately the university exams of my other sister Rae conflicted with the wedding dates. Had I known long enough in advance that there would be attendees from Glasgow I certainly would have adjusted the date. I missed Rae at the wedding. The family travelled to Lagos on the Elmina Palm, a Palm Line cargo ship, Captain Bunker in command. Unfortunately, when they arrived in Lagos enormous floods over a huge area blocked the direct route to the east, as a result of which all flights to Enugu were fully booked. It looked as if they too would be late for the wedding. These first-time adventurers in Africa decided to avoid the floods by driving far to the north before heading for Onitsha. Lorna tells the story of our father and the driver hiring young boys to push the car through great pools of water while our mother fretted about the safety of wedding presents as the floor of the car became flooded.

On a Saturday morning in the bank I announced my intention to cross the Niger and wait for the family at Asaba. I left my car near the car ferry terminal on the Onitsha side of the river and crossed in a small boat. I had not been standing on the other side for more than fifteen minutes when I saw a car draw up sharply a few yards away and my mother stumbled out and came rushing towards me. Later I heard the story of the journey and the approach to Asaba when my mother pointed out to my father a young man standing at the road side. She was saying to him, 'You should get a pair of white shorts like that... oh, oh it's Calum. It's Calum. Stop. Stop the car.'

So much for the so-called dark, impenetrable Africa. I timed the journey of my parents to within fifteen minutes and we met at the side of the road.

My parents and sister stayed with me and Ron and Jane Deeley kindly accommodated Ans. Ans' phlegmatic brother stayed with the local priests. Jane hosted a dinner party at which she served her usual delicious turkey. She kept turkeys in the back garden and they would come trotting to her when she called them. She liked to respond to compliments about the tender meat of her turkeys by revealing her secret. The turkeys were always given a relaxing shot of brandy just before they were dispatched by Job the gardener. What she did not know was that, although she shied away from watching the beheading, I happened to have had an unobserved view from my house of the demise of this particular turkey. I knew where the brandy had gone and it was not down the throat of the turkey. I never disabused her of the efficacy of her secret for producing tender turkey meat and I presume Job continued to enjoy the perks of an executioner.

The wedding was held in the Onitsha Cathedral, which had been built on the site where the first mass had been celebrated on Christmas Day 1885. It went off without a hitch and they allowed me, a non-Catholic, to participate in some of the ceremony. Ans' brother assisted the local priest. Armando Rogero was my best man, with my sister and the wife of a colleague the bridesmaids. Jane Deeley and my mother calmed the agitation over flowers, wedding dress and hair that could not be coiffured exactly as desired. Ron walked Ans down the aisle and gave her away. After the wedding Ans and I drove in Stephen Okonkwo's decorated Mercedes to the reception at the bank's large bachelor quarters, where a mix of expatriates and bank customers celebrated what the local paper dubbed the wedding of the "darling of the traders". (I have the cutting from the *Nigerian Spokesman*, the local newspaper, to prove it!) During the reception my Protestant mother whispered to me about Ans' brother, the catholic priest, 'He's just like a normal person.'

'Almost,' I replied.

In the evening Ans and I left in my bright red Morris 1100, the only one in Eastern Nigeria, Armando had assured me, when I bought it. We drove to Enugu and stayed at the government rest house. Next day we drove a further 170 miles to Obudu Cattle Ranch 5,200 feet up on the Obudu Plateau and close to the Cameroon border. The ranch had been developed in 1951 by a Scot called McCaughley and in our day was rather basic. It has now been developed into a major resort called Obudu Mountain Resort, complete with cable cars and new buildings. With Boko Haram now active in the area it may not be the best place for a holiday. At the ranch we pretended to be an old married couple despite the confetti that spilled from every garment and Ans' question about sugar in my tea. No milk, no sugar, ever since Denmark. We spent a week at Obudu, the longest I could bear to be away from the office, even though we were enjoying fresh strawberries, the cold and rainy afternoons, the horses and the log fires in the evenings.

Married and Happy in Onitsha

Dead yesterdays and unborn tomorrows,
why fret about it if today be sweet.
Omar Khayyam

In my time in Ghana and Nigeria it was generally accepted that house servants had to be replaced when a bachelor married and a wife appeared on the scene. It was never clear to me if the need for their departure was the fault of the servants, who disliked the disruption of the perfectly happy arrangement they had enjoyed when it was they who decided what had to be purchased, what was to be served at mealtimes and what needed cleaning and when, or if it was the fault of the new wife who did not like being told, 'But master likes it this way.'

Whatever the truth, it was decided that my servants had to go and go they went, unhappily but pacified by a generous severance payment. I came home one evening to be introduced to Sunday William, our new cook. I greeted him as genially as I could despite the fact that even this diminutive man himself could never have claimed to cut an impressive figure. As soon as he was well out of earshot I asked, 'Why in the name of God did you hire him? There were half a dozen candidates.'

'He was honest. He said that the only thing he could cook was porridge. His previous employer taught him.'

'Oh well, that is great. I am a Scotsman. I can eat porridge three times a day.'

'Oh, for heaven's sake, you don't understand. In addition to being honest, he admits he knows nothing. All the others know everything, so they say. I can show Sunday how to cook and do things the way I like them done.'

'Ah! Good luck with that.'

As things turned out, we had good luck indeed. Sunday, an Ibibio, for any that care, proved to be the best house servant I ever met, anywhere, either mine or anyone else's (well, perhaps excepting Ah Wong in Kuala Lumpur). Honest to a fault, cheerful and eager and able to learn whatever he was shown once. He was loyal and caring and in due course, a lover and protector of our children. To fast forward, when my wife was leaving, at the start of the Nigeria-Biafra war some years later, she said to Sunday on the doorstep, suitcase in hand, 'Sunday, please look after master.'

And Sunday did look after me. One day, in the very early days of the war, on the way home from the bank I stopped at the grocery store and bought potatoes. It was a long way for Sunday to walk to and from the store, particularly with a heavy load, and in any case I was not sure we would ever be able to buy any more potatoes. I heard no more about it for a couple of weeks until the next time I was in the store when the owner said he was doubtful about selling anything to me. I was astonished.

'What do you mean?'

'Two weeks ago your cook came in here and was very annoyed with me. He showed me the basket of potatoes he had brought with him and asked me what I meant by selling these to you. He told me that I should know that his master is in charge of the bank and does not know anything about potatoes.'

Apparently Sunday then picked out a new supply, examining each potato, one by one, making sure he got whatever he regarded as the very best and then walked home in the hot sun with his heavy load.

From time to time I have used the expression 'my Africa'. I called it that, not to annoy today's angry young men of Ghana or Nigeria, but in recognition that I lived in Africa in very different times; I do not judge the times better or worse, just different. On the very few occasions I have attempted to talk on a blog to young men in Ghana, and I doubt I'll ever try again, I have been cursed and reviled for what they seemed to think I was in the 1950s and 60s.

'You colonial bastard.'

'You were just exploiting us.'

'You took a job that should have been ours.'

'You treated our people like dogs.'

Certainly there was no truth in that last accusation even if there might have been some in the others. It became very clear to me that many people have difficulty in judging or assessing actions and deeds in the context of the times in which they took place. This applies to most of history. I was a young man in Ghana and Nigeria and yes, I was very glad to have a job in Africa. But, I did believe I was doing my job well and I harboured not a doubt that in my own very small way I was contributing to the advancement of the country and its people, both in Ghana and Nigeria. Certainly an African could have done my job and in due course an African did. But perhaps, just perhaps, I helped that person, a little, to do it well when the time came.

Apart from the small difficulties only to be expected when two mature adults who for years have ploughed their own independent furrow begin to live together, the next few years, for me at least, were very happy ones, full of great stories and one near-tragedy. This was when my wife of a few weeks suffered an ectopic pregnancy which required an operation to put right. The Spanish brain surgeon, yes that is right, a brain surgeon, at Ihiala Catholic Hospital left her in the recovery room bleeding internally until I, sitting by her side waiting for her to recover consciousness, questioned the ever-increasing pulse rate recorded every ten minutes on her chart. The young nursing assistant said she did not know what it meant and that her job was simply to make the record. I shouted for Sister Doctor, a nun and not the surgeon, who came immediately and ushered me out of the room with considerable urgency. The two expatriates who had volunteered as donors in case blood was needed – the only ones, European or African, with the right rare blood group who would volunteer – had been sent home to Onitsha, some thirty miles away. When the bleeding was discovered the volunteers somehow were stopped on the road and turned around. Sister Doctor cut Ans' leg open to find a vein because all the others had collapsed. The French volunteer, whom I knew only slightly, gave two pints of blood there and then and Lawrie Daw, accepted as a donor only because there was nobody else of the right blood group and despite his bout of jaundice some years before, gave a pint. He thereafter claimed kinship and ignored having given Ans jaundice within a couple of weeks of his donation. The bank, bless it, had a special drug flown in from Europe and in Ihiala within two or three days. I have never forgotten that it was called fibrinogen and was intended to help stop bleeding. I was not pleased to have been barred from the room while a priest gave the last rites and I was very angry with him when I found out what he had been doing. Did he think that a Protestant, particularly a non-practising one, would damage the efficacy of his 'wee prayer' as he called it? Ans' brother, the priest, had been sent for from Ghana but the crisis had passed by the time he arrived two or three days later. He was still phlegmatic.

There was a potentially dangerous event one evening as I was driving back to Onitsha at about 8 or 9pm, having made my daily visit to Ans, who spent a couple of weeks recovering in the hospital. It was pitch-black and the road was forested on either side. I could see the lights of cars well ahead of me swerving as if to avoid something. Three or four cars did this until I arrived at the spot and saw a twisted bicycle and two bodies lying on the road, a man and a woman, apparently having been knocked down. One of the things that had been drummed into us in Nigeria was never to stop at an accident, particularly at one you had caused. There had been a history of aggrieved villagers taking severe revenge on perpetrators. This certainly flashed through my mind as the two bodies appeared in my headlights. One appeared to be moving slightly. How could I just drive on? I passed them and pulled into the side of the road and got out of my car. The man was breathing. The woman looked dead. I tried to stop the next three or four cars to enquire if there was a hospital or clinic nearer than Ihiala, from whence I had just come. Nobody would stop. As seems to happen in West Africa, certainly it used to happen in Ghana and it happened then on that deserted road in Nigeria, people appeared out of the trees as if from nowhere. Within a few minutes there was a group of ten or fifteen people and voices were beginning to be raised in anger towards me. This was starting to look ugly. And then, to my great relief, an old man spoke up and said, 'It was not him. I saw it. It was a lorry.'

People in the crowd told me where there was a clinic with a doctor and I raced there in my car only to find the doctor in his bungalow having his dinner. He said he was too busy to come to see people who were probably dead. A road accident really was not his business. I promised to make his life and reputation miserable if he did not come with me. He followed in his car and when we arrived at the spot a few minutes later he seemed pleased to tell me that both casualties were dead and I had wasted his time.

When I arrived in Onitsha I went directly to the police station to relate what had happened and to ask the police to inspect my car. The desk sergeant did not seem to want to take the trouble, but I persevered. Then I had to insist that he make an appropriate entry in the log book. It was lucky I did. A few days later a police constable came to the bank to ask me the number of my car and if I had been on the Ihiala road on the night of the accident. Somebody, probably one of the ones who had refused to stop, had taken my number and made a report. I was able to refer the constable to the log book in the police station and I never heard any more about it.

Sunday's wife had delivered a baby girl and he came to ask me what I thought about a name for the new arrival. I asked him what he had in mind and he said, 'Grory.'

'Sunday,' I said questioningly, 'Is Grory a traditional name for a girl?'

'Yes master, in the Bible, Grory Hariruya.'

'You know what, Sunday? How about Elizabeth? All same the queen.'

So, Elizabeth it was and I wrote a blue airmail letter addressed to Her Majesty, using the words exactly as Sunday would have written them, if he had been able to write. In due course back came a letter addressed to Sunday with a Buckingham Palace crest on the envelope. A lady in waiting had been directed to tell him how pleased Her Majesty was and that she hoped the baby and mother were well. We had the letter framed and it hung in Sunday's room.

If he could write! Sunday could remember a recipe he had been shown once. He could go to the market and come back with a dozen items, tell you the price of each one and give you the change exact to a penny. I know I can't do that. Sunday had never had the opportunity to learn to read and write but that did not mean he was not a very smart man.

Job the gardener, past middle age and the turkey executioner, was very different. Indeed, he was an old rogue, but a loveable old rogue and not a particularly competent gardener. Ans would ask him the local names for different flowers and a standard reply would be something like, 'Ah, madam, we call dis one yellow flower.'

Coming home unexpectedly from time to time I would find Job asleep behind the garage. Once again I would fire him. He would be at work the next day because Ans would not let him go. Job and I would have a laugh about women who could not be controlled and Job would commiserate with me, confessing he had a similar problem.

One incident involving Job I hope to remember to my dying day. I had asked a plumber to fix a leaking water pipe in the garden and was showing him the offending tap. Job, finding any excuse not to be working, was looking on and giving unwanted advice. The plumber needed a washer, which he called 'a leather'. Job was sent on his bicycle to the market with a shilling to buy a leather. A couple of hours passed and there was no sign of Job. We started to worry. Then, in the distance I spied him wheeling his old bicycle up Egerton Street towards the house and balanced on it, with great difficulty, was a ten-foot bamboo ladder. Job said he had bargained as hard and as long as he could but I owed him another shilling because he could not get the price down below two shillings! The plumber and I laughed until we cried, while poor Job looked on mystified.

Job's prized possession was his old bicycle. It was a bit of a wreck but almost certainly the most valuable thing he owned. One day, Job was late for work, later than usual that is. His bicycle had been stolen and he had been forced to walk all the way from town. He was not to be consoled. Next day I came home for lunch followed by a bank lorry with a brand new Raleigh bicycle on the back, fitted with a light and a bell and a carrier over the back wheel. The driver unloaded it and I told Job and Sunday and Jimmy, all of whom had come to see why there was a lorry in the driveway, that I had bought this shiny new bicycle for myself.

Job immediately volunteered to teach me how to ride it. When I mounted and rode up and down the drive everyone clapped. Who would have believed that a white man could ride a bicycle? When I dismounted I handed the bicycle to Job and told him it was his. To this day I can see that old man with tears in his eyes and writing this I have tears in mine. I never bought myself so much pleasure for so many years for so little. We who have so much.....!

Another person who was in our compound every day was Michael the carpenter. He occupied one half of the back to back double garage. His half had been turned into a workshop long before my arrival and Michael was on the payroll at the bank as a messenger. At first I was a bit shocked by this irregular situation but I soon came to understand how practical it was and how much money it saved the bank. Many of the desks in the three branches were made of wood and Michael maintained these, repaired them and made new ones when needed. He also carried out other repairs at the branches and in the bank homes. He made mosquito screens for the doors and windows of our house. Michael was an excellent carpenter; indeed, he was a cabinet maker and could copy store-bought items so perfectly it was difficult to tell his finished product from the item he had copied. The reputation of our carpenter was known within the expatriate community and Michael always had a list of jobs to be done. He could undertake these on his own time or on the bank's time when there was nothing to be done for the bank. So although his pay as a messenger did not properly reflect his skills, he was able to supplement his income from private work.

The executive director's office in Lagos had approved the business case I made for the purchase of two Morris lorries. What we bought, of course from my friend Armando at CFAO, were two chassis which consisted only of the engines, the cabs and the framework at the back. Michael, the bank carpenter, and I took one chassis to the people who built and fitted the wooden structures which formed the passenger carrying areas of the ubiquitous mammy wagons. I asked them to make and fit a structure I had designed with a lockable cage in which to carry specie boxes and which included special fittings to chain and secure the boxes. Comfortable seats for the police guards were to be placed outside the cage. Part of the deal was that Michael was allowed to watch every part of the operation. After the first lorry had been completed, Michael, now an expert, built the second one. One lorry went to the Central Bank in Enugu every weekday to deposit our surplus cash and the other was used daily to bring cash to the main branch from the two other branches in town. I was pleased with and proud of our two lorries and the one built by Michael was every bit as good and as safe as the professionally-built lorry.

It was common in my day in West Africa for members of the bank staff intending to overnight in a particular town to telephone the local bank manager, even if they had never met, to ask for a reservation to be made at the local rest house. Of course, the usual response, as the caller expected it would be, was, 'Oh, the rest house is awful. Come stay with me.'

So I was not surprised when a man I had never met called with just such a request. He was passing through Onitsha on his way north. I invited him to spend the night with us. Apart from the normal courtesy, I was keen to meet this legendary character who went by the name John (Camel) Wright. He had been a tea planter in East Africa and now worked for the Kano branch of our bank. He was the only man I ever knew to receive a camel allowance; thus the nickname. His job was to inspect and, I suppose, count the bags of groundnuts stored in huge pyramids and against which the bank made loans. To do this he travelled about on the back of a camel. Wright arrived at our house in Onitsha driving himself in his Land Rover, which was festooned with jerry cans, chains and other apparatuses (I really thought that should be apparatusae, but my New Oxford says not). Sunday and Jimmy rushed out to bring his suitcases into the house. But he would not let them touch anything. Indeed, he had no suitcases and he explained that he never let anyone handle his bedroll. He hoisted this large bundle onto his shoulder and I directed him upstairs to his bedroom where he spread it out on the floor. At dinner that evening he regaled us with interesting details of his recent journey to England. From Maiduguri he had travelled north through the Sahara by way of Tamanrasset to Algiers, in a caravan on the back of a camel; or perhaps on more than one camel. He never said. After dinner when we moved from the dining table to have our coffee, Wright picked up a magazine from the table by the side of his armchair and screwed a monocle into one eye. I forget which one. Poor Jimmy! He had never seen anything like this and was trying with one hand to balance a tray with cups and coffee and milk and sugar while serving with the other and manfully attempting to contain his surprise. When all had been served he disappeared into the kitchen. Then Sunday appeared, apparently to put dishes away. This was never done in the presence of guests and was always left until the next morning and then it was Jimmy's job. I could see Sunday trying to sneak a look over his shoulder as he put dishes into a sideboard in front of the brick-red wall an Italian friend had painted for me as a wedding present. But the sideboard was in the wrong place for him to get a good look. In the end, he closed the sideboard door and walked over to where Wright was sitting, took a look and rushed back to the kitchen. Next morning I was obliged to remonstrate with Sunday and Jimmy.

'No laughing in the kitchen loud enough for guests to hear.'

In April 1964 we went on leave, first to Scotland to stay with my parents. I borrowed my father's car and we drove to Heerlen in the South of Holland, where I met my wife's family for the first time, other than her phlegmatic brother. I was glad to be able to thank my father-in-law for the medal he had sent me before the wedding. It had been adapted from a small plastic tag on a package of Kraft cheese and was marked in black ink "For bravery". I have it still. Why not? I earned it!

My father-in-law was a lovely man; he and his wife were honoured as "Righteous Among the Nations" by Yad Vashem for having hidden Jews in their home during the Second World War. I knew a little of the story from Ans who, as a child old enough to understand, had often been fearful of the situation. I asked him how he could have taken such risks with his own children in the house. His only answer was, 'How could I not?'

During the holiday Ans and I drove to Turin to meet Armando, the best man at our wedding, and his family. Memorably, we all went to see Juvé play. Unlike previous leaves when I had been single, this one seemed to be over all too soon. We returned to Onitsha on 29th July 1964.

We were quickly into the familiar routine and soon Ans and I were invited to lunch on a Sunday with the chief of a nearby town. I warned her that the fare might be a little unusual and I was surprised by her apparent concern. Although always trim, Ans was a good eater, better than I. In later years, particularly in Hong Kong and Malaysia, she often saved the honour of the family by her ability to keep eating long after I had been forced to retire from the fray. Our hosts were always well pleased with her. I knew she had eaten local food in Ghana so her worry about the Sunday lunch surprised me. Perhaps it was because she was pregnant. We plotted strategy as to what we would do if various things were served. On the fateful day we were seated at a table laid with a beautiful white linen tablecloth and sparkling cutlery and glassware. The first course was chicken noodle soup. Then came a mild chicken curry and a plum duff pudding with custard. The only unusual thing was the presentation on our departure of a live goat, which the chief's boys put into the boot of my car.

Time passed quickly until Ans left for Scotland for the birth of our first child, Margareta. She was called Margaret after my mother with an 'a' added to satisfy the Dutch. When she was older she became Maggie. The nurses in the Queen Mother's Hospital in Glasgow, knowing only that Ans was from Nigeria, were surprised when she produced a white baby.

While Ans was in Glasgow awaiting the birth of our daughter I was at work in Onitsha. One day I received a telephone call asking if I would like to have an African Grey parrot. Somebody was "going for bush" and would bring back parrots. If I wanted one for ten shillings I should be at Gerry Cartwright's house at 5pm. Naturally, I was late. When did I ever finish work at five o'clock? By the time I arrived all the parrots but one had been taken. The last one, mine, was so young it had only a few wisps of feathers. However, Ugly (how could he have been named anything else?) thrived under gentle care and grew a fine spread of feathers, despite which the name stuck. The only problem was that Ugly did not know he was a parrot. He was friendly and could be handled without any fear of a bite. He loved to flutter down from his perch and waddle across the carpet to where I was in my chair reading a newspaper. If I lowered the paper and looked at Ugly he would stop in the middle of the carpet, in full view, and put his head under his wing. If he could not see me I could not see him. On arriving he would climb the back of my chair and nuzzle my neck and ear. Ugly became a wonderful talker, imitating various voices. After Ans had been back for a few months Ugly learned to call out in a perfect imitation, 'Sunday, coffee please.'

In due course Sunday would arrive from the kitchen bearing a tray with coffee and finding Ans not there at all, would laugh, 'Dis parrot, he too too cleber.'

There are many other stories about Ugly's speaking but unfortunately he came to a very sad end. Some years later Ans and I went for a walk with the children, leaving Ugly on his perch on the stoep. Wild dogs came into the garden and, although Job the gardener was there, the dogs jumped and knocked Ugly off his perch and killed him. We were heartbroken and I wonder about keeping wild birds and animals, although we did have another parrot in Canada. It was no match for Ugly.

When Ans and Margareta returned from Scotland, with Margareta less than six weeks old, I felt it my duty to attend mass at the cathedral on a Sunday to help with the child, who most certainly could not be left with Cornelia the nanny, according to Ans. I thought we had hired Cornelia for just that purpose. I need not have taken the trouble because help was rarely needed in the cathedral. No sooner had we sat down than our blonde-haired baby daughter was spirited away by the nearest local lady and passed from lap to lap. The ladies liked to stroke Margareta's soft, almost white, hair that was nothing like the hair of their own children. Often we did not know where in the huge cathedral our daughter was. We never worried, knowing she would be well looked after.

Although many other religions were represented and there was an Anglican cathedral, Onitsha was, and I presume still is, a very Catholic town. The Catholic missionaries had arrived first and had done their work well. Joseph Shanahan was bishop from 1905 until 1931. He was known to have travelled the area on a motorbike, taking out his false teeth to amuse the children. His successor, Charles Heerey, eventually was appointed archbishop. He died in February 1967 and his funeral in Onitsha was something to behold. Shanahan and Heerey were Irish and Heerey, whom I remember well, was more like a farmer than an archbishop. He used to greet me whenever he saw me with a hearty, 'How's the missis?'

Heerey's successor was Francis Arinze, his former coadjutor bishop from 1965 to 1967, and a very different kind of man. Born in Onitsha and enormously well-educated, Arinze was the youngest Roman Catholic bishop in the world at age thirty-two. I remember finding him sitting on a stool in the middle of the staff area of the bank. Somebody had let him in but seemed to have abandoned him. I expressed my surprise and asked him if I could help. He said he had come to buy some travellers' cheques. I told him I would get them right away and asked what denomination he wanted. Without hesitation but with a small grin, he replied, 'Roman Catholic, of course.'

Francis Arinze became a cardinal in 1985 and at one time his name was being bandied around as a potential Pope. I was pulling strongly for him, not that I had a vote. But I thought that if he became the Pope I could dine out for years to come on my travellers' cheques story.

On one of the occasions during my time in Onitsha when I relieved the branch manager for several months, Nigeria, without warning, declared a ban on imports. I sought clarification from our people in Lagos. Surely the ban did not involve goods already ordered with payment guaranteed by letter of credit. Oh yes it did, I was assured. But how could this be? I had issued letters of credit to exporters in Europe and the Far East guaranteeing they would be paid if they put their goods on a ship bound for Nigeria. How could it help Nigeria if payment had to be made even if the goods were never imported? The answer from my people in Lagos was, for all intents and purposes, 'Sorry old boy, that's the way it is.'

I have never been a great worrier about the decisions I made once I had made them. I always knew I had decided based on the best information I had at the time and that my decisions had always been in the best interests of the bank and its customers. But on that occasion I worried and worried some more. Once I checked I realised I had committed the bank to pay out over £9 million, equivalent to about £170 million today. How was I to persuade my customers to pay for their documents if they knew their goods could not be landed? I foresaw unprecedented losses. What on earth was I to do? The letters of credit were irrevocable, but I cabled all the exporters advising them of the ban and asking them not to ship. But why should they care? To be paid all they had to do was put the goods on a ship and send the documents to their bank. Over the next few weeks I worried myself into a painful ulcer. Sister Doctor said, apparently without too much sympathy, I could do as she told me or in a few months she would cut out half my stomach. She instructed me to eat steamed fish and rice pudding. For the next few months Ans enforced the regime, although I am sure she did not know the cause of the suspected ulcer. No doubt in the earliest days of our marriage I had been obsessed with the bank and my work and probably I brought too much of it home. After all, before our marriage there had been little else in my life. So, in response to a protest, I agreed that I would try to leave the bank at the bank. With few lapses I did the best I could. During all the agony about the letters of credit, mental as well as physical, there was not a word of advice or instruction from bank offices in London or Lagos. A very few exporters returned the letters of credit unused, two or three said they would not ship but most said nothing, as they were fully entitled to do. Documents duly arrived and I was fearful when the first ship called at Port Harcourt, carrying goods that supposedly were not to be allowed to land. A couple of customers paid for their documents and told me not to worry. This was Nigeria and they would find a way to work things out. And they did. The authorities in Port Harcourt were not about to allow a Lagos directive to deny the East the goods it needed. Every shipment that arrived at Port Harcourt was landed and cleared despite the embargo and all my letters of credit under which goods had been shipped were paid for in full. We went on leave with the problem resolved and me still on my awful diet. The pains went away. They say worry does not cause ulcers but something certainly gave me hell in Onitsha.

During our leave in Glasgow we celebrated the birth of our son Malcolm one year, one month and one day after the birth of his sister. If he had been an American he would have been called "Malcolm Johnston IV". His son is Malcolm V. We, and the doctors in Onitsha, had decided on the Queen Mother's Hospital in Glasgow as a birthplace for both children as a precaution in case Ans had another problem with excessive bleeding. A bonus was that if either child wanted to play for Scotland they would be well qualified.

After Ans and Malcolm were home with my parents I took the overnight train from Glasgow to London to report to head office, as was required. I often stayed at the Cumberland Hotel near Marble Arch and I remember that in the earliest days in the 1950s it cost £5 5 shillings for a room for the night and a taxi from the hotel to Heathrow Airport cost £5. I like to tell taxi drivers this because last time I was in London, some years ago, a taxi to the airport cost about £50 while a hotel room cost several hundred. How did things get so out of kilter? On my 1966 visit to London I was walking towards Piccadilly late one evening after having left a theatre when I ran into Mike Venn, a former colleague from Ghana whom I had not seen for a few years.

'Good lord,' he said, 'let's go somewhere for a drink and a chat.'

I had no idea where to go at eleven at night in London and neither did Mike, but fortunately, or otherwise, a scurrilous little man wearing a cloth cap sidled up to us and in an Irish brogue asked if we wanted to find a club to have a drink.

'Sure.'

He led us to a nearby back street and down some steps where we each paid £1 to become members of a club in a dingy rat hole. At the bar Mike ordered a whisky and I received strange looks when I asked for a soft drink. Mike had little time to discover that his very expensive whisky was rotgut with plenty of water added before a couple of heavily made-up women were trying to climb onto our bar stools. We abandoned our drinks and got out of there fast. I would not be telling this story except that it involves

Lord Barbour, who became chairman of the Conservative Party and later was chairman of Standard Chartered Bank. Mike and I had been invited to a lunch at the Standard Bank headquarters in London, together with everyone on leave from the bank in West Africa. Standard and BWA had amalgamated the year before. We were now SBWA. During the pre-lunch reception, the day after our fortuitous meeting, I saw Mike Venn and wandered over to join his small group which included Lord Barbour. I have been told that it was he who gave encouragement to John Major's early political ambitions which led him to 10 Downing Street and a stint as prime minister. If so, Lord Barbour had an eye for a winner but he never said anything to me except, after I introduced myself, to ask in a plummy lordly voice, 'Do you know Mr. Venn?'

I couldn't resist and to Mike's very obvious discomfort I replied, 'Yes sir, we are members of the same club.'

Had Lord Barbour enquired further, which he did not, I hope I would have had the wit to say, 'Tarkwa Club, sir, in Ghana.'

After taking Malcolm to be baptised in the Netherlands, where we had to persuade the Dutch priest that Malcolm is a proper name for a saint, derived from Colm Kil who became Saint Columba of Iona, we were happy to be back in Onitsha on 2nd June 1966.

The time in Onitsha with the two children in our lovely little home set in its large garden with Sunday our cook, Jimmy the steward, Cornelia the nanny and Job the gardener was, no doubt, the happiest time of my life. Ans seemed content helping the nuns in the pharmacy. My long spells in charge at the bank during the leaves of the various managers and in between changes of manager added to my contentment. I played football and tennis at the Onitsha Sports Club, which was across the road from the house. I travelled with Onitsha teams to play cricket in Enugu and rugby in Port Harcourt where I cracked a rib when the scrum collapsed on me on the iron-hard ground. How could life have been any better?

War in Biafra

Cry Havoc and let slip the dogs of war.

Julius Caesar

William Shakespeare

It would take many volumes to do justice to a history of Nigeria. For those who do not know the country to gain a glimmer of an understanding, it is essential to accept that Nigeria was cobbled together for their own purposes by the British. Its regions were never truly united in the minds of the people. Tribalism and regionalism reigned and still cause difficulties today. On top of that is another factor, which overrides everything and is irrefutable in my opinion; that fact is that the Igbos of Eastern Nigeria, generally, have been more progressive, better educated and more commercially successful than any of the other peoples of Nigeria. This has caused a great deal of trouble over the years.

While we were happy and very content with our life and me with my work in the friendly community of Onitsha in Eastern Nigeria, I was not unaware of the disquieting events in the country. In January 1966 a military coup failed but caused the deaths of the prime minister and prominent politicians. Major General Aguiyi-Ironsi opposed the coup, took command and restored order in

Lagos. He announced in May 1966 that Nigeria was no longer to be a federation but simply a republic. Even though he included many restraints and delays to the process it is asserted that this announcement was the cause of rioting and bloody massacres of Igbos in Northern Nigeria, during which about 3,000 were killed. However, it has also been said that the conduct of some Igbos at the time of the January coup had been provocative and had created great ill-feeling towards all Igbos.

Despite the growing tensions we were glad to arrive back in Onitsha in June 1966 and to be greeted by the friendly faces at our house and in the bank. Soon after our return Colonel Chukuemeka Ojukwu, an Igbo, who had been appointed Military Governor of the East by General Aguiyi-Ironsi, called on his people, the Igbos, many of whom had fled, to return to their homes and jobs in the North. He said that the killings in the North had been part of the price to be paid for the ideal of One Nigeria. In June 1966 General Aguiyi-Ironsi began a tour of the regions, seeking input as to the future of the country. In July I was shocked to learn he had been arrested and killed by mutinous soldiers from the North. In the North and West, Igbo soldiers, officers and other ranks, were rounded up by their Northern colleagues and killed. The motive was said to be revenge because of the lack of any disciplinary action against the mutineers of the January coup. Lieutenant-Colonel Yakubu Gowon, who maintained he was not connected to the coup, although there is said to be some evidence to dispute that, took command of the army even though he was not first in seniority. He insisted he was trying to hold things together. However, the killings went on after he was in command and after he said they would stop. There is said to be evidence that the mutiny, with or without Gowon, had the objective of organising the secession of the North. When Colonel Ojukwu realised what was going on he interceded in favour of a united Nigeria and the British and Americans put pressure on Gowon, who announced a continuing effort to unite Nigeria. This is thought to have been a last-minute amendment to the original plan. Why did they not all just let it go? The North would have ended up as a cut-off-from-the-sea rival to Burkina Faso.

The Igbo soldiers in the North and West, officers and other ranks, who had managed to escape the killings, began to filter back to the East, disguised as civilians. With them came the awful news of the killing of their colleagues.

At a meeting of representatives of the military governors of the regions of Nigeria on 9th August 1966 it was agreed that all troops should return to their home regions. Northern troops were allowed to leave the East with their arms and ammunition but, according to Philip Efiong, Igbo officers were removed from prison in Benin and killed on 12th August. Later in the month twenty-two were executed at Ikeja. Northern troops did not leave Lagos or the West.

In September the dreadful happenings in the North were brought home to me forcibly. Igbos began to arrive in Onitsha, having fled their homes in the North. Truck loads were packed so tight with people that the dead were held upright by the living. The bellies of women had been ripped open. It was clear that killing gangs were afoot in many towns in the North and Igbos were being hunted down, raped and killed. Tales of unbridled horror and savagery were brought back to the East by those who escaped. I remember the frustrated rage of the staff and of my customers. I have no doubt this was common throughout the East and my own feelings were running high. How could it have been otherwise? There were some retaliatory acts of violence against Hausas in the East but from all accounts these were isolated instances. The order was given by Colonel Ojukwu that all Northerners were to be given police protection as far as the border with the North. The great majority left safely.

As the violence against Easterners spread into the West and Lagos more refugees fled home to the East, abandoning all they owned except for what they could carry. Most were silently absorbed into their towns and ancestral villages. They were looked after and provided with accommodation by relatives and friends. The final estimate of those who returned was close to 2 million people. It is thought that over 30,000 Igbos, men, women and children, died in the North, the West and Lagos. Of course these figures are disputed.

The Easterners, arguably, had been the strongest proponents of a united Nigeria but now there arose from the people of the East a great call for secession. 'If we cannot live in Nigeria why should we be Nigerians?' However, Colonel Ojukwu is said to have hoped that some solution could be found to avoid splitting the country. A meeting of the Supreme Military Council, including the military governors of the four regions, North, West, Mid-West and East, was held in Aburi, just north of Accra in Ghana, on 4th and 5th January 1967 in what had been Nkrumah's country hillside retreat. The meeting, which was to become known as the Aburi Accord, agreed that Nigeria should remain a single country but as a confederation of the regions.

From the bank's offices in London and Lagos nobody gave those of us in Onitsha the impression that anything about the political situation worried them. Apparently we were expected to carry on as usual and it was about this time that the bank sent a young man to Jos in the North of Nigeria for his first tour of duty. He was to be one of several assistant accountants. His name was John Roy Major, future British prime minister.

By March 1967 the federal government under Gowon had made no move to implement any part of the Aburi Accord. Colonel Ojukwu, said to believe that Gowon had no intention of doing so, insisted that the East, if left with no alternative, would pull out of the Federation. In May 1967 Gowon imposed a partial blockade on the East, cutting off postal, telephone and telex services and banning flights to Enugu and Port Harcourt. We were all but isolated from the world. Later in May Gowon published a decree dividing Nigeria into twelve new states, which meant the East was to be separated into three small parts. On 30th May 1967 Colonel Ojukwu, having obtained a unanimous mandate from the 335 member Assembly of Chiefs and Elders, responded by proclaiming the East of Nigeria to be *An Independent Sovereign State of the Name and Title of The Republic of Biafra.*

I hope the reader will understand that my summary of events is exactly that. It omits many pertinent facts, including arguments about wages for those forced to flee from their homes and jobs, rights to oil revenues, involvement of foreign countries and a myriad of intriguing sub-plots, including the first African to win a gold medal at the Commonwealth Games. He shot and killed Nigeria's first prime minister. Eventually he was shot at the stake, not for killing the prime minister, but as a Biafran army officer convicted of treason. My summary, wholly inadequate, is intended only as a backdrop to the personal story of my family. For any interested in all the details of what turned into an incredibly horrible civil war, there are many accounts, most of which present the story from the point of view of one side or the other. Each side contradicts the details, actions and motivations described by the other. If you have to read only one, my personal preference is for Frederic Forsyth's *The Biafra Story*. Forsyth makes no bones about being a supporter of Biafra, as I was. Mark my words, it will be a very long time before the name and concept of Biafra is forgotten and perhaps it never will be.

Back now to early 1967, when the bank manager in Onitsha was transferred and I was hugely disappointed to be told that a new manager would arrive within three or four months. Once again I was to act as manager in the meantime. I knew my record was good and I hoped that as soon as the new manager had settled in I would be transferred. I wanted a branch of my own, where I would be left long-term, but I greatly disliked the thought of leaving Onitsha. I felt that I had been the driving force behind the major improvements we had achieved over the last few years. Nevertheless, I carried on, glad to be in charge once again.

I believed the prospect of war was becoming ever more likely. A customer asked me to open a letter of credit for the importation of several cases of shotguns. I refused.

'You know very well that it has been announced that all ships are required to call at Lagos before coming to Port Harcourt and that cargoes will be inspected. I am sure the authorities will not let guns come to the East.'

'Ah,' he said, 'so you support the Federal Authorities.'

'How can you say that? You know me and you know I have been here for years. I have never worked anywhere else in Nigeria. But I am sure that guns will not be allowed to reach the East.'

'If you do not open my l/c I will report you. You are not on our side.'

'Mr. N., to hear you say that upsets me. This is what I will do and it is against my better judgement. I will open your l/c, under protest, provided you prepay it and accept the risk that the cargo will not reach Port Harcourt.'

'Good. I accept and will make the deposit.'

'It is not a deposit. It is prepayment in full and the cost will be for you even if the guns are not on board.'

He prepaid and in due course the documents arrived evidencing that the shipment from Europe had been made. The documents were delivered to him. Soon thereafter he stormed into the bank with several assistants, accusing me of tipping off the authorities in Lagos about the guns, which had not been on board when the ship arrived in Port Harcourt. I most certainly had not done any such thing. Nevertheless I was required to attend the police station on several occasions over the next few months and was very aggressively grilled each time. I will not expand on the abuse to which I was subjected because I know that it would not have happened in normal times. Nothing more came of the matter but it was the first inkling I had that relationships between expatriates and locals had changed. Instead of being a trusted friend I was now suspected of being in league with the other side.

On another occasion I was called to the police station late one afternoon to vouch for a European official of one of the trading companies. Having secured his release, I was amused the next morning to be told by a senior clerk in the bank that he had been involved in a citizen's arrest the previous afternoon. A strange European had been driving slowly up and down New Market Road looking left and right. It was all very suspicious, he said. I was pleased to be able to explain that the man, an official of a large trading company in Lagos, had been unexpectedly delayed in Onitsha and had been looking for a place to buy a shirt in order to be presentable when he came to the club that evening. This may seem amusing now, but it is a very good indication of how tense everybody was. Biafrans may have been waiting for the war, as in a song popular at the time, but nobody really knew what war would bring or how we should behave in anticipation of it.

A more frightening incident happened early in May 1967. On a Saturday morning a young soldier burst into my office at the bank, using his automatic rifle to prod the back of an obviously terrified chubby white man who trembled in front of him. The soldier looked like a teenager. He was agitated and his eyes were popping. He may well have smoked a "little something".

'Dis man is a spy,' he yelled.

'Take it easy,' I said. 'Who the hell are you?' I asked the captive.

He gave his name in a quavering voice and said he was from a confirming house in Manchester or Birmingham.

'Look,' I said to the soldier, 'I know about this man. I have a letter from England introducing him. I'll show you.'

I came from behind my desk and walked across the office to a filing cabinet on the other side, leaned down and opened the bottom drawer. As I did so the soldier bounded three steps towards me and, giving the drawer a mighty kick with a dusty boot, closed it on my hand.

He yelled as he pointed his gun at me, 'You are defending the enemy, you are under arrest. You are under arrest.'

I raised my hands in surrender and retreated behind my desk.

'Okay, okay, what do we do now?'

'You will come to the bridgehead with me.'

'Oh, I can't do that. I am very busy here and there are customers waiting to see me.'

As I spoke I managed to press the button under the top of my desk. I guess I must have lowered my hands. The button did nothing except ring a buzzer outside the office door to summon Godwin, the senior and trustworthy bank messenger who sat there.

'You must come with me or I'll shoot you,' the soldier shouted.

I thought he might just do that but I was hoping he was as frightened as I was but not frightened enough to pull the trigger. Godwin entered and looked startled when he heard the soldier threatening to shoot me.

'This is Godwin,' I said. 'He has known me for years. He will tell you what a fine chap I am.'

As I spoke I signalled to Godwin, giving him the sign of money by rubbing my thumb and first two fingers together. The captive had crumpled onto a chair in front of my desk and while Godwin engaged the attention of the soldier I picked up the telephone and dialled the number of the police station. A lady answered and I said quietly, 'This is the Standard Bank manager. I have a soldier in my office threatening to shoot me. Can you help?'

'Hold on please,' said the lady, at which point the soldier saw me holding the telephone. Leaning over the desk and prodding me firmly in the stomach with his automatic rifle he yelled his instruction that I put it down. I complied with alacrity.

Godwin continued explaining what a fine fellow I was. The
telephone rang. Thank God; the police. But it wasn't. To my horror
I heard my wife saying, 'We have been invited to the Cartwrights
this evening. Is that okay for you?'

'Yes.'

'What time will you be home this afternoon?'

'Can't talk now.'

I put the telephone down. Eventually, after a good ten minutes
or more and without the help of a letter of introduction, Godwin
convinced the soldier that I was not a threat and nor was his
prisoner. He had secured the release of both of us for the price of
£5. The soldier departed with more money than, probably, he had
ever had at any one time. A very relieved man from Manchester
or Birmingham and an acting bank manager fished out cigarettes.
The shaking hands of the former captive would not allow him
to get a match close to the end of his cigarette. I helped with my
monogrammed S.T. Dupont lighter.

'What in God's name were you doing to get yourself arrested?'

Apparently he had been taking photographs of enamelware
in the market and had suffered a citizen's arrest as a possible spy.
The citizens had detailed a passing soldier to take him to the
bridgehead, the local military headquarters. However, the captive
had managed to persuade the soldier to bring him to the bank
where the bank manager would vouch for him.

'I thought that if I couldn't get the money we are owed I could
at least show my boss the enamelware. It never occurred to me that
enamelware in a market stall could be a military secret!'

'You have to understand we are on the verge of a war. People
are very jumpy and highly suspicious, particularly of foreigners.
Believe me, nothing like this would have happened in Onitsha in
normal times.'

As we sat chatting, smoking and trying to recover from the
ordeal, the office door opened and I could see Godwin directing

two very large policemen. Comically, they were struggling to side-step through the doorway. The lead policeman had his left arm through the left arm of a soldier and the second policeman had his right arm through the soldier's other arm. The soldier, with his automatic rifle on a sling over his shoulder, was being transported facing in the opposite direction to the policemen. When they had lined themselves in front of my desk they turned the soldier round to face me and explained that they had been instructed to rush to the bank where a soldier was causing trouble. As they came up the steps at the front door this soldier was coming down.

'Is dis de man?' one of the policemen asked, triumphantly.

'Oh no,' I explained. 'Oh no, that is not the one.'

'Are you sure?'

'Yes. Certainly he is not the one. The troublemaker, he smaller, darker with black curly hair,' I said, waving my hand around my head.

The policemen seemed very doubtful but after further assurances they released their dark, black-curly-haired captive who, a few minutes before, had been threatening to shoot me. He gave me a sort of half-smile as he left. The policemen departed to look for a smaller, darker soldier with black curly hair.

The pudgy enamelware man looked at me quizzically.

'Why did you say that was not the man?'

'There was absolutely nothing to be gained by getting him into trouble. Do you think I want half of his regiment showing up at my house aiming to make my children orphans?'

When I arrived home I had to explain my abruptness on the telephone. That was one occasion when what happened at the bank did not stay at the bank, although I did try to make the incident sound more hilarious than it had been.

A few weeks later the new manager and his wife arrived. This was his first tour in Nigeria, having worked in Ghana for fifteen or more years. He was laconic, very laid back and made no effort to take over the reins. He seemed mystified by what was going on all around us and did not appear to appreciate the seriousness of the current situation. I found it strange that he did not want to take control. Whenever I took on a new responsibility I could barely contain my impatience to be in charge and to get on with doing things my way. A few mornings after his arrival, and with me still in charge, I came to the bank, early as usual, and was surprised to find about a dozen people waiting outside the main door, which was not due to be opened for nearly an hour. Other people were lounging against the store of our neighbour, a watchmaker, whose memorable sign said he was a "Doctor of all Clolcks".

I asked a man I recognised, 'Why are you here so early?'

'Mr. J, we hear SBWA is going to close. I need to take my money.'

I assured everyone that we were not going to close and that we had plenty of money in the bank. But I was worried. The branch took in a great deal of cash every day, because of the large number of traders paying in their daily takings. Every weekday we sent a lorry to the Central Bank in Enugu with the excess cash, usually about £100,000 in notes and £10,000 or £20,000 in coin. We sent twice as much on a Monday. That morning, I gave instructions not to load the lorry until we could see exactly what was happening. By mid-morning we had on our hands a full-blown run on the bank. I was told that a loudspeaker van had being doing the rounds giving out the false information about SBWA and Barclays closing. The local bank was the suspect but I had no proof of that. Funnily enough it was the local bank that ran out of cash first and they telephoned to ask if they could borrow some. Fat chance! I sent someone to see what was going on at Barclays and was told they were allowing only a handful of people into the bank at one time. They had a large angry crowd outside their door. Barclays soon ran out of cash and I refused to let them have any of ours. We allowed everyone into our bank so that although the customers were packed like sardines in a tin there was no crowd outside to bring further attention to the situation. I ordered a pile of notes to be stacked up at the back of the row of cashiers' cages, well out of reach of customers but in full view and under the watch of an officer and a couple of bank messengers as guards. I told them all not to move from their post or blink their eyes. They were armed with a large bag and instructions to scoop the notes and run like hell for the strongroom at the first sign of trouble. There was a risk, but I believed the risk of panic was greater if customers thought they might not be paid. I wanted everyone to see we had plenty of cash and hoped all would stay calm. Earlier I had sent one of our lorries to the Central Bank in Enugu to bring back more cash and until it arrived I told the cashiers not to stop paying out but to count every note three times and to go as slowly as they could without causing a riot. I walked among the crowds of customers. Pushing my way here and there I talked to those around me, trying to assure them we were not about to close and that we had plenty of cash. I was unable to persuade anybody to leave without their money.

The run went on for days. I no longer remember the numbers but our very substantial deposits, tens of millions of pounds, were withdrawn until we had little in the way of deposits left. Nobody came to pay off their loan before we closed.

All banks in all towns in the East suffered runs and many were obliged to close temporarily, having run out of cash. In Onitsha none of our branches closed. The executive director, Donald McLeod, telephoned to say he was coming from Lagos on tour to get a handle on exactly what was going on. I had been reporting daily, giving the numbers and I assume my colleagues in other branches had been doing the same but I am sure that it was difficult for people in Lagos to really understand the situation. My new boss and I met McLeod and his assistant at our side of the Niger bridge and I jumped into his car to lead him to the manager's new bank house while my boss followed in his own car. I was astonished when McLeod asked me who the person with me was. Seemingly my boss had not thought it wise to make his number with the executive director when he passed through Lagos.

A few days before McLeod's arrival I had bought the front page of the Onitsha newspaper, the *Nigerian Spokesman*, and had announced that local management assured our customers that SBWA was not about to close and that we had enough cash to pay everyone. McLeod asked why I had said local management. I told him I had no idea what he intended to do and I had left room for him to say I had been wrong. I never knew what he thought about that but he seemed pleased with all the various steps I had taken, although he appeared very puzzled as to why the new manager had still not taken over.

A couple of weeks later I was no longer in charge of the bank but I often discussed the political situation with members of the expatriate staff. One had a wife who thought she should leave Onitsha because it was going to be unsafe for her to stay but the husband did not want her to go. Another husband wanted his wife to go but the wife did not. It seemed that my wife was one of the few without a strong opinion. She said simply, 'I'll do whatever you decide is right.'

On Saturday morning 27th May 1967 I decided. I called Ans on the telephone from the bank and said, 'Ans, it is not safe for you and the children to stay in Onitsha. God only knows what is going to happen to this country but whatever it is I know that you and the children will be better out of it. Be ready to leave in two hours. I am taking you and the children over the bridge to Benin and putting you on the plane to Lagos, from where you can go to Heerlen or Glasgow. Pack what you will need for a few days. You will have to leave everything else behind.'

I then told the other married expatriates what I was about to do. They agreed that all the women and children should leave with us, except, that is, the wife of my boss. He did not see the need for his wife to leave. We decided to form a convoy of three cars driven by myself and two other husbands. Then I telephoned Lagos and spoke to the deputy executive director who told me I was creating a huge problem.

'Why on earth do you think they should leave and what are we to do with them all here in Lagos?'

'I don't know. Put them in a hotel until you can get them on planes for Europe.'

'But, my goodness, aren't you just panicking? Things will settle down.'

I recalled my conversation with this same man some years before when I had asked him to arrange to get a special injection against rabies shipped to me in Onitsha. A dog had died and had been diagnosed as having had rabies. Every man, woman and child in the block of six bank apartments claimed to have touched that damn dog. The standard treatment then was a debilitating course of three very painful injections administered through the ribs. If nearly every member of my expatriate staff had to go through that ordeal as well as the wives and children I would have difficulty keeping the bank open. I had been told that there was a new treatment involving a single injection administered in the arm and I asked for it to be procured and sent to me as quickly as possible.

'Why should we be doing that? It's a storm in a teacup,' said the deputy executive director.

'You're right,' I said. 'It probably is, but if we happen to be wrong, when the first child dies I'll have the mother speak to you.'

The injections were in Onitsha within a couple of days.

So now I was arguing with the same man about what he was going to do with four wives and three or four children. I ended the debate by saying, 'You can have them met and looked after or not, as you see fit, but they have confirmed seats and will be arriving this afternoon on the plane from Benin. I'll warn them that they may have to fend for themselves.'

'Oh, all right,' he answered, 'but I am sure this is not necessary. Let it be on your head.'

'Good. Thanks.'

The convoy left on time. We were stopped for inspection by armed soldiers not long after leaving the bank where we had assembled and again at the approach to the almost mile-long bridge on the outskirts of Onitsha. This bridge, spanning the River Niger, had been built by Dumez, the French construction company, in about six months between 1964 and 1965 at a cost of £6.75 million, although it was rumoured that not all of that went into the bridge. It certainly provided a more convenient way of crossing the river than the car ferry and the numerous small boats and large canoes which in earlier times had been the sole means of getting from one side to the other. In Onitsha we considered the bridge a wonder of its time. With the wives and children we crossed over to the far side of the Niger where we were questioned again, this time by Mid-West soldiers. The armed guardians on both sides seemed a little unsure what they were looking for and were not threatening. They appeared to be satisfied with our answer that we were going to Benin to put the women and children on a plane for Lagos because they were going home on leave. By prior agreement we were at pains not to suggest that anyone was running away. We enjoyed a pleasant and uneventful trip to Benin. The sun was shining and the roads were quiet. It was fortunate we did not know then that on 23rd April, just a month before our trip, a Fokker F-27 had been hijacked when flying from Benin to Lagos and forced to land in Enugu. And so, after tearful farewells at the airport and having watched the departure of the Fokker F-27 taking our families away, for how long we did not know and could not guess, we were relieved to think them out of whatever danger was to come.

The husbands decided to return to Onitsha as quickly as possible. Once there we would head for the club. No need to hurry home to wife and children this Saturday afternoon. However, there was a problem. Once my car had been emptied of suitcases it became obvious that my briefcase was in the boot. It should not have been there. Sunday, always happy to help, must have put it in the car with the suitcases. I said nothing until the women and children had left, but then I confessed to the others that we would need to find a quiet place to burn some documents. I was a member of a small committee of expats in Onitsha, supposedly very hush-hush. We had drawn up a plan to protect our families and ourselves until we could be rescued if we were cut off and in danger from out of control Federal forces. We had discussed helicopters and boats on the River Niger we hoped the British authorities would send to rescue us if necessary. The plan was to defend the textile factory which was close to the bridge and which had space in the grounds for a helicopter to land. Liam O'Brian, boss of the factory, of course was a member of the committee. We intended to stock the factory with food and water and other essentials, funded by a loan from my bank. My copy of the plan was in my briefcase and might well be regarded as highly suspicious. It could land me and perhaps all of us in trouble if discovered during one of the searches we were sure to encounter on the way back. This time my briefcase would not be hidden under suitcases. We were able to stop at a quiet stretch of the road and I put a light to the papers. And so on to the Onitsha Sports Club, to be met by jeers and catcalls from the well-lubricated late Saturday afternoon crowd. On 27th May 1967 our wives and children had been the first to leave Onitsha, or, so far as we knew, the East of Nigeria, and we were called panic-mongers and chickens.

Three days after our trip to Benin the catcalls stopped. On 30th May 1967 the founding of the country of Biafra was announced and the bridge was closed on the Biafra side. On 1st June 1967 the government in Lagos retaliated by closing the bridge on their side. The Niger Bridge did not reopen for civilian traffic until late September 1967 and then only for a day or two, when Biafran soldiers and civilians used it to retreat from Asaba to Biafra, immediately after which several spans were destroyed to prevent invaders using the bridge.

The British High Commission in Lagos ordered all non-essential British subjects out of the East. To leave Onitsha and to travel to Lagos everyone, including the wife of my manager and all the European bank staff, other than the manager and myself, had to be driven about 110 miles to Port Harcourt, passing through almost countless roadside inspections by army, police and anyone who decided to set up a roadblock. Once in Port Harcourt they would wait, most in uncomfortable conditions, for a suitable cargo ship, on the deck or in the hold of which they would spend about thirty hours before arriving in Lagos. About 800 expatriates of all nationalities from all over Biafra left on 20th July, packed in every available corner of the Italian freighter the *MV Isonzo*.

I found out later that the bank people in Lagos looked after our families very well. But within a few days, when at last it became obvious to those in authority that the situation was serious and not about to blow over quickly, our families were shipped off to Europe. My wife took our children to her parents in Holland and as the war escalated and we were cut off the bank supplied families with whatever news they had of us. Although I was drawing my salary in Onitsha as usual, I did not know until it was all over that the bank sent funds to my wife from time to time so that she was not without money. So far as I remember I was never asked to account for this double payment. In any event, my baby son had left Onitsha with his nappy stuffed with as much foreign currency as I could afford to buy and could get my hands on and I knew that my parents and in-laws would help my wife with money if that became necessary.

Although I heard nothing from the Port Harcourt manager, who was supposedly the senior man in the East, I tried to keep in regular touch with middle-aged Mr. Hailes, the manager in Enugu. One day while talking to him, with him assuring me all was well, I heard through the telephone an enormous bang.

'What on earth was that?' I asked.

'Oh, we are being shelled again,' he said in his calm, very proper English accent.

'Where are you?' I asked. 'Oh, I am in the office. Don't worry. I am fine. I am under my desk.'

By late June most of the remaining Europeans had left Onitsha. No need now to defend the factory. There were no families to safeguard. Indeed, so far as I knew, apart from a few remaining Catholic priests and nuns in the surrounding towns and villages, there was me, my laconic laid back manager and Henri Jellinek, an Austrian commission agent who seemingly was still trying to collect the money he was owed. At the bank there wasn't much to do. The market was very quiet and the country was surrounded and embargoed. No goods were coming in. We suffered air raids perpetrated by Nigerian commercial planes piloted, we believed, by white South Africans. We could see their arms as they leaned out the doors to drop homemade canister bombs, most of which seemed to land in the river. In Onitsha at that time the army had nothing but small arms with which to defend the town and each low-flying plane caused a noisy but almost useless fusillade. One night, hearing a loud bang in my garden I did exactly the wrong thing. I stuck my head out of the bedroom window to see what was going on. Fortunately it was the watchnight with his shotgun and a large metal dustbin.

'What are you doing, watchnight?'

'Ah, master, I am shooting into this bin to make big noise.'

'Why are you doing that?'

'If de plane dey for up hears me he will tink we have big big guns and he go away one time.'

It was all rather sad. Simple people facing a war they did not really understand even although they knew the cause and felt strongly about it. A popular song said, 'Ojukwu, give us guns to fight a war.'

Unfortunately Ojukwu did not have too many guns to give and few could anticipate the horrors to come. However, at this stage we were all confident of victory. Right was on our side and the small inconveniences, such as sitting at home trying to read by candlelight or being stopped in my car three or four times on the way home from work, seemed not too great an imposition given what was at stake. However, I never did become entirely comfortable in the presence of teenage soldiers brandishing automatic weapons.

My house had been built on land where, since before 1912, the bank branch had been situated. The centre of town had moved and the branch had followed. The land had then been used to build two very nice houses. At the back of my garden was a strongroom, with a large door complete with a combination and two key locks. Probably it had been too much trouble to knock it all down when the bank with living quarters above had been demolished. A small anteroom had been built to protect the door, which appeared not to have been touched in years; It took real strength to swing it fully open. I managed to gain access to the workings by removing the back and I spent many hours cleaning rust off the bars and stripping and oiling the locks and the brass combination tumblers so that everything worked perfectly. I was not sure why I was taking the trouble but it gave me something to do and the strongroom became useful to store an airgun left with me by Mac Fullen, a departing member of staff. He could not leave it lying in his apartment and certainly he could not carry it with him. I, with my reputation with the police as a possible enemy sympathiser, certainly did not want to be caught with it.

One evening in my house, listening by candlelight to Radio Hilversum on my shortwave radio, I decided to ask them to play a record for my wife in Holland. I drafted a letter giving them details of my request, including the name and identifying number of the record taken from my own copy. But how was I to get the letter out of Biafra? A few days later, by sheer luck, I met a nun who was leaving via Port Harcourt and who agreed to take the letter. I have always imagined that she secreted it in her wimple. Whether or not she did that I'll never know, but it makes a better story if she did! Sure enough, some weeks later I heard the announcement by Radio Hilversum of the receipt of a letter from Biafra written on the letterhead of the Standard Bank of West Africa. I was shocked. How could I have been so silly as to use a bank airmail letter? Anyway, they played "My Love is Like a Red, Red Rose" sung by Kenneth McKellar with the lines, for those who do not know what is arguably the second most famous of Robert Burns' 368 songs:

And fare-thee-weel, my only Luve!
And fare-thee-weel, a while!
And I will come again, my Luve,
Tho' it were ten thousand mile!

Nobody from the bank ever mentioned the letter heading. I doubt that anyone in head office was listening to Radio Hilversum.

Escape (Desertion)

I hated myself for going.
Why couldn't I be the kind of person who stays?
Jonathan Safran Foer

Ans and I, like many others, regarded our bank quarters as our home and furnished them as we would furnish a home anywhere. Practically everything we owned, wedding presents, silverware, photographs, records and paintings, was in our home in Onitsha. I had bought a beautiful oil painting from our friend Ben Enwonwu, a famous local artist who had entertained us in his elegant apartment in his home village and who had dined in our house. One of his sculptures is owned by the Queen and a painting by him sold in London in 2013 for £193,000. The painting I bought from him cost me £1,000. As there was little to do in the evenings and no light in which to do it, because, in case of air raids, we were forbidden to use anything but candles, I spent many evenings packing everything we owned except what I needed for daily life. I had plenty of time and so I was careful to make a record of every item with my estimate of its current value. When the task was completed I stored everything in the now renovated strongroom in the garden.

The war had started in earnest on 6th July 1967 when Federal forces shelled Ogoja in the Northeast of Biafra. On 14th July the university town of Nsuka, about seventy miles from Onitsha, fell to Federal forces. On 9th August, about two o'clock in the morning, I was wakened by what turned out to be the sound of a Biafran motorised rifle brigade with over 3,000 soldiers led by Brigadier Victor Banjo on the road to the Niger bridge. The seizure of the Mid-West was accomplished within hours but instead of continuing immediately to Ibadan and reaching Lagos by 10th August, which were his orders from Governor Ojukwu, Banjo delayed in Benin from where he withdrew on 12th September without firing a shot. Federal troops did not arrive until 21st September.

On 19th September 1967 Banjo was called to Enugu to explain himself and is said to have confessed to his leading role in a plot to assassinate Governor Ojukwu, among other objectives. On 22nd September Banjo, Lieutenant-Colonel Ifeajuna, the gold medal-winning high jumper at the 1954 Empire and Commonwealth Games, and two other officers, having been arrested, tried and found guilty of treason, were executed by a firing squad. Banjo was not an Igbo, but as a personal friend, had been trusted by Governor Ojukwu.

In September it became public knowledge in Biafra that the British and American governments and their agents were very firmly on the Federal side and were supplying arms and ammunition. I became concerned about public wrath and worried even more about my safety. In Onitsha, other than Catholic priests, whom I never saw, my boss and I were the only Brits left. Also still there was Henry Jellinek, the Austrian commission agent. I travelled to the bank each morning, rarely left the office for any reason and travelled home in the afternoons. Usually I was stopped by soldiers at roadblocks three or four times in my journey of about a mile each way. I was careful not to say or do anything to irritate them and when asked to 'climb down' from my car I did so promptly and without complaint.

The news grew grimmer by the day. We heard reports of Federal troops running wild in Benin and killing Igbo civilians. By 30th September the Biafrans were defending Asaba on the other side of the Niger. We could hear the guns. It looked to me as if the Federal troops would soon cross the river. I discussed things with my boss – in fact we talked about little else.

'Look,' I said, 'we need to have a plan. If the Federals come at night you will be at your house and I will be at mine. We would be safer together, acting as witnesses. Unless, of course, they shoot us both.'

'My God! Surely you don't think they would do that?'

'You know about the announcement I heard on the radio. Any expatriate found in Biafra will be treated as a mercenary and shot.'

'Yes, but the embassies protested and it was changed to say that only expatriates found to have been helping Biafra would be treated as mercenaries.'

'Sure. But I don't know what helping means. I assume that if I am found manning a gun at the riverside that would be helping.'

'But what,' said my boss, 'if you are found running a bank and keeping the economy functioning? Would that be helping?'

'I don't know,' I replied, 'but what I do know is that an eighteen-year-old soldier carrying an automatic rifle might not pause long enough to make a reasoned decision. And I am not sure he will have heard the latest order. Let's play it day by day. If the invasion comes at night the noise of the defence should give us plenty of time to get to the bank. All the focus will be on the river. We can shelter in the locked strongroom. There is a hatch to the bookroom that will give us a way in and out. We can stick our heads out and carry on when things calm down. I'll tell Henry to try to get himself here as quickly as he can.'

I desperately wanted to stay but I thought long and hard about what my wife and children would do if I were dead. I had a little life insurance, but certainly not enough for my wife to raise two children. I knew the grandparents would help and despite our plan I agonised about what I should do. I had been told months before by the executive director in Lagos that I was to use my own judgement and leave if and when I felt I should do so. It had been made clear that under no circumstances did the bank want me to put myself in danger. The trouble was I did not feel I should leave this bank and the people I had worked with and with whom, together, we had made the place run like clockwork. I thought my duty to my employer, and to my Biafran colleagues who could not leave, was to stay. But I thought it was my duty to my family to leave.

On 4th October 1967 the Federal troops entered Enugu, sixty miles away, and their colleagues in Asaba began shelling Onitsha. The far banks of the Niger were limned by the flashes from gun barrels. On the 5th I told my boss, 'Time to go. They will be here any day now, either from Asaba or Enugu, or both. I don't trust them not to shoot us when we come out of hiding. We need to head south to Aba tomorrow. We will be okay there for a while. If Port Harcourt is closed we can find a way out through the creeks.'

My boss owned a big and heavy Peugeot. My car was a small Morris 1100. We decided we would use his car for the journey. I contacted my friend Christopher Uba and he bought my beautiful little car. The price was a good deal for him, or at least he thought so, and better for me than abandoning the car to the Federal troops. I hope Christopher was able to protect himself, his family and the car from the hell that came to Onitsha. I could not bear to say goodbye to the staff, particularly the bright young men and women I had hired. I felt I was deserting them and left my boss to hand his keys to L. E. Okafor, the man I suggested he appoint to be in charge. I went home to give Sunday six months' pay. I told him I thought he should try to get his family to his home village.

'But master, what about the house and the furniture and Madam's things?'

'Sunday, to hell with the house and Madam's things. Look after yourself and your family. Take anything you want and can carry. But don't take so much that you can't travel. And Sunday, thank you for everything. Good luck. I'll find you when I get back.'

When my wife had left with the children I had sold her car and paid off Jimmy and Cornelia and told them to go to their villages where they would be safer. There now was nothing more for me to do but leave. And so I deserted my post next morning on 6th October 1967 at about nine o'clock.

I had been able to find Henry and we also had with us in a convoy of three cars a German who had escaped over the bridge from Asaba and a young Sikh with a turban. I have no idea from where he arrived or how he came to be with us. As we left, shells were falling but mostly close to the river, where I suppose the Federals were trying to knock out the defences. My last view of Onitsha was Zik's statue, at the top of New Market Road. He had a car tyre round his neck. The streets were packed with people, all heading away from the river, and the main road was thronged with vehicles headed south. There were roadblocks every few hundred yards formed by oil drums, tree branches and debris of all kinds. The barriers were manned by civilians armed with cutlasses and they were shouting, 'Stay and fight.'

Cutlasses were being waved as persuaders. It was chaotic and not a pretty sight.

After passing through several checks we came to a more official-looking barrier not more than a couple of miles from town. It was guarded by soldiers who arrested us. They did not say why and we did not argue. Four of us were driven to the police station in our cars and Henry, for some unexplained reason, was taken to the military headquarters. I don't think there was any reason for our separation other than the panic and utter confusion all around us.

For a couple of hours we sat in the police station, where nobody seemed to know what to do with us or even why we were there. So far as I remember we were not accused of anything and we just sat quietly, barely speaking to each other, while the chaos around us escalated by the minute. Eventually a man in the uniform of an army lieutenant-colonel turned up.

'Where are you going?' he asked.

'We are headed for Aba,' my boss replied.

'Good,' said the officer. 'I am headed there too. I'll get you released and we can join forces.'

I kept very quiet. I was suspicious of this man who wanted to join forces with people he knew nothing about. He did not ask why we were in the police station, but perhaps he had made enquiries before he spoke to us. He was told we could not leave without Henry and he undertook to fetch him. When he returned with Henry I felt reassured that he appeared to have some level of authority. He said he was from the Mid-West and had been the paymaster of the Nigerian Army. When we were outside the police station we found that he had a Mercedes and with him were two very young-looking private soldiers, each of whom had a .303 rifle. The colonel posted one soldier in the back of my boss's car with me in the front passenger seat and the other soldier in the rear car of our now four-car convoy. The soldiers were ordered to point their rifles out the windows at roadblocks. We set off with the colonel driving the lead car. When we came to the first roadblock he leaned out the window, waved a revolver and shouted, 'Clear the road.'

The road was cleared and we proceeded like this through at least a dozen roadblocks, the scenes around which appeared unorganised, chaotic and far from reassuring. Twice the colonel fired a shot in the air when the road was not cleared quickly enough to suit him. The distance between the roadblocks increased and we began to relax. We passed Ihiala and it looked as if we had made our escape from Onitsha. Then a column of four or five open military jeeps sped past us. Soldiers, wearing military police armbands, were clinging to the sides and back of each vehicle in addition to the three or four seated inside.

'There's an emergency somewhere,' I said.

And then, a hundred yards or so ahead of us, the jeeps pulled up and blocked the road. The soldiers leaped off even before the jeeps had come to a full stop. They levelled their rifles at us and formed a semi-circle into which we drove and pulled up. As we were stopping I turned and leaned over to the driver's side of the back seat and grabbed the rifle of the soldier behind and forced it down onto the floor, where he let it go. Then I got out of the car with my hands high above my head. I am not sure now of the order in which the worries flooded my brain, but it went something like this; *shit, if the colonel resists we are all dead. What is the soldier in the back of the car doing? Is he getting out without his rifle?* I turned and shouted to him, 'Leave the gun.'

My mind raced. *What about the soldier in the last car? Who is telling him not to resist? Christ, what is the colonel doing?* Fortunately, as I looked around, I could see everyone getting out of the cars with their hands up. The colonel was out but his hands were only halfway up. I could not see his revolver because I was on the passenger side while he was getting out of the driver's seat of the car in front. I was very worried about what he might do. Going through the checkpoints he had seemed hot-headed, to say the least. A sergeant, who appeared to be in charge, shouted, 'Get them together.'

Whereupon, with rifles poking us, we were herded into a group and thoroughly and a bit roughly searched. We were all very quiet and I was glad that the colonel said not a word. We watched under close guard while the cars were examined carefully and a number of weapons removed from the boot of the Mercedes. Our bags were opened and searched, after which we were loaded back into our cars with a soldier behind each one of us. I had a rifle poking the back of my neck. I presumed the others were in the same predicament. The colonel had been arrested by a sergeant and we were all forced to drive to a police station not far away with jeeps in front and behind. We drove through a gate into a police compound on the edge of a small town. The station had a wall round it with a grassy lawn in the middle and a few buildings round the perimeter.

'Climb down,' the guards yelled and we were lined up with weapons menacing us. Things seemed a bit dangerous but then we were told to sit on the lawn. The guards withdrew to what seemed like a safer distance. So, having asked permission, and under close scrutiny we broke out our flasks and sandwiches and pretended not to be worried. Stiff upper lip and all that, even though we were only two Brits and three foreigners. At least one of the foreigners could be relied on, I thought. The Sikh. I wasn't sure about the other two.

After an hour or so we were called to sit in a single row on benches outside the office of the senior policeman who would interview us and apparently decide our fate. The colonel and his two soldiers were immediately ahead of me and the rest behind me. I became exceedingly worried when I overheard the colonel whispering to his men, obviously giving them instructions. The colonel had told us he was from the Mid-West but it transpired that his soldiers were Igbos born in the north of Nigeria. The Mid-West army had proved to have divided loyalties, with some officers and men loyal to Biafra and others siding with the Federal government. *What if this guy is a saboteur headed to Aba to do some damage or even make an attempt on Governor Ojukwu's life?* I thought. The interrogation was aggressive, verbally but not physically. It was carried out by a policeman who, I think, was an inspector or a lieutenant. If the situation had been less serious it would have been funny. The inspector, if that is what he was, had a peculiar clipped mannerism and sported a most unusual headdress, seemingly unsuitable in the heat of Nigeria. His cap was made of leather and had fur-lined ear flaps which were pinned up to the top of the cap. For some reason his attire and mannerisms made me think of a young Jerry Lewis, the comedian, and lacking another name for him, that is what we called him, but not to his face. After a couple of hours, following lengthy telephone calls, of which we were aware but could not overhear, it was decided we were to be sent to Owerri for "further interrogation". Our passports had been confiscated and were to be handed back to us one by one by Jerry Lewis. He called my name and I gave him a simple thank you for returning my passport. That courtesy was not enough for the portly Austrian Henry Jellinek. When his turn came he stepped up smartly to the desk of the funny policeman in a remote outpost in Nigeria where our lives had been threatened and still seemed to be in some danger. Clicking his heels in the best Teutonic fashion, Henry bowed and presented his business card while saying, 'If ever you are in Vienna.'

I dared not laugh.

We were loaded back into our cars and once again I had the cold steel of a rifle jabbing the back of my neck. I felt very far from my wife and children and I worried again about an accidental discharge; both into me and out of me! As the gates of the compound opened it became clear that word had gone round the town. Mercenaries had been captured. A large crowd lined the path out of the police station. There arose a chilling chant; 'Kill them. Kill them.'

The chant was accompanied by hands beating on the roof of the car.

As we were under close escort the trip to Owerri was uneventful apart from the constant worry of an accident with a rifle. Because of our police and military escort we had no trouble at the roadblocks, except that we encountered a lot of curiosity and some hostility. I hoped that none of our guards would attempt to curry the favour of the crowd by shooting one of us. On the way darkness fell and when we arrived at Owerri it must have been about seven in the evening. We were shown into a large room and were told we were to be questioned by the head or director of military intelligence who, very fortunately for us, just happened to be in town. Otherwise we might have been there for days. The colonel and his soldiers were dealt with separately somewhere else. When the director arrived I stepped up first to prove I was not a mercenary. I produced my driving licence, issued in Onitsha and renewed there every year for the last four years, and I suggested that Chief Isaac Mbanefo would vouch for me. And that was that. I do not remember what the others told me they had said but whatever it was it was considered enough and we were advised we could proceed to Aba. Apparently the colonel had been told the same thing but, amusingly, he arrived in our room and complained to the director that he would not travel in the dark unless we accompanied him. Our journey to Aba was uneventful and our arrival memorable for only one thing. We had told Jamie Lister, manager of the bank in Aba, that we were coming and my boss and I were to stay at the bank house. When we pulled into the driveway late at night Jamie was angry with us. He said it had been inconsiderate of us not to have let him know we had been delayed. He then proceeded to give us a detailed lecture and a demonstration about the use of the water heater which needed to be switched off after use. When he left us alone our laughter probably came as much from relief as from the excessively detailed water heater instructions.

I have read a good deal about the Biafran war and have found several references to the person I am reasonably sure was our colonel. I believe he was Major Morah, paymaster of the Nigerian Army. In May 1966 he was promoted to temporary lieutenant-colonel. An article, said to be part of an American diplomatic dispatch, which now can be found on the internet, states:

In the evening of 22 September, the Mid-West paymaster, Col. Morah, from Eze near Onicha Olona, offered an American expatriate in Asaba £3,000 if the American would arrange for Morah to get $5,000 upon his arrival in the United States. This would have been a profit of about $3,400 to the American. The offer was refused. Later on September 25, Morah disappeared with £33,000.

In fairness to Colonel Morah, if indeed he was our man, I saw no evidence of a bag of money when we were searched and other references to him say that he became the paymaster of the Biafran army and fought gallantly for Biafra.

I need not have left Onitsha on 6th October. An estimated 700 men and boys had been massacred in Asaba by Federal troops on 7th October. Two divisions of Federal troops crossed the Niger in boats on 12th October and in an act of pure vandalism set fire to the Onitsha market. They were allowed to advance into a carefully-staged ambush in which they were soundly defeated and forced to retreat back across the river. Onitsha did not fall until March 1968.

On the morning of 7th October I awoke in the bank house in Aba and was happy to learn that Jamie had made arrangements, which were somewhat uncertain, for a boat to take us from Ikang through the creeks to Cameroon. We were to be joined on the trip by a motley crew including a couple of Catholic priests and the deputy British High Commissioner together with one of his staff. The latter two had been released from house arrest in Port Harcourt a day or so before. But first we had to get to Ikang. We set off on the morning of the seventh and the journey took us through Ikot Ekpene and Calabar. At Ikang we abandoned the cars. My boss gave his keys to a driver from the bank in Aba in the hope of recovering his Peugeot at some time in the future. The trip had been largely uneventful except that we had picked up along the way an Irish lady and four children. She was the wife of a local judge and seemed not to have any transport or food and she had no passports for two of the children. At Ikang we were processed by the authorities and I still have my old passport stamped IMMIGRATION POST IKANG NIGERIA with NIGERIA crossed out in ink and BIAFRA substituted. My entry permit of 2nd June 1966, although it was to Nigeria and numbered LA/3532/66, was carefully detailed by hand in the body of the exit stamp and was stated to have been withdrawn. The stamp is dated 7th October 1967. I found it odd that one country was withdrawing the entry permit to another country, but I did not comment. One never knew what might rouse the ire of the authorities.

After clearing immigration, we went looking for our "boat" and found it to be a very large motorised canoe with a small cuddy cabin. We were soon underway and concerned about being chased by the Nigerian Navy, which was blockading all sea approaches. At Ikang the mouth of the Cross River is about twelve miles wide and we had to get to the other side without being spotted by a Nigerian gunboat. But before long we were in the creeks, where there seemed little chance of being detected or followed. I remember the priests taking occupation of the cuddy cabin, the most comfortable accommodation, and there may have been more than two of them, because a bridge game in which I did not take part was soon in progress. Before long we were well into the creeks, surrounded very closely on either side and overhung by mangroves. We would pass openings to channels on the right and left and suddenly take a turn that looked no different from several we had just passed. I could see no markings of any kind and have no idea how the captain decided which turn was the correct one. In the late afternoon, we were stopped by a large submerged tree blocking the narrow creek. Worried about being stuck there indefinitely, several of us waded in and tried to move the tree or lift the boat, without making the slightest impression on either. I remember feeling like Humphrey Bogart in the film *The African Queen*. Defeated, I poked my head into the cuddy cabin and told the priests we had done all we could. We were stuck and it was now up to them to pray. I don't know what they did, but within fifteen or twenty minutes the tide rose and we floated over the log. Why did the captain not tell us this was about to happen? I imagine he just wanted to see white men panicking and making fools of themselves. One of the priests was known as the 'sweary priest' and I believe he was famous in Nigeria for his peculiar language skills. I don't know if he offered any prayers on that occasion but I am now sure the tide was going to rise whatever anyone said or did and I am just as sure our captain knew that.

After darkness fell about 6pm we spent a most uncomfortable seven or eight hours, during which most of us sat upright on wooden benches with no back, very like passengers on a mammy wagon. One of the Irish lady's youngsters fell asleep and collapsed into my lap, making it difficult for me to move and thus doubly uncomfortable. We arrived in the wee hours of the morning at a palm oil plantation in Cameroon, which I think was owned by United Africa Company. The staff there received us most kindly considering the ungodly hour and found accommodation for us for what remained of the night. In the morning we all emerged from the chalets in which we had slept, mostly looking dishevelled and in the clothes in which we had retired. I was struck by the ridiculous appearance of the British High Commission assistant. He emerged in freshly-pressed slacks, a striped seersucker jacket and a red bow tie, greeting everyone as 'old chap', as if we were attendees at the Oxford and Cambridge boat race instead of refugees in the jungle. I thought of our policeman, Jerry Lewis, and decided that there are men in every culture worthy of a caricature.

Later that day, 8th October, we all reported to the authorities in Lobe, a tourist destination where a waterfall splashes into the sea. In anticipation of a possible departure from Biafra through

Cameroon I had applied to the Cameroon Embassy in Enugu for a visa and my passport shows that a six-month visa number 135/67 was issued on 25th August 1967. Nobody else in the group had a visa but it did not seem to matter. We were refugees and were admitted without question. All of us were conscious that our loved ones did not know where we were and indeed had not known for some weeks. I was keen to get to Duala to find a flight to Europe. Strangely there is nothing in my passport about leaving Duala or my arrival in or departure from Libreville in Gabon, half a degree north of the equator. The lack of stamps in the passport may have had something to do with the fact that we had with us the two children who had no passports. Once again we all claimed refugee status and told the four children not to stand still but to be unruly, something probably a little foreign to these well-behaved children; we all milled around until the frustrated officials waved us through the checkpoints. From Libreville we took an overnight flight to Paris, where we arrived on 10th October. There my passport was stamped and there I left the Irish lady attempting to contact the Irish Embassy. No doubt she was rescued. She wrote a letter to *The Times* a few days later condemning the British for supporting the Nigerian Federal Authorities.

That same afternoon I was knocking on the door of my in-laws in Heerlen in the South of Holland and hugging my wife and children. From time to time and not infrequently in the previous months I had wondered if I would ever see them again. Although I had spent much of the time on the journey from Libreville thinking about the bank in Onitsha and trying to imagine what the staff were doing and what problems I had left them to face, the first look at my children told me why I had abandoned Onitsha.

Goodbye Africa

Do not grieve when something good ends.
Be glad that it happened.

Jeffrey Fry

After a couple of weeks in Holland, Ans and I with the children flew to London where I reported to head office. I was received kindly and was asked to pick up from Mappin & Webb, in Old Bond Street, a gold Omega watch presented to me, not by the executives of the bank but by the directors, for service above and beyond the call of duty in Biafra. I was pleased to receive it but sorry ever since that it had not been engraved. I was asked to plan to return to Lagos in January 1968. At home in Glasgow my parents made much of Christmas with the children.

The bank had offered compensation for what they thought we had lost but I held onto the hope that all our possessions would be safe in the strong room at the house in Onitsha and we would recover everything once the war was over. I made reservations on the *MV Apapa* sailing from Liverpool. We all enjoyed the relaxed sea trip, during which the children starred in the fancy dress competition. But we were glad to arrive in Lagos on 25 January 1968. I knew that the wait to be processed by immigration, to pick up our luggage in the enormous baggage hall and to get through customs would be long and hot. We were to go ashore immediately after breakfast and on leaving the table Ans picked up a ripe pear which she felt would provide some needed liquid for the children; the fashion of walking about with bottles full of water costing more than petrol had not yet taken hold. The man at the customs desk confiscated the pear as a prohibited import and we saw him eat it as we struggled later to leave with all our baggage. There had been no comment about the Biafra stamp in my passport.

I was to take up the post of accountant of Marina branch, the main branch in Lagos. This was a senior post but it had been made clear to me that as soon as the war was over I was to return to the East. I hoped to be appointed on a long-term basis to the top job in Onitsha.

Although I loved the work, life in Lagos wasn't much fun. The traffic was awful and bunches of armed soldiers roamed the streets, appearing more threatening than they probably were. I knew that Ans disliked Lagos. She did not mix with the other wives and would not attend the coffee mornings hosted by the wife of the executive director, who, no doubt, was under instruction from her husband to have a look at her and report back. Ans contented herself with the children and the house and with ensuring that things ran exactly as she wanted. To give her a break in June 1968 I arranged for all four of us to fly to Accra for a long weekend with a rugby team. Once there we avoided the game and I was pleased to introduce Ans to my great friend Joe Ryan. Joe had arranged for me to hire a car, although in those days there were no car hire firms, and we drove to the east of Ghana and arrived without prior warning at the station of Ans' brother the priest. Apparently the local children had discovered his many middle names, one of which was Elizabeth. Laughingly they referred to him as Father Elizabeth. Unaccountably, he did not seem surprised to see us. He was still phlegmatic.

I looked forward to returning to Onitsha, but I began to realise, to my distress, that Biafra was going to lose the war. Nigeria was being supplied by America and Britain and other European countries with arms and ammunition and, some said, with military advisers. Biafra was encircled, cut off and was being starved. In addition to all this, suddenly one day I realised, almost as a revelation, I could not go back to the East. I had run away when I was needed most. What was I to say?

'You have managed without me through the hell of the last few years. Now I have returned to tell you what to do and how to do it.'

I knew the people I had worked with in Onitsha did not need me or anyone else. What should I do? If I refused to go back to the East or, more likely, if the Easterners refused to have me, I thought the bank would find me a place somewhere in Nigeria. But Nigeria was going to have two demobilised armies with no jobs to give the former soldiers. Things were going to be unpleasant. An alternative would be a posting somewhere else in Africa. If I had been a single man that would have been great, I loved Africa, but now I had a wife and children. I needed to do something to make the future more certain for the family. I did not want to work for a bank in Scotland, even if one would employ me. I knew I would never get a suitable job in The Netherlands. We liked the idea of Australia and even more of New Zealand, but they were so far away from Europe and our families. As it so happened, in Lagos we lived one house away from the residence of the Canadian High Commissioner to Nigeria. He and his wife provided us with a good deal of information which made Canada seem inviting. I did not find out until much later that his statistics, particularly financial, were a good deal out of date. In a peculiar twist of fate, just when I was trying to evaluate Canada as a possible destination where I could become the bank manager in a little country town, where we could raise our children and I could continue to be the kind of community banker I wanted to be, I saw an advertisement placed by the Bank of Nova Scotia (which now trades as Scotiabank) of which I knew nothing. Nevertheless, I wrote to the address in London, England.

Even the head office of SBWA in London had admitted that conditions in Nigeria were difficult and had shortened the tours of duty to ten months in Nigeria and two months at home. Soon this was changed to five months in Nigeria and one month at home. These were my terms and I am not sure if they applied only to senior officers or to all expatriates. In any event, after less than eight months we left on 8th September 1968 for home leave, during which I attended a pre-arranged Scotiabank interview in London with a man called Baker. I was unimpressed and I got the distinct feeling that Mr. Baker had been unimpressed by me. No offer was made and I assumed that was the end of it. I determined to enjoy our home leave, partly in Holland and partly in Scotland as usual. To my surprise, a couple of weeks later I received a letter from Scotiabank informing me that Mr. Earl Forcey and another bank official would be in Glasgow and would like to interview me. Fortunately, I was in Scotland at the time of the interview or my life and that of my wife and children would probably have been very different. I went along to the Central Hotel in Glasgow and enjoyed a very long interview, during which we swapped Ghana, Biafra and Cuba stories. Scotiabank, in Cuba since 1906, was one of only two banks to reach a mutually satisfactory arrangement with the Cuban government, which nationalised all other foreign banks in December 1960 without compensation. Che Guevara, appointed director of the National Bank of Cuba in November 1959, sold Cuba's gold reserves, then held in Fort Knox, and transferred part of the proceeds to Scotiabank in Toronto. No doubt this provided the bank with some leverage in the negotiations. The story told, which I learned much later in my career, is that Bobby Kennedy, then American attorney-general, telephoned

Scotiabank's president and admitted that the Americans had been listening to the telephone conversations the bank had been having with the Cuban government. He suggested that Scotiabank share the proceeds of Cuba's gold sale with the American banks that had been nationalised without compensation. Sorry, but no! My interview in Glasgow went well and lasted so long that my car, parked at a meter, was adorned with a parking ticket when I returned. I wonder if it is too late to submit an expense claim.

I had advised Mr. Forcey that I was not available for at least six months. I did not feel able to walk out on my employer without giving adequate notice. Forcey was ambivalent about this and I thought it might queer my pitch. However, in due course I received a written offer of a job in Canada starting at Can$9,000 per annum. Even on the out of date numbers I had received from the Canadian High Commission this salary clearly did not recognise the seniority I had achieved, but I decided that although it was a huge backward step this was a life move that I should make. I was confident I would soon demonstrate I was worth much more. So I thought!

We all returned to Lagos by air on 27ᵗʰ October 1968 to start my ninth and final tour of duty in Africa. I soon handed in my resignation with the five months' notice that would take me to the end of my tour. My colleagues were mystified. How, they asked, could I give up such a good senior position? The executive director, Mr. McLeod, never spoke to me again.

To add to my distress at the thought of leaving Nigeria, we heard from Sunday a couple of weeks before we were due to depart. He had turned up at the Calabar branch of the bank and asked if they knew my whereabouts. He and his family had made it to his home safely and all were well. I sent some money to keep Sunday going for a couple of months, together with a message saying how sorry we were that we were leaving and that we could not bring him to Lagos as he had asked. I said that Sunday should keep in touch with the branch at Calabar and I would send an address as soon as we had one. To add to the misery of leaving we learned that the strongroom I had so carefully refurbished had been breached through a wall, presumably by the Nigerian troops who had been stationed in Onitsha for so long. Without question the bank paid what I asked in recompense for the loss of everything we owned, but of course the current value I had placed on things bore little relation to replacement cost. And how do you value precious wedding photographs and presents?

The day we were leaving I went to the library to return some books and outside I saw an old Hausa trader sitting with his wares spread out before him on a rug. I fell in love with a carving of an old man with a stick in one hand and a begging cup in the other. Repeating the stupidity of my departure from Ghana, when I bought an elephant table on the dock, I bargained for and bought the almost three-foot high carving. Then I had to rush home and persuade Pat next door to box it up and ship it to us whenever we had an address in Canada.

We almost missed the flight out of Lagos. Anticipating possible traffic problems, roadblocks and searches by soldiers, I had arranged to leave home very early and for us to rest in a day room at the hotel next to the airport. In the taxi, on the way, I asked Ans if she had the air tickets. Assuming my question was meant to scare her into thinking I did not have them, an obviously all too common silly trick I used to play, she said she had them. I did not realise she was just fed up with my joke and we did not discover that neither of us had the tickets until we were comfortably lodged in the hotel room with the kids enjoying a television programme about how to clean a meat safe. In those days there were no electronic bookings that could be referenced on a computer. One needed to have the ticket. I hired a taxi and bribed the driver to rush back at breakneck speed to the house. I collected the tickets from exactly where I had left them on the dressing table in the bedroom and made it back to the hotel in time for the flight. It is better to be lucky than smart. I built a career on it.

We left Nigeria for good and it did not escape me that the date was 1st April 1969, All Fool's Day. Not for the first time in my life, and with a heavy heart about leaving Africa, I wondered what I had let myself in for. This time it was more serious. I now had a wife and children to worry about. As we sat in the plane waiting to take off, I thought with great sadness that I would never again enjoy the wonderful heady smell of the earth in our garden in Onitsha as it was wet by the first rain after the dry season. And never again would I have the pleasure of strolling through the Onitsha market being greeted as a friend by my customers or of witnessing a beautiful sunset or a fearsome electrical storm over the waters of the River Niger.

Glasgow, Toronto, New York and Port of Spain

18

In America nothing is bad luck. It is somebody's fault and if you hire the right lawyer you will be compensated.

Calum Johnston

By May 1969 we were waiting in Glasgow for my Canadian papers to arrive. My mother asked, 'What will you do if the papers are not approved?'

'Don't worry about it. I have an offer of a job and that makes it routine.'

I was less confident than I sounded and it certainly did cross my mind that we would be high and dry if the papers did not come through. From the information I had been given by the Bank of Nova Scotia I was aware that I could join the bank's pension plan without a medical if I did so before the age of thirty-five. Although I believed I was in good health I remembered the malaria, the dengue and particularly the typhoid fever and thought I should avoid a medical if I could. I was thirty-four. I wrote to Earl Forcey to say I was hoping my papers would come through in time for me to be in Canada in July before I was thirty-five. He replied immediately and told me to sign on as a member of the bank staff at the bank's Glasgow branch as soon as I liked. I remember feeling that this consideration augured well for my future relationship with the bank and I felt a little more confident about having made the change of employer at my age, even though, clearly, I had given up a lot of seniority to do so. I spent a couple of weeks in the Glasgow branch reading every manual I could get my hands on. I was not impressed by the management and thought about what I would do if I could persuade the bank to send me to manage the Glasgow branch instead of the Englishman then in that position. My papers came through and I flew to Toronto alone on 24th June 1969. I had advised Earl Forcey of my flight details and as I expected he met me at the airport and took me to the Westbury Hotel. This was normal Africa procedure. I did not learn until later that it was a kindness on Earl's part. In general, in Canada the bank did not care where you came from each morning or where you went every evening after work. Overseas with Scotiabank it was different.

Next morning I walked down Yonge Street and turned right at King Street and into the building at 44 King, that I came to know so well and regarded as my headquarters for the next twenty-eight years, even when I was at the other side of the world. By mid-morning I had completed all the paperwork and had been directed to a department where I found Hugh Buckeridge, who had worked in Onitsha with BWA before my time, and who was remembered there, and Bill Matthews, who had worked with me in Onitsha, and Gordon Wylie, a former SBWA Liverpool employee. I was to work with a group headed by a non-banker, a time and motion expert. To my utter dismay he told me to find a project and to start work on it.

'What kind of project?'

'Anything that you think could be improved.'

I thought of a couple of things about his department that could be improved! However, this was not the time to have a big mouth. I sat down at my desk for a few minutes and thought of

Nigeria and Sunday our cook. I decided to go downstairs to the branch on the ground floor. After finding the right counter for sending wire transfers I asked the young lady standing there if I could send money to SBWA in Calabar, Nigeria. She reacted as if I had asked to send money to the moon. It took the clerk most of an hour to figure out how to accomplish the task. This involved looking in several books and consulting with two different people.

I went back to my desk, knowing exactly what could be improved. I got hold of copies of the manuals that the lady had consulted and found them confusing and unhelpful. Within a couple of weeks I had gathered the information about all our correspondent banks and the instructions for dealing with them. I had drafted the pages for a manual and completed the task of making it simple to find out how and where to send funds. The design was largely as I remembered the book used for the same task in SBWA. I also made a list of where we needed additional correspondent banks. Only when this had been done and the work submitted for approval was I told that my manual had to be split and accommodated in two separate binders.

'Why on earth should there be two binders? This is one complete manual that tells people all they need to know.'

'Well, you see, Mr. (and I forget his name. He was an elderly gentleman) has been working on this for a couple of years now and the binders for his work were ordered some time ago and are here. We need to use them for your concept which we agree is much simpler.'

I wonder, if you want to send a foreign wire at Scotiabank, if the clerk will be looking at my work, updated I hope, but still in two separate binders. However, probably it is all computerised. No doubt binders have gone the way of my fondly-remembered bound ledgers.

I had rented a small bungalow at Highland Creek, on the fast train line from Toronto. The people at the bank were surprised.

Apparently, I was supposed to rent an apartment. I had two children and I was not going to do that. I bought a second-hand Ford Falcon station wagon and amused the salesman by suggesting that he should give me a discount because I was paying cash. He said he would prefer me to finance the purchase because that way he could make a little more money. This was my introduction to the world of credit for everybody for everything. In due course I was happy to meet Ans and the children at the airport. We were soon settled in.

On the weekend of the Caribana Carnival, when all the people of Caribbean origin living anywhere within reach of Toronto gather for a great festive weekend, the four of us took the train into Toronto. Malcolm, now aged three, was thrilled when we alighted into a sea of black faces.

'Hurray. We're back in Nigeria!'

We were learning about life in Canada and enjoying Toronto; a fine city to bring up children, or it was then. Ans, easily identified as "foreign" by the wide-open windows in our little bungalow and the blankets hanging out to be aired, was asked by a passing neighbour, 'What does your husband do for a living?'

'He is a banker,' said Ans proudly.

The neighbour answered condescendingly, 'Well, as an immigrant, you have to take what you can get.'

Bank employees were not viewed in the light to which we were used. And, indeed, I was a little worried about the fact that we were spending every month more than I was earning, even though I felt we were living very modestly. Ans kept house frugally. Although I had sufficient savings to cover us for the foreseeable future I decided to try to earn a little by undertaking a telephone survey for, as best I remember, a dollar or two for each completed survey about transport in Toronto. What an ordeal, particularly for somebody who knew little about Toronto except how to get to work and back. Ever since that experience I have had sympathy for people who telephone at seven in the evening asking if I have time to answer a few questions. They always assure me it will take only a few minutes and, although I know better, I usually agree to participate.

By August I was part of a team trying to modernise the bank's Wall Street, New York, office and from August to December 1969 I flew to New York every Monday and flew home to Toronto every Friday. I was aghast at what I found in New York. The place was more outdated than SBWA in Lagos. The work was difficult, but the most difficult thing was to try to persuade a taxi cab to take me to La Guardia airport on a Friday afternoon. I learned to get in before declaring my destination but that didn't always work because cabs would cruise with their "in service" light off, slow down and ask my destination. When I said La Guardia, they took off without a word. Traffic was so bad that they did not want to make the trip. I learned to leave the office earlier and earlier on a Friday. While that made it easier to get to the airport it did not get me home any sooner. We often sat in the plane for two or three hours waiting to take off. The man on the night shift at the information desk at Toronto came to know Ans' voice. When she asked about the flight number he would say, 'Sorry Mrs. Johnston. They are still on the ground at La Guardia.'

It was often close to midnight before I was home. Eventually I told the bank enough was enough. Apart from the fact I was losing at the very least two half days of work every week, in the office I was just that guy from Toronto. If I was to accomplish more I needed to move to New York and become a full-time member of the staff. So, after cutting down our first real tree and celebrating our first Christmas in Canada, I hired a U-Haul trailer and we drove to New York. Earlier I had told my colleague, Brian Hurst, that he was mad to live so far away from the office and that I would borrow his car and drive to New York, turning back as soon as the area didn't look too inviting. I ended up in Larchmont, ten minutes closer to the office than he was! Not following the advice that later I always gave to young men going abroad, which was to let their wife choose the house, I rented a house next to the home Al Jolson was said to have built for his paramour. I was on tenterhooks when we pulled up outside but fortunately everyone was pleased with my choice. I loved Larchmont and would have been happy to remain there for ever if I could have earned the same locally as I was now earning on Wall Street, almost twice as much as I had started on in Toronto six months earlier. Larchmont, in Westchester County, was a happy little town with convenient church, schools, yacht club and beach at the end of the street. We had wonderful neighbours in the Robbs, next door, and the Perrys, a few houses down. No doubt these parents were confused when their children started calling cookies biscuits. Ans insisted that there were no cookies in our house and the American children soon learned that it paid to ask for a biscuit. Ans knew very well that in America a biscuit is more like a scone but... well, I would never dare suggest she was a little stubborn in some things.

The one drawback to Larchmont was that it took me one and a half hours on the train and subway to get to the office and a lot longer if it rained heavily. If it snowed there might be no way home at all. I tried driving to the subway but gave that up and passed the time on the train studying business management courses. In the office we made headway. I remember walking round to all the various departments asking for the paperwork on any problem dating from yesterday or before to be thrown into a large basket. Today's problems belonged to the department and were to be solved today but the old ones were mine. I was staggered by the number of enquiries about lost funds, duplicated payments, missing payments, mismatched payments and assorted other problems. I had a basketful. I hired an experienced banker and created a department called Investigations Department, for which I was reprimanded by Toronto. Who was I to create departments? Within six months they had a similarly named department in Toronto. We simply took each problem, entered it in a book, gave it a number and worked on it until we solved it. This might involve looking in the dungeon of a storeroom for vouchers that were years old to determine who had done what. I well remember Peter Godsoe, who much later became chairman of the bank, telling me he would eat his hat if I recovered $50,000 from Chase Bank that we had paid out a couple of years before on their instructions. I proved we had never been paid. Not only did I get the $50,000, but I recovered interest on the funds based on the convention in New York that no matter who was at fault whoever had held the funds would pay interest. I think the rate at that time was 6% per annum. I should make it clear that Scotiabank was no worse than most of the other banks in New York and that the other half of all our problems existed at another bank, and more often than not, the problem was the fault of the other bank.

Our bank in Trinidad had been incorporated locally. It maintained an account with our New York office. I was sending statements of their account to Trinidad but I knew from the lack of any enquiries from them they were not reconciling the statements with the account in their own books. The process is exactly like reconciling the cheque book of a personal account with the statement sent by the bank. After failing to get any response from Trinidad I complained to Toronto and told them they needed to do something before things got entirely out of hand. To my surprise I was told to come to Toronto to discuss the matter. What was there to discuss? Once there I was asked if I would go to Trinidad to reconcile the account. I was astonished. This was basic banking, or, as they say in North America, Banking 101. You match the entries in your account with the entries on the statement and query anything that cannot be matched. Surely they had somebody in Trinidad who could do that. Apparently not. I said I could not go to Trinidad.

'My wife is unwell and I cannot leave her for the few weeks that this will take. After all it has been many months since the account was opened and not reconciled.'

In the end I was told I could come home every weekend and reluctantly I agreed to go. After checking in at the upsidedown Hilton in Port of Spain where one took an elevator down to the rooms from the reception floor, I made my way to the main branch in Port of Spain. There I met Brian Nicholson, the accountant, and against whose uncle, a priest, I had played football in Onitsha. I told Nicholson I needed to say hello to the manager, an Englishman. Brian was most reluctant. He did not think the manager would want to see me over such a routine task. So routine, I thought, that nobody in Trinidad could do it! I told him that although I agreed what I was about to do was a clerical job there was no way I was going to sit in a branch without being introduced or introducing myself to the manager, even if it was to do no more than say good morning. And that is all I was allowed to say. At the door of the office, Brian, apparently afraid to enter, said who I was and what I had come to do. I got no further than the door before being dismissed with a curt, 'Good. Carry on.' And this, I thought, by a man who was unable to reconcile a bank account. Even if he had nobody to do it in a branch with forty or fifty on the staff he should have done it himself. Apparently he was too high and mighty for that. I got the job done in three weeks, including showing Errol Calendar how to continue where I left off. Errol took me home for lunch one day and his wife served me a nice dish of chicken and rice with an added chicken foot; the kind of thing we used to scare our young sisters with by pulling the ligaments and articulating the claws. To this day I am ashamed to say I made no attempt to eat it. Sorry Errol. I did not know how, never having encountered this in Africa. I went home only once during my visit. It seemed excessive to travel more often, even if the bank had agreed. When finally I went home I brought Ans a beautiful gold cameo brooch set with seed pearls, too expensive for my salary at the time and purchased at a jewellery store in the hotel. Ans wore that brooch almost daily for many years until I detected it was no longer in view. It was something I had given her and I was out of favour.

Ans was ill and had to go into hospital. Rodney Little most kindly agreed that his wife Mia, a marvellous Italian lady, would come from Boston, where they lived, to look after the children and me. We had known them in Nigeria and accompanying Mia was Livingstone, a grand African Grey parrot whom we had last seen in Onitsha.

Other visitors to our home in Larchmont, with whom Ans coped well, were my parents and sisters, her own parents and her uncle and aunt, sundry friends and acquaintances who stopped over for a night or two and my Great-aunt Annie, my grandmother's sister, whom I used to fetch from New Jersey and who seemed to like to stay with us for a week or two from time to time. She was good company and told us the story of being sent by her parents to America in 1909 at age sixteen with her fourteen-year-old brother Tom. They said on the ship's manifest that they were seventeen and sixteen. Fortunately, according to the manifest, they both declared, 'No,' when asked if they were polygamists or anarchists. They were to be met in New York by an aunt who did not turn up. Between them they had $45, most of which they were supposed to send back to Glasgow for the next part of the family to use for their entry to America. Annie used a little of it, she said, to get the pair of them to Manchester, Connecticut, where she found a job in a bakery for Tom, thinking that at least he would be able to eat.

Towards the end of my two years in New York I set an assistant the task of organising stationery and the ordering of it, which was as disorganised as it always had been in Africa. Unfortunately, in his enthusiasm to get everything in one place, he made the mistake of removing a small personal supply maintained by a senior

American officer, who seemed to do little other than work on his own investment portfolio. He was outraged, and I am sure it was he who objected to my appointment as agent administration. I had been informed by the incumbent that the post was to be mine. Peter Godsoe had been promoted to Toronto and returned to New York to tell me that I was not to have the promised appointment, but he never said why. I did not really care and did not ask. I had believed he was coming to fire me. In any case a few weeks before I had been head-hunted, out of the blue, to head up the international division of New England Merchants National Bank in Boston. I never found out how my name had come up, but I had been to Boston for interview, where the chairman said, 'You are just the man to put straight our international department in a year.'

'Sorry,' I said. 'I am not the man for that. It will take me two years.'

The chairman clapped his hands in approval and, remarkably, took me upstairs to introduce me to the man who would be my number two and showed me the corner office overlooking the Charles River that was to be mine. They were to pay me twice what I was earning, but they had to procure a green card as I was in the United States on an H specialist visa. That meant they had to advertise the job all over America and explain convincingly why every truck driver who applied was not suitable. While I waited I reorganised the letter of credit department in Scotiabank's New York agency.

The time came for our return to Canada. New England Merchants National Bank told me they were still working on my green card and that they would not give up. My Great-uncle Sam said he had political connections and a word from him would sort things out in no time. I declined his offer, not wanting a job that might make me obligated to a politician. I hired a mover and witnessed as efficient an operation as I ever saw. Three or four men descended on the house like locusts and in short order everything was wrapped, packed and taped. We drove to a ranch house on five acres we had rented in King City, a few miles north of Toronto. I could have purchased it for $300,000. It might as well have been $3 million. I did not have $300,000. There are now five or six houses on that land. Something clicked in the minds of the kids when we crossed the border into Canada. Later, every time we drove from King City to Toronto they would ask, 'Are we still in Canada?'

At the bank I was put to work doing menial clerical tasks in the Caribbean Regional Office. When an officer went on holiday I volunteered to fill in for him. I was finished with his day's work before lunchtime and even after scratching around for things I could do usefully, I had to pretend to be busy for the rest of the day. I pestered the man in Personnel, a cadaverous-looking chap never without a cigarette, who asked me to think about Trinidad. I told him I did not need to think. I would go, but only for the top job there. He was aghast. How could I suggest such a thing? I told him I had met the top man! I asked for a branch somewhere and was told that would not be possible. I had not been long with the bank and would not know the right forms to use! I understood then why he was in Personnel. I called on him every week. Eventually he telephoned me at home on a Friday when I was on holiday for a week during a visit of my mother and he said he had a posting to offer.

'You will either love it or hate it. Come see me Monday.'

'Please tell me now.'

'Oh no, I need to see you in person.'

Pleading did not help. Why on earth did he not wait until Monday to call me? I decided that whatever the offer turned out to be I would give him no reaction and ask for time to think, keeping him on the spot for a while.

When I met him, he offered the position of special representative. I was to go to Hong Kong to open our first office there. I asked for time to think and suggested a month in spite of the fact that in my mind I had already accepted and with great pleasure.

'Oh, good lord, no. I must have an answer soon.'

'Well, you see, the salary you offer is not enough and I would need an allowance to buy the right clothing for the family.'

'But Hong Kong is not tropical, it is sub-tropical.'

'Exactly. The family will need light winter as well as tropical summer clothing.'

In the end acceptable clothing allowances were agreed for each member of the family and a couple of thousand a year added to the salary. I would have gone without either the increase or the allowances. I was confident Ans would not object, although I did go through the formality of asking her. However, despite the terms having been agreed it turned out that I was to be interviewed by Hans Marsman, a wily old Dutch banker who was head of our European operations based in London and for the time being spearheading the push into Asia. If he didn't like me there would be no deal. At our first meeting in Toronto we talked of Africa and Indonesia where as a young man he had been a banker in conditions similar to those I experienced in Africa. I remember him telling me the joke about young bankers in Indonesia being held up by a highwayman and facing a demand for their money or their life. The answer was always, 'Take my life. I work for the bank and have no money.'

It was agreed I would go to Hong Kong. My uncle, William Jackson Johnston, aged twenty-two according to his birth certificate, although on the ship's manifest he said he was twenty-four and most remarkably had a passport that said the same, had sailed for Hong Kong on the *SS Morea* on 5th December 1924. Carrying out my family research many years later and long after Uncle Willie had died, it had fascinated me to look down the manifest, available online, and listen to echoes of the lost empire. Four or five young

Scots age twenty-one and twenty-two off to posts in Manila, Bangkok, Bombay, Shanghai and Sarawak. Most of them had sailed in Second Class but I was glad to see that twenty-two-year-old Mr. Livingston from Edinburgh, banker, bound for Bombay, was in First Class; as were a nineteen-year-old and a couple of twenty-year-old Englishmen who were joining China Customs in Shanghai. Malcolm Muggeridge, age twenty-one, who was on his way to Tuticorin (now also known as Thoothukudi) in Tamil Nadu in India to take up a job as a teacher, was also listed. I wonder if Willie ever knew, many years later when Muggeridge had become famous as a veteran of MI6, editor of *Punch* and a television personality, that they had sailed together on the long journey to the East.

Marsman went back to London and left me in Toronto celebrating with colleagues in Chinese restaurants and practising with my chopsticks. Many years later I learned that I had not been the first choice for the Hong Kong job. After Marsman had told the first man recommended by the personnel department that in Hong Kong he would have an amah to look after his children the candidate declined the position on the grounds that he would not have his children brought up by a communist maid! As Andy Rooney said, opportunities are never lost. Someone will take the ones you missed.

In Toronto I toured head office, asking as many senior people as would talk to me what they wanted me to do in Hong Kong. Invariably the answer was that once I got there I was to tell them what we should be doing. The bank had branches in Chinatowns in Toronto and Vancouver and I thought that the stationery department might have something in Chinese that would be of use. No luck. In desperation I asked if there were any bank matches I could have.

'Oh yes,' said the head of stationery, as I thought, glad at last to be able to help. He opened his desk drawer and from there took out a single book of matches with the bank logo on the cover and presented what he seemed to think was the Holy Grail. Before I left Canada my mother sent me a letter of introduction to Sir Sidney Gordon CBE, JP, whose aunt she knew. Sir Sidney, born in Glasgow, had accepted a position as an accountant in Hong Kong in 1947. Eventually, as a senior partner in Low, Bingham and Matthews, which became PricewaterhouseCoopers, Sir Sidney was the primary accountant to Sir Elly Kadoorie and Sons, the major shareholder in many companies in Hong Kong. Their portfolio included Hong Kong and Shanghai Hotels, operator of ten hotels in Asia with the Peninsula in Hong Kong the flagship. Also in the Kadoorie portfolio was China Light and Power, of which Sir Sidney was chairman. He became very close to the Kadoorie family and eventually became the group's chairman. Long after I had left Hong Kong I was pleased to learn that Sir Sidney, as a major force in the development of Hong Kong, had been awarded the Grand Bauhinia Medal, the highest award available to the Hong Kong government, at least until Hong Kong once again became part of China. So off to Hong Kong went the four of us, me with a book of matches and my letter of introduction. Guess which turned out to be the more useful.

I wrote to the chairman of the New England Merchants National Bank in Boston and thanked him for his generous offer and for his patience in waiting all through the months of trying for a green card. I told him about my appointment to Hong Kong and said that in view of the uncertainty about the job in Boston I regretfully had to decline his offer. It was probably a good decision. NEMNB became the Bank of New England and in 1990 suffered a loss of over $1 billion. Despite selling assets and laying off over 5,000 staff the bank lost a further $6 billion and was eventually closed. Of course, I might by then have been chairman and prevented the whole mess! In 2007 the Southern New Hampshire Bank and Trust was renamed Bank of New England but is in no way connected to the earlier bank of the same name.

Hong Kong

If you've 'eard the East a-callin',
you won't never 'eed naught else.

"Mandalay" Rudyard Kipling

I was a community, commercial and lending banker. I had never been in a representative office. In Toronto before our departure I asked if I could go to Detroit to visit the bank's representative office there. No. That would cost too much. I could have persevered and asked at a higher level and certainly would have received approval. Instead of asking I decided to go to Hong Kong via Tokyo, where the bank had a representative office. It cost a bit more for the four of us to spend a few days in Tokyo than for me to go to Detroit for the day, but it was as simple to arrange as telling the travel desk! To the amusement of my colleagues, because of the questions the kids had asked about still being in Canada when we drove from our home in King City to Toronto, I decided we would go by train to Vancouver and fly from there to Tokyo and Hong Kong. This would let the kids, and Ans and me, see exactly how big Canada is, or at least how big half of it is. It was a great trip in a comfortable little cabin with four beds and four armchairs which we furnished with an endless supply of little toys and colouring books. There was an observation car and, of course, a dining car but yes, it's a bit dull looking at all those snow-covered plains. But wait till we get to the Rockies, I would say. We got there just as it was getting dark and saw nothing until we were coasting down into Vancouver the next morning. We spent the day and that night in a hotel and I was glad of the chance to meet up again with Danny Kaneshiro, with whom I had worked in New York.

We arrived in Tokyo on 2nd December and left on the sixth. We were visiting Japan for the first time and before we arrived I had some serious reservations. Towards the end of the war my father, a voluntary ambulance driver in his spare time from the Home Guard and fire watching and his wartime job making Bofor 40mm anti-aircraft guns, had arrived home with Keith Burtenshaw. Keith had been freed from a Japanese prisoner of war camp and had been put on the first ship to get him away from the Far East. He had arrived in Glasgow to await transport to his home in New Zealand. My father was detailed to take him to a hospital but brought him home instead. He stayed with us for a week or ten days. Keith did not say much but what slipped out did not leave a very good impression of the Japanese. Keith told us that in the camp he and a friend had promised each other that whichever of them survived would be sure to tell the respective parents as much as they could about their son. Keith had the name and address of his friend's parents. Truth can be stranger than fiction. The address was in Glasgow. Keith was hesitating to make the trip because he had lost contact with his friend when either he or the friend had been moved to another camp some months before he had been liberated. Keith did not know if his friend was dead or alive. Eventually he gathered his courage and revealed the address to which my father was to take him. It was in the same street as the house of my grandparents. His friend's parents were happy to see him and pleased to say that they had heard from their son a few days before. He was in Australia waiting for a ship to bring him home to Scotland.

In Tokyo Ans and I were astonished by the courtesy and the efficient service we received in the Palace Hotel. I wondered if George Korenaga, the bank's Tokyo representative, who became a long-time good friend, had told the hotel I was some kind of prince or king of an obscure island. But in the coming years I discovered that the treatment we received on that visit was not unusual. During our four days in Tokyo we saw the sights, attended a tea ceremony, looked at ancient bonsai trees and I met John Roberts, the bank's man in Curacao, who was in Tokyo with a trade mission. He was impressed by the way our kids could sit, well-mannered, at a dining table and eat strange Japanese food. We could always take our children anywhere and rely on them to behave perfectly. And we did, and they did. One unforgettable experience in Tokyo was an earthquake. It happened while we sat in a marble-floored tearoom. Our elegant glass-topped table began to rattle and I noticed the large decorative palms in the room waving to and fro. The waiters with loaded trays carried one-handed high above their shoulders had stopped in their tracks and were standing as if rooted to the spot. The orchestra ceased playing and I grabbed a hand of each of the children, ready to run. But to run where? We were on the ground floor of a high-rise building in a forest of tall buildings. I sat still for ten minutes, which registered only five or six seconds on my watch. The shaking stopped, the palms ceased waving, the orchestra picked up where it had left off and the waiters moved again. Nobody said very much. I guess the Japanese are used to it. Of course, while in Tokyo I also had a quick look at the bank's representative office.

When we arrived in Hong Kong we checked into the Mandarin Hotel and were there for about six weeks. Next day I bought a car for the bank, a Toyota Crown. We took a whirl round Hong Kong Island, after which Malcolm asked if Hong Kong was bigger than Canada and Maggie claimed to have seen a 'garbage' in the harbour. Nearly right. It was a junk. In December 1971 Hong

Kong was buzzing. Taxi drivers, waiters, amahs and everyone else were playing the stock market. The economy was booming. If an apartment was advertised in the newspaper it was gone before the paper hit the street. Within days I had an office up and running in a suite in the Hilton Hotel, but we were still in the Mandarin, trying daily to find somewhere to live. One morning I received a call about an apartment in Baloo Paloo Road. I knew I was going to survive in Hong Kong when instantly in my head I translated Baloo Paloo into Blue Pool. The apartment was awful, but the landlady repeatedly said, 'But look at the beautiful fish tank.'

We had two connected rooms in the Mandarin and on Christmas Eve we looked in to the kids' room where they had been playing quietly, to find that Maggie had Malcolm fitted out with a cotton wool beard and was attempting to decorate the room. I felt awful giving my children a Christmas in a hotel room, all for the sake of the Bank of Nova Scotia. As a break from the Mandarin, on Christmas Day we had lunch in the ballroom of the Hilton Hotel. I don't know how many hundreds of people were there but so far as I could see we were the only Europeans. We were in our Sunday best with the kids in their kilts. As we left, Santa was presenting each child with a gift, which he took from one of two barrels. Malcolm maintained later that if that had been the real Santa he would have known that Scottish boys wear the kilt and would certainly not have given him a doll.

Eventually, in desperation we took over an apartment on the Peak that would be vacant for six months while the English tenants went on home leave. They walked out without emptying a cupboard or a drawer. The place was damp and miserable. Ans ended up in hospital with pneumonia and I tried to run an office and look after two children.

I was trying to rent more permanent office space. I telephoned Hong Kong Land to ask about their new building, Connaught Centre, where the upper floors were still being fitted out. At the time, Connaught Centre was said to be the most desirable business address, although later, because of its round windows, it became known as the house of a thousand arseholes and was said to have bad feng shui. The English property manager at Hong Kong Land said to me, 'Bank of Nova what? No. You would have to take an entire floor.'

I telephoned Sir Sidney Gordon, chairman of China Light and Power, to whom I had earlier presented my letter of introduction and to whose beautiful home we had all been invited the weekend before. I related my problem and he asked if I would be in my office in the next half hour. I looked at my empty diary and assured him I would make time to be available. Twenty minutes later Peter Hutson, a very senior man at the Hong Kong and Shanghai Bank, called me and asked me to explain my problem. I did and he asked if I would be at my desk in the next half hour or so. I confirmed I would. Within the half hour the same man at Hong Kong Land I had talked to earlier telephoned me. He said he understood that I wanted to rent some space in Connaught Centre. He had some room and if I came over to his office we could see if it would suit. I called on him. Neither of us mentioned our first conversation and I rented exactly the corner space I wanted on the otherwise empty twenty-second floor. Ah, Hong Kong. Like everywhere else. Not what you know but who you know. Now I had to fit out the space. I hired an architect and told the bank to increase my letter of credit so I could draw the required funds from HSBC. The very substantial amounts I spent, faithfully reported to Toronto, were never queried until the office had been completed and we had moved in. Then the premises department in Toronto came forward with some suggestions for the layout. I filed them carefully.

While all this was going on I was trying to determine what kind of business we could do in Hong Kong. A representative office has no cash, keeps no customer accounts but tries to find business to refer to branches of the bank. To be worth the effort any such transaction had to be of significant size. I decided to try to find some shipping loans. From the telephone book and other sources I compiled a list of shipping companies, of which there were many. I think, no I am sure, making cold calls on shipping companies, most of which had never heard of the Bank of Nova Scotia, was the most dispiriting time of my life. Sometimes I had to make two or three visits before I could inveigle the secretary guarding the door to let me meet the boss. Several times I found myself calling on a company from mainland China. There was no way to tell from the name and although I was received politely there was no hope in those days they would be permitted to borrow from a bank. At the end of each day I wondered how I could justify drawing my salary, except that I was representing the bank at two or three cocktail receptions most weekday evenings, as the many banks and large corporations in town hosted receptions for their visiting dignitaries. I did not enjoy the meaningless diplomacy and flummery of these occasions. In due course I learned to go in the front door, shake hands with those in the reception line, drop my card in the basket, meet anyone in the room who did not look like a competing banker and find my way out through a back door or even a kitchen without being seen, except, of course, by those doing exactly the same thing, all of us heading for the next reception. In preparation for two or three receptions after a day in the office and before going home, I learned to go to the barber's shop. There, for a Hong Kong dollar, I was allowed to sit in a chair for ten minutes with a couple of hot towels on my face. This was the second-best deal in Hong Kong. The best was a ride on one of the ten Star Ferries which transported thousands of people daily across the harbour from Tsim Sha Tsui in Kowloon to Hong Kong Island and back. The fare in 1972 was, I think, HK$0.50 (about US$0.10) for the upper deck and HK$0.25 for the lower. A ride on the upper deck should be on everyone's bucket list even though the fares for the ten-minute ride have soared to HK$2.50 (now about US$0.35) and HK$2.00.

In April 1972 I received a telegram telling me that my father was in hospital and not expected to live for more than a day or two. He had not wanted me to know he was so ill. He thought I had enough on my plate in Hong Kong, so I had no warning. Marsman, my boss from London, was already on his way for his first visit to me in Hong Kong. I hesitated for only a second. Ans would take care of Marsman and give him the list of appointments I had lined up. Dickie the bank driver would take him to where he needed to be. I caught whatever planes would get me home the quickest and travelled through Tokyo, Frankfurt and London. I went straight from the airport in Glasgow to the hospital. I think my father knew I was there; he blinked his eyes when asked by the nurse to acknowledge my presence. He was semi-conscious at best and breathing very harshly. I asked a young doctor if there was anything he could do to make things easier for him. He said there wasn't and that my father was an old man and wouldn't last long. The doctor was right about how long he would last. My father died at about four o'clock next morning while I held his hand. The person the doctor had called an old man was sixty-six years old. As I heard the death rattle I told him I loved him. I hope he heard me even if, as I thought about how his drinking and resultant aggression had affected my childhood, I was not sure it was true. With the passage of time I have mellowed and become less judgemental. I have learned that in life most people do the best they can with the cards they are dealt. But some try harder than others.

I was back in Hong Kong within a few days. Ans had done well and Marsman seemed happy with his visit. While I was away the tenant of our leave flat had returned early from home leave in England and he had had the unbridled cheek to ask to reoccupy his apartment before the end of the lease. Ans was delighted to say goodbye to the awful place. When I got back I found her in rooms at the Hilton with the kids and the amah. The children were attending the German Swiss School and it did not matter if they went down to school from the leave apartment on the Peak tram or up on it from the Hilton. After her first week at school Maggie had told me she would be dumb all her life because she did not understand a word of German, the language of tuition. Within weeks she was doing well and in three months was getting top marks for diktat. Malcolm managed, unsupervised, to write and post a letter in German to his Opa in Holland, whom he loved dearly. He told him he had a pistol that could *scheisse*. Opa treasured that letter and forgave the transposed i and e. Indeed, he enjoyed them and happily showed the letter to all the patrons when he next visited the barber. We soon found an apartment on the third level of a three-storey block of six apartments at the very top of the Peak. In those days that apartment and its neighbour were the two highest apartments in Hong Kong. We looked down on the clouds and on the planes landing at Kai Tak airport.

The next important visit from head office was from the chairman. I met Mr. and Mrs. Ritchie at the airport with a Rolls Royce. When he asked where the car came from I told him that Murray MacLehose, the governor of Hong Kong, was on home leave, which was true. I didn't say that the Rolls Royce had been hired from the Mandarin Hotel, which also was true. The chairman walked into the new office in the Connaught Centre and when he saw the wall of tartan behind my desk he turned to me and said, 'You bloody Scotsman.'

'Chairman,' I replied, 'it's the Nova Scotia tartan and there was enough left over for new kilts for my children.'

Again this was true. Never tell your chairman a lie, even if you feel you do not always have to tell him the whole truth. However, for many years to come the chairman from time to time did call me a bloody Scotsman, in a good-natured way, I hope. I always took it as a compliment. His stereotyped opinion of me was reinforced in Hong Kong when I dismissed our hired car halfway through the morning and reminded the driver to tell his boss not to charge for the full day. The chairman asked how we were to get to the next appointments and I assured him I had arranged them to be within walking distance of each other; easy to do in Hong Kong. Ans and Mrs. Ritchie were to use the bank car but soon found they both disliked shopping and sat in the Mandarin drinking coffee. I took the chairman to lunch with the chairman of the Hong Kong and Shanghai Bank. The table was laden with silver and the room was awash with white-gloved waiters. Afterwards, I told the chairman the story of the silver. When the Japanese arrived during the war the servants hid it all in the air-conditioning ducts and the Japanese never found it. I suggested to the chairman that we should get some silver for his dining table in head office in Toronto. I was rebuked sharply.

'We are not that kind of bank.'

And we were not. Recently a reporter in Canada mentioned in an article that when he visited the head offices of banks in Canada it was common for him to be offered cocktails or tea or coffee but when he visited Scotiabank's head office he was offered a small bottle of water. I think the ethos that pervaded the bank in my days with Scotiabank came from the origins of the bank in the Maritime Provinces and from having had for many years the benefit of a down to earth chairman like Ritchie. He had worked his way up from a clerical position to top dog. And top dog he was. But you could talk to him. You could pull his leg, but only a little! He was the chairman and our panjandrum after all and you did not take too many liberties. Our Maritime customers also influenced the bank. I remember the story of a dealer in tea from the Maritimes who came to lunch in Toronto. He asked for a cup of tea and was horrified to be served the wrong brand of tea. The wrong brand was any brand he did not sell. He very kindly said he would send us a case of good tea. True to his word, soon after his visit a very large case of tea was delivered. A week later the bill arrived.

During the chairman's visit to Hong Kong we held our own reception with the chairman and Marsman in attendance. A favourite memory of that event was of seeing Ans in a beautiful high-necked black dress designed for her by Johnson Dong, who provided her with several stunning outfits during our time in Hong Kong. Towards the end of the evening a Japanese guest was pressing Mr. Marsman to visit Japan. Marsman replied coldly that he had been a guest of the Japanese on a previous occasion. That ended the conversation. No need to explain that he had been a prisoner of war. That was the only time Marsman ever made any reference to it in my presence. Some years later at Marsman's retirement party in London, the chairman looked around the assembled guests and reminded Marsman that he had given instructions that this was to be a bank affair, as much to introduce the new man as to say farewell to Marsman. The Japanese banks were to be invited. Where were the Japanese?

'I don't know,' said Marsman. 'I just don't understand it. I sent the invitations round half an hour ago.'

In Hong Kong I received a telex from the chairman alerting me to the forthcoming visit of a director of the bank who would be travelling with the adult son of a famous Canadian business family. I was to be sure to look after them. As usual, Sir Sidney came to my rescue and to help me fill in one morning he arranged a trip to the Kadoorie Extension Experimental Farm at Pak Ngau Shek in the New Territories. This was and is an interesting place concentrating on crop production and animal husbandry, now called Kadoorie Farm and Botanic Garden. After a quick tour of the farm our trip was to include lunch with Sir Lawrence Kadoorie, who later became Baron Kadoorie. I felt sure that our director would relish having lunch with one of the richest men in Hong Kong, to say nothing of Sir Sidney. However, the rather stuck-up pain in the neck said there was no way he was going to any farm and I was obliged to ask Sir Sidney to forgive me for cancelling at short notice. The young businessman was quite upset and apologetic and later he sent me his bread and butter letter as did everyone I ever hosted in Hong Kong, other than the director and the premier of British Columbia. I found the latter and his party standing on the street and wondering what to do after leaving a reception. I took them to a favourite restaurant and gave them dinner in a private room.

In Hong Kong it annoyed me to be sending business to branches of the bank and I had told the chairman we needed a finance company in Hong Kong; nothing big, just enough so that we could put some business on our own books and make enough to pay the expenses of the office. He wasn't so sure about it but when he got home he sent me a bank draft for $10,000 and said I should do with it what I could. It became the capital. The months passed and business was picking up. I allowed the representatives of the Canadian private schools, who recruited in Hong Kong each year, to use my secretary and our spare office as a base. Through them I met several wealthy people who were considering sending their kids to school in Canada. I began to take deposits for Vancouver branch and arranged for them to grant some mortgage loans. But the first big deal came unexpectedly one afternoon. I had called on a very wealthy, important and well-known Chinese businessman and had been pleased to meet him in person after having tried for an appointment for some time. A few days after my visit he telephoned and said he remembered that I had mentioned that my bank was a big dealer in gold (only the biggest in North America). Could I buy 15,000 ounces for him personally and advance him the largest loan I was able to make against the security of the gold?

'Certainly, I could do that,' I said with confidence, although I had no experience of Toronto's gold department which I had never even seen. I had done nothing with gold since I used to sell one-ounce squares to artisans in the Gold Coast in 1956 for the equivalent of US$35 an ounce plus a small commission. I collected my wits and decided I would not ask this man for a written order. I knew his word was good, although I was sure my head office would have wanted me to trouble him for something more formal. I telexed Toronto giving all the details I could think of and asking if they needed anything more. I did not want this deal to go wrong. Then I waited. It was about 4am in Toronto and I was sure that when somebody arrived and saw my telex and with whom I was dealing they would rush to the chairman to let him know. I lacked experience of head office and head office functionaries! There was a twelve-hour time difference between Hong Kong and Toronto. By ten at night my time I had received no response. So I telexed again asking for assurance they had everything they needed to put the deal though. No response. At 3am my time, still without a response, I telexed, 'To hell with you. I am going to bed.'

I drove up to the top of the Peak, too tired to be hungry. But I could not sleep. This was a deal for nearly $2 million with one of the most important men in Hong Kong, whose name was known the world over. (I am a bit worried about confidentiality even after all these years, but there are a few men to whom this could refer.) Although not a huge deal it was a door opener. By 5am I was back in the office. Waiting for me was a telex telling me that 15,000 ounces of gold had been purchased. I forget the price, but it was about $120 per ounce. I was asked to remit almost $2 million in payment. No mention of the loan. I telexed back asking about the loan. No answer. I decided that 80% was a safe amount to lend against gold in our own strong room. I contacted Jack Keith, the manager of one of our branches in London, and asked him to borrow 80% of the total in the eurodollar market in the name of the bank and then on lend it at the same rate to the Hong Kong finance company but to remit the funds to Toronto. Then I created a loan agreement out of my head and had the secretary type it up. I telephoned for an appointment with my customer. He was gracious, as always, and pleased with the deal and happy to give me a cheque for the 20%. By about 3pm that afternoon I was dropping with sleep and, having convinced myself that all the ends had been tied up, I was ready to go home for the day. The telephone rang. It was my gold customer. He liked the way the transaction had gone. Could I repeat it today? Another 15,000 ounces. I did it all again, with the same result, except that I did not wait in the office for half the night. About ten days later approval for the loans came in. I was authorised to lend 75% of the value of the gold, not the 80% I had already advanced as loans on the books of the local finance company. I telexed back saying I had been obliged to fund the purchases and had granted loans of 80% and I was not about to disturb the customer. A gentle rebuke came back reminding me that I had no authority to make such loans. A more experienced man would have accepted that Marsman had been obliged to send the rebuke and would have filed it without comment. However, always aggressive, I telexed Marsman, saying that he needed to get somebody else out here who had less pride in the bank and who wouldn't be embarrassed to tell a customer that we could not put two parts of a deal together in less than ten days. The wise old bird telexed back, 'Johnston keep your shirt on.'

I never heard any more about it. To jump ahead in time and end this story, the price of gold went down and I was obliged to ask the customer to top up the margin. This he did instantly and without hesitation. I got to know him well enough to be invited with my family on his yacht for day trips from time to time, as were many other bankers, all of whom, like me, were glad to say they knew him, even if he was rarely on the yacht with them. I had left Hong Kong when the price of gold rose to something like $190 an ounce and I telephoned to say I was nervous for him. Would he not think of taking his substantial profit? He laughed and said he was waiting for $200. Gold hit $200 an ounce briefly a few weeks later in 1975 and he sold, taking his profit of nearly $2.5 million. Pocket money for him, of course.

On the home front we were a lot happier in the apartment at the top of the Peak and the children continued to go to and from school alone on the Peak Tram, riding with the tourists and the amahs going to and from work. On Saturday afternoons we took the children to Billy Tingle's club at the cricket ground in central Hong Kong. The main purpose of the club seemed to be to let the apartment-bound children of Hong Kong run about on grass. The cricket ground was removed long ago to make room for more skyscrapers.

In April 1974 the chairman visited us again, on his way to the Canton trade fair. I don't think I did my reputation any good by taking him and Mrs. Ritchie to Happy Valley racecourse as guests of HSBC in their private box. That alone did not do me any harm but once there I proceeded to back three winners in a row at good odds simply by picking names that appealed to me. One choice I remember was prompted by Ans' red hair. I don't think the chairman believed that was the only time I had ever been at the racecourse and that I knew nothing about the horses I had picked. After that day out, and as the four of us walked back to his hotel after dinner, the chairman suggested that I take up the management of our branch in Kuala Lumpur. I was surprised and explained that, although he thought that things had gone well in Hong Kong, we were just at the beginning. I was starting to know a lot of people and to be known. Sir Sidney and his brother had fast-tracked my membership of the exclusive and elegant Hong Kong Club, of which I am still a member. I knew who to call and people called me. Although Ans was not very happy living in an apartment I was now enjoying my life and work in Hong Kong and could see great potential. I dismissed the idea of going to Malaysia and the chairman started to talk to Ans.

'Just think about the better quality of life in Kuala Lumpur, in a house with a garden.'

'You shouldn't talk to me about it. You need to talk to the boss,' Ans responded.

'I thought I was the boss,' said the chairman.

No more was said during his visit but when he returned to Canada Mr. Ritchie telephoned me and suggested that I take the family to Kuala Lumpur for the weekend to have a look, as if KL was just around the corner and not 1,600 miles away. Lesson one in the book of corporate survival is if the chairman asks you to have a look at something, you go to have a look. So, at the end of April 1974 the four of us went to KL for three days. The branch was small, with about thirty on the staff but, clearly, although it had been open only for about eighteen months it had a large loan portfolio. That was attractive to me. I have always considered myself a lending banker and had been making loans since I was twenty-one. A house with a garden was attractive to Ans. And although I would be very sorry to leave Hong Kong, once it had penetrated my thick skull that it wasn't just a whim and the chairman really wanted me to move to KL, for no reason he ever made clear, there was never any doubt that I would do just that.

It was decided that we would move to Kuala Lumpur in August after our home leave. However, my assiduous courting of the Bank of China had paid dividends. This had included calling on them on days of special celebration and drinking a good deal of Maotai at dinners to which I had been invited and had reciprocated. Ans and I were invited, together with half a dozen other bankers and their wives, out of the many in Hong Kong, for a two-week tour of China as guests of the Bank of China. The tour was to commence on 3rd September 1974. This was a couple of years after Nixon's visit and few people had seen much of China beyond what used to be Canton. We were to move to KL direct from home leave in Europe and Ans, wisely, felt she could not leave the children in a strange country for two weeks with colleagues we did not really know, and she did not want them to have to fly alone from Europe to Malaysia. I am sorry that Ans did not have what was then a memorable and unique experience of a visit to China. Why she

could not have flown back to Europe to collect the children I do
not remember. Perhaps it had something to do with getting them
into school at the start of the term. In any case Ans had decided
and I went to China alone.

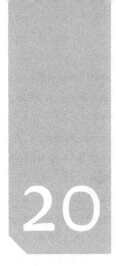

China

China is a big country, inhabited by many Chinese.

Charles de Gaulle

On 3rd September 1974 I joined a small group of bankers and their wives at Kowloon Station, from where we left by train for the one-hour journey on the East Rail Line to Lo Wu on the border between Hong Kong and China. The party, so far as I remember, consisted of the Hong Kong representatives of one other Canadian bank, three Japanese banks, a Dutch and a Scottish bank, most accompanied by a wife. No Americans. The party was escorted by the two senior men from the Bank of China in Hong Kong, Mr. Chen and Mr. Wang.

In Lo Wu we walked into China over the bridge, now moved and maintained as a historic monument. We were shown into a waiting room from which Messrs. Chen and Wang disappeared briefly. When they returned they had shed their impeccable Western suits and silk ties and were now wearing the ubiquitous modified Zhongshan suits known in the West as Mao suits. We never saw a Chinese man or a woman dressed in anything else during our fifteen days in China. We saw very few non-Chinese. Most children were Young Pioneers and wore the triangular red scarf with plain uniforms. Mr. Chen was the top man at the Bank of China in Hong Kong, although we suspected that somebody lower down the ranks was probably the political man who was really in charge. As Mr Wang later became chairman I am guessing that he was the one with the direct line to head office. Mr. Chen was a tall, sturdy man, always elegantly dressed in Hong Kong in the best of Western clothing, and it was strange to see him in little more than a peasant's outfit, even if it was an outfit also worn by Chairman Mao.

Our party was joined by Tao, Wang, and Li, who were to be our guides and translators. The director of China International Travel Services had come from Peking (to use the terminology of the day and as used in the official itinerary provided by Bank of China) to meet and welcome us. He made a point of saying that it was his first visit to Lo Wu in eighteen months. There were several long speeches of introduction and welcome, something we would become used to during our trip. At dinners in the evenings there were many toasts to friendship and co-operation, with an occasional shout of, 'Gahn bay,' which means dry glass, and so glasses had to be emptied in one go. I soon noticed that when making a toast our host for the evening would hold up his glass of Maotai but having made the toast, as we downed our Maotai, frequently he would put down his glass and pick up a glass of water. I learned to do the same, but only when it suited me. Maotai is a very strong sorghum-based liquor brewed in South West China but, certainly during our visit, ubiquitous throughout the country. I have heard Maotai described as tasting like kerosene. I don't know who drank kerosene to make the comparison, but I agree that Maotai is probably an acquired taste. I worked hard to acquire it in Hong Kong in furtherance of my ambitions to get close to the Bank of China and to become Scotiabank's go-to man for all things Chinese. I foresaw great opportunities for business in China at some time in the future. Although I could not predict when that time would come, I felt sure that eventually it would arrive. I wanted to be part of it.

It is difficult to remember now how excited I was in 1974, how honoured and privileged I felt and how unknown China was to us all at that time. Twenty years later China did not seem so different to anywhere else. Waking up in a five-star hotel in Beijing one might have been in a five-star hotel anywhere in the world, except that the service was better in Beijing. In 1974 China was undeveloped and very different. What has been accomplished in the years since is more than remarkable, although in some areas there remains much to be done. I have no doubt it will be accomplished, although the recent creation of unproductive infrastructure and high levels of debt suggest there are problems on the horizon.

At Lo Wu we proceeded through customs without any trouble or delay and without having to open our cases. I changed some US dollars at the rate of 1.99 yuan for a dollar. The rate for a Canadian dollar was 1.96 yuan. Renminbi is the name for China's currency, but the notes are expressed in yuan; just as the currency of the UK is sterling but the notes are expressed in pounds. Largely through currency manipulation by the Chinese government the yuan would fall to a low of over eight to the US dollar by 1995, making Chinese goods cheap for foreign buyers. As I write the rate is over six yuan to the US dollar.

After taking one hour off our watches we enjoyed a pleasant lunch, during which we tried to get to know our guides/interpreters but without learning much about them. They did open up later in our stay if any of us managed to get one of them on his own and without any other Chinese within hearing. Then he might whisper, 'Gang of Four.' Otherwise they were always very guarded in what they said about almost anything we asked. As dedicated "China watchers" most of our group knew all about the Cultural Revolution that Mao had launched in 1966 with the objective of purging the remnants of capitalism through violent class struggle. The revolution was declared to be over in 1969 but it had reduced the economy to a disastrous state, despite which communist ideology had continued to be more important than productivity. In 1973, the year before our visit, Mao's wife, Jiang Qing, the leader of the Gang of Four, who had political ambitions of her own as Mao's health declined, started a very public campaign to weaken the political position of the moderate Premier Zhou Enlai. There was a great deal of uncertainty and tension in the air. This lasted until the arrest of the Gang of Four in 1976. In 1974, while we wanted to have the latest inside information, we knew that as foreigners we needed to be very careful, both for ourselves and for our hosts. Mostly we were.

I have notes of every arrival at the next stop on the itinerary and of every departure, together with train and plane times and details of meals. I will spare you most of that. Let me say only that over the next fifteen days we visited (again using the spelling on the official itinerary) Kwangchow, Peking, where we spent six days, Nanking, Shanghai, Hangchow and back to Kwangchow. We all felt very privileged to have been invited by the Bank of China to see as much of China as we did. Often when we alighted from our little bus a crowd would gather quickly and many who had probably never seen a Caucasian before would applaud as if we had accomplished something just by being there. In a way we had, being among the very few to have been invited. We always returned the applause. Although I was told that China anticipated a great increase in the number of tourists visiting the country and that I should provide comments on hotels and restaurants and the sights we were taken to see I do not recall ever being asked. I was reluctant to be critical in case of causing offence. Not that there was a lot to be critical about. Some of the hotels were very old and run down but it was clear that efforts had been made to make them clean and comfortable. The employees at hotels were usually smiling and helpful, if they could understand what we wanted. Few could speak English and none of our party had more than a few words of the Cantonese we had learned in Hong Kong, not that that Cantonese was much use in most of China.

We arrived in Kwangchow, formerly Canton, at the new and impressive railway station and were bussed to the Tung Fang Hotel, where the room doors had locks that could be operated only from the inside. So, when not in the room, the door was unlocked. Was this a way to demonstrate to us, and to visitors to the Canton Fair, that there was no crime in China?

Next morning, on a visit to the Red Cotton Silk Factory, we saw silk being woven. There was little response from any of the employees to smiles and none to questions. All production was sent to a central agency, so nobody could tell us what percentage was for export. Presumably all of it went for export because I saw no silk anywhere in China. I began to understand about centralised production; a system under which factories produce goods but have no idea what is to happen to them or what markets they are serving. This understanding was reinforced throughout our visit to China and this was the great conundrum for the Chinese government. How do you relax things sufficiently to create a more competitive and realistic system without losing control of the whole shebang? The government has relaxed the system considerably since 1974 but is still very much in control.

That evening we flew to Peking in a Boeing 707 in beautiful condition. Contrary to my expectations there were three rows of First Class seats. Perhaps they were for party members. We sat at the back and enjoyed a banana for an in-flight snack followed by a hot towel. Peking airport building, from the runway, looked like an American city hall with wide stone steps. As in Kwangchow airport there seemed to be nobody there but us. The good road to Peking looked as if it had been cut though a forest. Except for one bend, it had been built on a straight line from the city to the airport. It was after ten at night and in the first half hour of our drive we saw two cars, one going in each direction. After a midnight dinner I was glad to climb into bed in the Nationalities Hotel. It was much cooler in Peking and there was no air-conditioning. I went to sleep with the windows open. I woke at six in the morning to a cacophony of tinkling bells. I had to rise and look out the window to understand this incredible but not unpleasant noise. Thousands of bicycles were streaming past on the wide boulevard just below my window, ten or more abreast and in an unbroken column as far as I could see. Every rider, for some reason that was not obvious to me, was ringing his or her handlebar bell. It was a nice reminder that I was in China.

Because of rain our itinerary was changed and we went for a ride on the subway. It was not particularly deep but very clean. The carriage was modern and air-conditioned but with very basic seats. Our coach was locked to keep out local people and I took the chance to ask why, if there is no crime, all bicycles have a lock. It was admitted that there is still a 'class struggle' but also because bicycles are all very similar and locks prevent the accidental removal of the wrong bicycle. I found the use of the 'class struggle' terminology interesting particularly as the second part of the answer seemed convincing and sufficient.

At an agricultural commune where 42,000 people lived I questioned the chairman. After considerable evasion eventually he told me that he had been appointed to his position after being the sole nominee of the department controlling communes. At this commune and at factories and work places we visited later there was always great emphasis on the progress made in recent years.

'Before, we had only one tractor. Now we have ten,' was a common theme everywhere. This could apply to cows, pigs, machines or houses. It was difficult, indeed almost impossible, to get any reaction from the workers, other than those detailed to be our hosts, but everyone seemed happy enough in their work although there did not appear to be any great rush to produce.

On a visit to the Great Wall, about two hours from Peking, I found the countryside to be very like Scotland. Somehow, it was not quite what I expected. The Great Wall, the Forbidden City and Tiananmen Square were exactly as you now see them on television but in 1974 it was a thrill to be there in person. In the Forbidden City and the Temple of Heaven, where the emperor had prayed each year for a good harvest, it was easy to imagine the glorious places they once had been. At the University of Peking one of the Japanese members of our party was gushingly expressing his admiration for the buildings when one of our hosts leaned over and whispered to me disdainfully, 'And they stabled their horses here,' in reference to the Japanese occupation.

In Nanking we were taken to a hospital and I guessed immediately that formerly it had been a mission hospital. I had seen dozens very like it in Africa. I was surprised to be allowed into an operating room where three procedures were underway simultaneously. In a chair like a dentist's chair an elderly man was having something hammered out of the roof of his mouth. When the hammering stopped he told us through a translator that he looked forward to going home for his dinner. Another procedure was an open-heart operation and, although gowned and masked, I was astonished to be allowed to witness it. The face of the patient was hidden behind a cloth screen, but her heart very obviously was sitting on her chest, beating nicely. Behind the screen the lady was awake and talking. It was explained that she and the other patients had been given only a mild sedative in addition to intense acupuncture. Later we were introduced to a man whose hand had been reattached after an accident. The scar that circled his wrist was obvious and he showed me how he could move his fingers. Quite clearly, as well as the barefoot doctors, there were some very skilled surgeons among the 300 doctors at the hospital.

On 12th September we flew to Shanghai. Our plane was an old four-engine turboprop Ilyushin 18. I thought my last day had come when smoke poured into the cabin from the luggage racks above the seats. Within seconds I could not see more than two or three seats ahead of me. It took only a minute to realise that it was not smoke but condensation from the air-conditioning system. A minute is a long time when you are contemplating your death in China.

Shanghai was very different from Peking. Shops in Peking rarely had anything in the window and if they did have one or two articles there was no attempt to dress the window and make an attractive display. In Shanghai I could feel the repressed capitalists bursting to express themselves. Shop windows were attractively dressed and there was a general hustle and bustle that was lacking in Peking. Although nothing to compare with what happened in later years in Shanghai, one could see cranes and equipment and the beginnings of the efforts to build the infrastructure. I thought it marvellous to be walking along the Bund on the west bank of the Huangpu River and to be looking at the famous and iconic buildings. Surely my uncle had known many of them in the 1920s and may even have frequented some of them when they had been used for the purposes for which they had been built; now the former shops, banks and embassies were drab offices, except, that is, for the original famous Cathay Hotel, functioning again since 1956 as the Peace Hotel and still with the Old Jazz Band. The members of the band looked as if they had been there since the days of the Cathay Hotel and well they might have been. They were ancient, but, remarkably for 1974, still producing decadent Western jazz.

Over the fifteen days we were given many opportunities to see performances by children. We were always impressed by the discipline of the various routines and the charm of the children. However, a highlight was a visit to the Children's Municipal Palace in Shanghai, the former home of the Kadoorie family, called the Marble Palace. The grandeur of this home was breathtaking and seemed not to have suffered at all from being a residence where children could learn to excel in their particular discipline. On arrival, my hand was grabbed by an eight-year-old who welcomed me in English and called me uncle. He led me to a small zip line which we both negotiated. Later we were told that the children we were observing as we went from room to room were just 'normal children' but I suspected, and the evidence was there for all to see, that they were gifted children selected from all over China for intense training. We saw and heard youngsters playing violins like masters. In another classroom kids spoke English better than our translators and when we came to the table tennis room I was soundly whipped by a boy who could barely see over the table.

At one banquet towards the end of our visit our party was divided, with two or three of us at each table. The table next to the one at which I sat somehow got ahead of us in the order of courses being served and had learned that the meat in the last course put before them had been dog. The ladies, particularly, were not pleased. When our course came several of my colleagues refused to eat it, but I had often eaten goat in Africa and did not see that dog could be much different. I ate and found the meat stronger than chicken but perhaps not as strong as goat. In answer to my question about what kind of dog I had eaten I was told, 'just general dog.'

In Shanghai we met two young Scotsmen who were said to be the only resident Europeans except for an ancient Polish or Russian lady who had refused to leave. One lad represented the Hong Kong and Shanghai Bank and the other the Standard Chartered Bank. They were desperate for any reading material we could leave for them and they told us that neither was allowed to leave China until his replacement had actually arrived. I gathered that the only business done in either of their branches was fed to them by Chinese banks.

As our visit came to an end I had very mixed feelings. I was anxious to get back to my family which was camped in the Hilton

Hotel in Kuala Lumpur but very sorry indeed to leave China. I admired the country and the Chinese and was very keen to learn more about everything in China. The awakening was not as obvious as it became a few years later but I felt sure I had detected something that would grow and would be of interest to the whole world. I wanted to be part of it on behalf of Scotiabank and was sorry I was leaving Hong Kong. I hoped I could find a way to get back there after a year or two in Kuala Lumpur. That never happened, except for visits. And I was very sorry not to be in Hong Kong in 1997 when my regiment played a leading role in the final handover ceremony; a ceremony at which a well-publicised picture of a Black Watch soldier revealed the answer to an age-old question.

As the years passed, wherever I was, I worked on my connections with China. In Jamaica I paid my respects to the Chinese Embassy when Chairman Mao died and in Toronto when the Bank of China opened a representative office I made friends with their representative. When they opened a branch and needed a clearing agent I suspect that the bid I signed was little or no different from that submitted by the other Canadian banks. But Scotiabank's bid was signed with my Chinese chop and we became the clearing agent. When Mr. Wang De-yan, my friend from the China trip in 1974, visited New York in 1989 as chairman of Bank of China I persuaded Scotiabank's vice-chairman to fly with me to New York to host a reception and dinner in a private suite at the Waldorf for Mr. Wang and his party. A great time was had by all. In 1991 Bank of China produced a glossy coffee table book to celebrate the eightieth anniversary of its founding; 271 pages, mostly photographs, with not more than about a dozen non-Chinese shown and few of those named. I was happy to find myself pictured in my wood-panelled office in Toronto, and named, shaking hands with my friend Lei Zuhua of Bank of China in Beijing and sharing a double page of five photographs featuring Henry Kissinger, the prime minister of Luxemburg, the chairman of Bank of America and Sir Charles Bauer, an executive director of Jardines. As I told my chairman, in China such things did not happen by accident.

My great disappointment came in 1991, when Scotiabank was invited to partner a major Chinese bank in a joint venture. I have little doubt the invitation came because of my efforts over the years. I was sent to Shanghai to negotiate but my chairman insisted that I take with me our man in Hong Kong. The negotiations went well. It was clear that the Chinese bank intended to funnel business to the joint venture. It seemed to me a great opportunity for Scotiabank to be among the first and the few to have a significant operation in China. Towards the end of our talks I risked a small joke. The main man for the Chinese bank was named Mao and I suggested that he should chair the new joint venture (which was probably going to happen anyway). There was the slightest pause then everyone roared with laughter. Chairman Mao. Then Mr. Mao responded. He said that since my name was Johnston I could be his tutor. I guessed that this was a clever reference to Reginald Johnston, the tutor of Puyi, the last Emperor of China.

I travelled home very pleased and excited about what I saw as a great opportunity for my bank. However, to my great disappointment my chairman, Mr. Ritchie, wanted nothing to do with the idea. He would give no explanation and I could not move him. I felt sure that our man in Hong Kong, as was his wont, had picked up the telephone and called the chairman. I have no idea what he said or what his motives were, other than, perhaps, that he did not want anyone else treading on his territory, even his boss. I told the chairman that it would have been a great deal better if he had scotched the idea before he sent me to China.

Malaysia

> Without doubt, Malaysia is the
> economic star of the Muslim world.
>
> **Martin Jacques**

I arrived in Hong Kong from my trip to China on 18th September 1974 and on Thursday the 19th flew to Kuala Lumpur to find Ans and the children ensconced in two very comfortable rooms in the beautiful Hilton Hotel. Malcolm had been ill and Ans rejoiced in her sensible decision not to leave the children with our colleagues. I was happy to be reunited with the family.

On Sunday 22nd September I flew back to Hong Kong and spent the week handing over formally to my successor, a rather strange man, to say the least. And he had a recently arrived strange Canadian-Chinese assistant who, before I was told he was coming as assistant representative, had written to many important people in Hong Kong to say, 'Dear Uncle, I have been appointed our bank's representative in Hong Kong,' forgetting the 'assistant' and as if I and our office did not exist. His strange letter prompted several calls asking me if I was leaving and who was this tin man who had dealt this low blow?

I returned to KL on 27th September and on my second day there, being driven by Hassan, the bank driver, I was thinking that I would never find my own way around this city. Then I saw a street I remembered. I was beginning to get my bearings. I was glad to tell the driver that I recognised Jalan Sehala and that we had passed it before.

'Yes Tuan,' said Hassan, 'Jalan Sehala means one-way street.'

I was anxious to get to grips with my new responsibilities. However, I could not get my predecessor to sit down for more than a few minutes. He was racing round town buying furniture to fill the remaining space in a container he intended to ship to Canada. He had introduced me to the staff and that was as much of a handover as I received. He was soon gone, and I started to look at the loan portfolio. The procedure was that I had to make a list of the loans for which I would not take responsibility; in other words, a list of the loans I thought were not fully collectible. I would still have to do my best to collect, but if I could not, I would not be the one whose name was associated with the loss. When I worked in head office I had seen managers take a couple of months to submit their list. That was not my style. Within a week, working very long hours, I had examined every loan and the supporting documents. Although I did my best to keep the list as short as possible, it was enormous. I had never seen anything like it. This was the worst loan book I had ever seen.

In the aftermath of post-election racial riots in Malaysia in 1969 a new economic policy had been introduced in an attempt to disassociate the Bumiputras, in other words the sons of the soil, from agriculture. At a time when Bumiputras made up 53% of the population, with Chinese at 35.6%, Indians at 10.6% and others at 0.8%, economic activity appeared to be in the hands of the Bumiputras to the extent of only 2.4% with other Malaysians at 33% and foreigners at 63%. The new policy aimed at changing these figures to 30%, 40% and 30% over the next twenty years. Modest targets were set for banks to increase gradually the percentage of their loans to Bumiputras. My predecessor, starting from zero, felt that he could arrange his portfolio to have 50% of the loans to Bumiputras; a noble, if unrealistic, objective at the time. There were not enough viable Bumiputra businesses to which good loans could be made. He overreached, and I inherited the consequences. But not all the problems had resulted from his noble intentions and not all bad loans had been made to Bumiputras.

I sent in my list. Soon I was advised that Don Lindsay, the general manager now in charge of the Far East, and based in Manila, would visit me. On the day he arrived he first wanted to go through the loans. In fact, that was all he wanted to do. One by one we pored over the files. After about an hour he asked where the washroom was. As he left my desk, where he had been sitting opposite me, he very deliberately turned his open briefcase round so that I could see a letter lying on top of everything else. Clearly, he wanted me to read it. The letter was addressed to him from the executive office in Toronto asking him to go to KL where it looked as if Johnston had gone off the deep end, or words to that effect. When Lindsay finished his review of all loans and overdrafts he challenged me for not having put more of them on my list, and he enumerated the ones he thought should have been there. I explained that I had tried very hard to keep the list as short as possible and if I thought I could work out of a difficult situation, even if it looked a bit dicey, I had not put it on my list.

'More fool you,' he said.

At the end of my first month in KL I was presented with a chit to sign for something like the equivalent of $200. This turned out to be the shortfall from the bar. I had seen the bar in the branch, really a couple of chairs and a large fridge from which staff and customers were permitted to help themselves to a soft drink or a beer. Staff members, at least, were supposed to pay for their soft drinks. Such an arrangement was a first for me and I had thought the whole thing peculiar but had more important things to worry about. I signed the chit but said I had seen no customers at the bar and I was not prepared to subsidise drinks for the staff. If there was a shortfall next month the bar would close. And close it did. I never heard a complaint or comment from a customer. The bar incident and a few others were indicative of how the branch had been supervised. We received a report of a missing cheque mailed to us and I was worried about the security of the mail. It arrived in a locked mail bag carried from the Post Office by a messenger. Letters were opened and the contents recorded by the Canadian assistant. There was no record of the missing cheque. Everything seemed okay until another cheque was reported missing. I was assured that the mail always arrived locked in the bag. One morning, surreptitiously, I followed the messenger to the Post Office. I saw him hand a key to the clerk who locked the bag and returned bag and key to the messenger. It transpired that the Post Office had lost its key. But everyone had felt comfortable in assuring me that our mail always arrived locked. We bought a new bag with two new keys.

In a safe I found an open envelope with a name on it that I later found to be that of a customer. The envelope was unsealed and inside was a handful of what looked like diamonds. The customer responded to my invitation and assured me the diamonds were genuine. He offered to sell me one. I declined and asked him to take the diamonds away and sign the receipt I proffered. He said he would prefer to seal them up and leave them, but I wanted his receipt there and then before he decided to say one was missing or a valuable diamond had been swapped for one of lesser value. He signed and took them away, to my great relief.

Before we were really settled in Kuala Lumpur I received a surprise invitation or at least Ans received it. She was invited by the owner to launch a ship in Tokyo. I had arranged financing for the new build while in Hong Kong. I was pleased with the invitation, which included me, because the owner had every reason and excuse to overlook us now that we were no longer in Hong

Kong. He also invited my strange Hong Kong replacement. So off we went to Tokyo on 27th November 1974 with tickets supplied by the ship owner. There were several memorable incidents on that trip, the first of which was seeing an excited group of Japanese ladies in the hairdressing salon at our hotel watching as Ans had her waist-long red hair washed and then seeing them all convulse in laughter as the hairdresser was unable to pin it back up. Ans did it herself to a round of applause. The launch the next day was exciting and nerve-racking. The procedure was that Ans had to cut a cord stretched across a block at waist height with a not very sharp silver, well, silver-looking, axe, which was later presented to her in a wooden case. We had been told that it was bad luck if it took more than one swing. There was lot of bowing and shaking of hands and the presenting of business cards and I was pleased that our host had honoured my request that he invite George Korenaga and Hiro Uhara, our Tokyo representatives. Eventually the time came to launch the ship. Ans pronounced her blessing and gave the cord an almighty whack. I was relieved to see it part. Far above us a wooden arm swung free and broke a bottle of something on the stern of the ship. A flock of doves and a host of balloons were released but the ship did not move. I wanted to rush forward and put my shoulder to it. But almost imperceptibly she began to slide, gathering speed as she went down the slipway. Within seconds the *Everjust* was in the water, making a great splash. Silently I asked the gods of the ocean not to let her turn turtle or sink. My request was granted. That evening there was a party at which the Japanese shipyard executives let down their hair! They were singing and dancing on tables. I had never before seen the very staid and correct Japanese businessmen at play but play they did. I didn't do so badly myself, with a rendition, tunelessly no doubt, of "I belong to Glasgow". I thought the Japanese would appreciate hearing about another shipbuilding city. During the evening Ans showed me a little box with a huge white natural South Sea pearl that the ship-owner, quietly, had given her. I told him we could not accept. He laughed and said he had already been offered $7 million more than the ship had cost him. Did I think that one pearl made any difference to the equation? And he said he had arranged our return tickets so that we stopped off in Hong Kong on the way back. We were to go to Lane Crawford and have the pearl set in a ring with diamonds. It would be done while we waited. I am sorry now that I resisted the recommendation of the jeweller and insisted on two very small diamond chips. I am sure my granddaughter will be sorry too when, and if, the ring becomes hers. She should get it now because Ans would never wear it, saying the pearl was so big that people would think it was plastic.

On the way back to Hong Kong our plane was diverted to Saigon for a reason I never knew or have forgotten. I remember the plane taxiing past hundreds, perhaps thousands, of war planes lined up on either side of the runway. It was an incredible sight. When we were allowed off the plane onto the tarmac we were directed to a staircase said to lead to a lounge and were told we would have to wait there for not much more than an hour. A very grubby and untidy-looking Vietnamese soldier standing at the foot of the staircase wanted to take our passports in return for a dirty and tattered landing card. I refused to give up our passports and Ans and I stood on the tarmac for the hour until allowed to embark once again. The other passengers had no trouble getting their passports back and Ans kindly refrained from calling me an ass. Saigon fell exactly five months later.

Back in Kuala Lumpur the staff of the branch was a mixture of Chinese, Malays, and Indians as well as the Canadian assistant. The different races co-operated and worked well together, on the surface. Underneath there was sometimes a bit of tension with one lot quick to point out any mistakes of another. I remember three of the Malay staff marching a young Chinese clerk into my office. He had made a bad mistake and they thought he should be fired.

The boy was in tears. He said his father would kill him if he was dismissed. He would never get another job. I was sorry for him but knew I could not leave the matter there. So I said I would fire him but that that would create a precedent. Anyone who made a mistake of any kind in future would have to be fired. It was agreed very quickly that a stern warning would be enough in this case. Over twenty years later during a visit to the branch I recognised him but, unlike other members of the staff I had known, he avoided me. I did not embarrass him by seeking him out, not that I would have mentioned the incident.

I was warned that the approach of Chinese New Year could be expected to bring an increase in bank robberies. This was the result of the Chinese tradition of making sure that all debts were repaid before the New Year. Apparently, some did not care what steps they had to take to honour the tradition. So, I trained the recently hired teller not to resist but to make sure that along with any funds he handed over he would be sure to include the bait money. This was a small bundle of notes, the numbers of which had been recorded and was kept only to hand over in a robbery. One morning from my desk on the mezzanine floor which was open to the banking hall below I heard a shout; 'Mr. Johnston, we have been robbed.'

I grabbed one of the two revolvers I had inherited from my predecessor and charged down the stairs. A staff member told me which way the robber had gone. I ran out to the street and saw a figure running about fifty or more yards ahead of me. I gave chase but soon lost him in the crowd. I found myself in the street with a loaded revolver. Returning to the bank I made sure the police had been called. After they had completed their enquiries and made notes I spoke to the investigating officer.

'So, what happens now?'

'Well sir, we really do not have much other than that the robber might have been an Indian. I don't think there is anything more we can do but we will take the adding machine which printed the figures on the wrappers round the notes. We might be able to make a match at some point.'

'Officer, the guard says he was hit so hard in the stomach that he is now coughing blood but I heard nothing, although he was standing one floor below me as I sat on the open mezzanine. If he had been hit so hard I would have heard something. Also, the teller handed out all his cash except the bait money, despite his training. I think if you lock them both up for the night you might know a bit more by morning.'

And they did. The guard and the teller confessed to having been in cahoots with the robber and they told the police he could be found in a nearby hotel. The robber was apprehended, and all the money recovered. However, the police held on to the notes and the adding machine. These were evidence, they said. Years passed and there was no prosecution. I understood why. The punishment for participation in armed robbery in Malaysia was death. Nobody wanted to see a lad barely out of his teens receive such a sentence, and certainly not I who knew him or the bank. We did nothing to press for a resolution and eventually, years later, our funds and the machine were returned and nothing more said. By the way, although I held a licence for the two revolvers, I turned them in to the police soon after the robbery. During the chase I had realised that if I got close enough to take a pot shot I might kill somebody. The *Pacific Stars and Stripes* newspaper of 30th Jan 1976 provided a brief report: "with a pistol-packing bank manager in hot pursuit".

On the home front we were reasonably happy. We had inherited a large house with pleasant grounds, but it really was not suitable for a family. The main reception room was large enough to host a hundred people and was complete with a bar. The rest of the two-bedroom house was small and cramped and certainly proved its unsuitability during the visit of my mother. We broke her stay by flying for a long weekend in Penang where Doctor Ong, father of a customer, courteously showed us the snake temple and other interesting sights. At a luncheon, held in the open air and hosted by yet another customer, my mother, normally a very fussy and conservative eater, ignored the flies and tucked in manfully to a host of exotic and, to her, strange dishes. When later I remarked on this to my sister she replied, 'Mum did that for you and you'll never know what it cost her.'

As well as the house and Trixie the beautiful German shepherd dog, we had inherited the amah, Ah Wong. She lived in the staff quarters with her husband, who had the never to be forgotten name of Ah Choo. I was tempted to call him Sneezy, but never did. Ah Wong was a cultured lady who could drive my wife's car to pick up the children from school when needed and who could give lessons on the piano. She worked to provide the funds to send her boys to university, one in Australia and one later in Canada. She and Ans divided the housework between them and grew to be great friends. Many years later Ah Wong came to stay with us in Toronto for a holiday. Her greatest pleasure was to sit in the back seat of my Cadillac with the Tuan acting as her driver.

Along with the Mercedes my predecessor had bought for the bank, presumably without permission, I inherited Hassan, the driver. Hassan, with his songkok squarely on his head and his smart salute, was proud to tell me of his twenty years as a driver with the British Army. While taking my mother to Malacca, Ans having declined to accompany her, Hassan insisted on a side trip to his home where my reluctant mother, not knowing what to expect, was most impressed by the local house built on stilts, with the orderly simplicity of it and with the charm of Hassan's wife and children. Hassan stayed in the quarters at our house but went home to his own family often for long weekends. During the week, without ever being asked, he would polish my shoes and Malcolm's shoes, but he would never touch the shoes of a female. We never commented on it and neither did Hassan.

The lease on the unsuitable house was due to expire before the end of our first year in KL. I waited in vain for the Indian landlord to remind me that I needed to renew, which I had no intention of doing. When I gave him a few weeks' notice that I would not renew, which the lease did not require me to do, he was so angry that he wrote to the executive office in Toronto to say that my predecessor had promised indefinite renewals. I realised that if I had found myself still in residence after the expiry of the lease I would have been obliged to agree to the increase in rent the landlord almost certainly intended to impose. We had found a partly-built three-bedroom house on Jalan U Thant in the district of Ampang, now thoroughly developed and host to a dozen or more embassies. In my day there were few houses on the street and the one that became ours was at the end of the development. Between us and the nearby kampong was bush. Once in residence I loved to hear the early morning call of the muezzin. The call to prayer seemed to start the day on a good note. When I found the house, about three-quarters finished, I discovered that the owner could do with some financing to finish it. I added a walled garden with swimming pool to his original elaborate plans and extended the servants' quarters. Then I authorised a nine-year loan which would be repaid by the rent from the nine-year lease. It was an okay deal for the owner because it solved his immediate problem and a great deal for the bank which gained accommodation for nine years at the same rent. However, it pained me later when I tried to persuade the bank to buy this excellent house in a great location, to always receive the same reply: 'We have a lease for x remaining years at the original rent. Why should we buy?' Jalan U Thant was a great neighbourhood and our house would be worth a fortune now.

Our first Christmas in KL was marked by the surprise of receiving at the house a dozen or more baskets filled with expensive food and drink sent by customers; certainly not the ones I was chasing to repay their loans. We did have some good accounts! I wrote to each one, careful not to offend, thanking them and explaining that it was not our custom in Canada to accept such gifts (only partly true I suppose, but how should I know? I had never worked there except in anonymous roles in executive offices). I suggested a gift to a charity in future. Next Christmas we received twice as many baskets.

Gradually the branch was becoming organised and the regional office in Manila was upset that my Canadian assistant had not received a renewal of his work permit and had to be transferred to Manila. I did not tell them the permit had not been renewed because I had not submitted the required application. I counselled Michael Lim, a nineteen-year-old staff member, and the quickest person on a calculator I ever saw, not to move into the now vacated office but to handle the functions of the departed Canadian. I watched as the staff performing the daily routine turned to Michael whenever they had a problem. After a couple of months I told him he was the accountant and should now move into the office. Nobody could complain because everyone realised they had accepted him in the role. Manila was not happy and the Canadian was transferred back after I left because my successor apparently did not feel able to cope without Canadian support. Michael, whose wedding Ans and I were happy to attend, eventually emigrated to Canada with his wife and children.

In March 1975 we were in Singapore for the opening of the branch there and early in 1976 I was advised that I had won the Chairman's Award. Ans and I had been invited to spend a week with the chairman in Jamaica. I had no idea what this was all about but soon discovered that the award was won mainly by branch managers in Canada who had performed well in a competition. I had not competed and I guessed I had been added to the list because of the mess I had sorted out in Kuala Lumpur. I later discovered that Jim Ross, our manager in Beirut, was also on the trip. I assume his name had been added as a reward for his great fortitude, as well as, no doubt, for his excellent banking skills. Branch managers from small towns in Canada rarely had an opportunity to meet the chairman and so winning the competition and an all-expenses paid trip to Jamaica was very special for them. International staff had many more opportunities to interact with the chairman and senior people in the bank and having to travel halfway round the world from one tropical location to another was not greatly alluring.

I have more than once heard my various promotions in the bank attributed to the good luck that came as the result of meeting frequently with the chairman and other senior officers in situations in which I would spend hours if not days interacting with them. I always agreed that I had indeed been lucky to have had the opportunities but would challenge my accusers to tell me what might have happened if the chairman and others, seeing me at close quarters, had concluded that I was an idiot. And such things can happen. I remember visiting a branch as a senior executive. On the first customer call with the manager I was standing with him on the street while he knocked on a door. Eventually I pointed out that the door had been nailed shut and clearly was not the entrance to anywhere. Later we proceeded to cross the town backward and forward spending more time in traffic than with customers. Next day we had arranged to fly to another branch. When we arrived at the airport the manager had no tickets. He said he had bought them days before but could not find them when we were leaving the branch. His credit card did not work and I had to buy the tickets for the flight. We soon found him a job to which he was better suited. So, exposure to senior executives can be a two-edged sword.

Not long after I had received word of the award and the trip to Jamaica my vice-chairman visited the region again. There was to be a conference in Manila, but he came first to Kuala Lumpur.

When I escorted him to his hotel room, which I always did for senior officials to make sure the room was to their liking and that there was nothing they needed, he asked me to stay for a minute. He then said, 'I want to offer you the jewel in our crown.'

'I beg your pardon, sir?'

'Kingston, Jamaica. It is the first branch we opened outside of North America. The bank has been in Jamaica since 1889 and opened there before we had a branch in Toronto. The main branch in Kingston is very large and very profitable and Scotiabank is the largest and best bank in the country. Indeed it is the only place in the world where we are number one.'

'Ah, now I understand the award and the trip to Jamaica.'

'Mr. Johnston, how dare you! You owe the chairman and me an apology. The award has nothing to do with what I am now offering you.'

'If that is the case, sir, then I apologise. But once again I am being moved just when I have things sorted out and I am ready to reap the fruits of my labour. Two years is not enough.'

'That may be so, but what I am offering you is a very substantial promotion. I want you to let me know when I see you in a few days in Manila.'

'Sir, I will be in Jamaica on the 28th of this month. I would prefer to let you know after that.'

'Very well, but you must not tell anyone in Jamaica about my offer to you.'

'As you please, sir.'

It was at the conference in Manila that Ans and I decided we would never again fly together without the children. We had left them in Kuala Lumpur with Ah Wong. That did not worry us but the thought of a plane crash with us on board was really too much to contemplate. So I went to Jamaica alone.

Once in Jamaica, near Montego Bay, I relaxed and watched my newly found colleagues enjoy the relief from a Canadian winter. On a solo trip to Kingston I saw the branch and met the deputy manager, who told me he was considering an offer to become the manager in a few months but was not sure he would take the opportunity. I remained mum as instructed and arranged to be introduced to a couple of schools on the pretence that, as a director of a school in Malaysia, which I no longer was, I was taking the opportunity to see how schools in Jamaica were governed. Priory High School satisfied me that the kids would receive a good education there. One memorable trip which I intended to be solo was on a horse to the top of a mountain near Montego Bay. The owner of my rented horse would not let me go alone and sent a boy with me on a second horse. It was a good ride up the mountain, but at the top it started to rain. There was a little bar there and I hammered on the closed and locked door until the owner opened for us. I gave the horse boy money to play the jukebox and to buy bread to feed the horses while Mr. McPherson, the bar owner, and I sampled some of the many bottles of rum arrayed on his shelf. He seemed pleased to have the opportunity to taste his own wares and to have some company doing so. We, of course, were comrades, if not relatives, because my grandfather was a McPherson, although of a fairer complexion. After a couple of hours the rain stopped and it was time to leave. I asked for a bill, never having discussed the price of anything. I decided that if the tally was over US$50 I would argue; if less I would pay with good cheer. Mr. McPherson, not having kept any notes, scanned the bottles on the shelf, muttering to himself, and declared that I owed him something in the order of US$7. The horse boy and I galloped down the mountain. Well, if not galloping we probably went more quickly than was wise.

Another memorable trip was on a train to a rum distillery where in a competition I won a bottle of rum. This I shared liberally on the train trip back to our hotel, during which I participated lustily in the singing. During the week there had been no sign of the chairman but on the evening of the train trip there was to be a grand dinner with the chairman and Mrs. Ritchie as hosts. With a couple of hours to get ready after the train trip I enjoyed a long shower and lay on my bed to relax for a few minutes. I awoke, for no reason I could discern, exactly at the time for the dinner stated on the invitation. I dressed quickly and entered the reception room a fashionable ten minutes late. I was the last to arrive and the chairman declared that he had been told I would not make it.

'Why on earth not, Chairman?' said I, stone cold sober. Once again, better to be lucky than smart.

I returned to Kuala Lumpur via Glasgow where I spent a couple of days, thus making a circuit of the world.

In August it was time for our annual leave, after which we would move to Jamaica. On his last visit the vice-chairman had mooted the suggestion that annual leaves to Europe or Canada were too expensive and that perhaps a local leave should be taken every second year. I countered by pointing out that my children were growing up with very little contact with their grandparents, aunts, uncles and cousins. While I was aware of all the advantages of international service, this was one of several disadvantages. No more was said. At the party for our departure and to welcome my successor I was thoroughly embarrassed to see a table at the entrance to the reception room in a hotel stacked high with parcels. There was no acceptable way to refuse the gifts that turned out to be for me and for Ans. Customers in Malaysia were exceedingly generous. It is a national trait and I was genuinely sorry to leave this beautiful country where we had made friends with people from all three common ethnic origins; the Malay who owned the button factory, the Chinese with the timber mill, the Indian who sold jeans and not forgetting the Chinese lawyer who worked for the law firm I appointed as the first Bumiputra law firm to represent a bank in Malaysia. He had a Scottish wife and a baby named Malcolm. I remembered also some of the good times; Ah Wong and Ah Choo coming home one evening after a visit to the cinema with a durian and all four of us jumping into the pool, the only civilised place to eat durian. Anthony Bourdain says of durian, "Its taste can only be described as… indescribable; something you will either love or despise… Your breath will smell as if you had been French-kissing your dead grandmother".

Another memorable occasion was taking my vice-chairman in a helicopter to Genting, where we met with a man whose two daughters had married two prime ministers of Malaysia, and although neither he nor we could know it at the time, years later his grandson became prime minister. We did not have a chance to talk much business because our host was focused on a television set watching the "thrilla in Manila", the third boxing match between Muhammad Ali and Joe Frazier. But the experience of the trip over miles and miles of dense jungle in the glass bubble of Genting's helicopter was not to be forgotten, although I still remember reflecting that if we went down into that jungle our chances of survival would be exceedingly small.

And so, once again, I was leaving just as I thought I was on the cusp of making great use of my contacts and my knowledge of the country. Not a good thing for the bank, I thought, but the steep learning curve in each new location was good for me. However, again I was wrenching my children from a school I believe they liked and were happy attending, as I had done in Hong Kong.

I have often wondered what harm I did to my children by dragging them round the world from school to school. Maggie started off at Montessori in Lagos, Nigeria, then both she and Malcolm had two years at the same school in Larchmont, New York, followed by some months at school in King City, North of Toronto. Then the German Swiss School in Hong Kong for two years with whatever pain there was augmented by having to learn German. When we arrived in Kuala Lumpur with little time to explore options we enrolled them in the American School, said by my predecessor to be the only possibility. I inherited my predecessor's directorship of the school and quickly became disenchanted. The school had great facilities but the teachers all seemed to be from California and, to me, had a very strange approach to discipline and learning. I soon resigned my directorship and we enrolled the children in the Garden School, situated in an old house in a large garden. It was the school for almost all nationalities other than American and most of the diplomatic kids were in attendance. The Garden School has now transmogrified into Taylor's International School, with the most amazing modern facilities and a great reputation for academic excellence. After KL both children attended Priory in Kingston for two years. Maggie and Malcolm both finished their schooling in Toronto. Oh, my poor kids. What did I do to them? Maggie came home from school in Toronto after one of her first days there, age thirteen, excited to tell us that there was a girl in her class who has lived in the same house all her life! I take some comfort from something said by Kurt Hahn, the German founder of Gordonstoun School in Scotland, who opined that, "It is the sin of the soul to force young people into opinions – indoctrination is of the devil – but it is culpable neglect not to impel young people into experiences". I am pleased and grateful that, in the end, both my kids went to university and turned out to be kind, thoughtful parents comfortable with and certainly not inimical to any race or creed. I am immensely proud of them.

Jamaica

Jamaica full of ghetto, but boy, I tell you:
me never see it like that.

Damian Marley

On my return to Kuala Lumpur from the award trip to Jamaica I telexed my vice chairman:

'Despite what I learned in Kingston I accept your offer of the management of the main branch.'

How could I have turned down such a promotion even though Kingston seemed far less attractive than Kuala Lumpur? And of course, Ans had agreed although, to be fair, not really knowing exactly what she was letting herself in for. So, after leave in Holland and Scotland in August 1976 we arrived in Kingston. I had done everything possible to make arrangements to ship our beautiful dog Trixie to Jamaica but, apparently, there was no way it could be done. Jamaica did not want dogs that might bring some unknown disease to the legions of unwanted scabrous curs roaming their streets. Fortunately our vet in Kuala Lumpur, who had a son about the same age as Malcolm, whom Trixie adored, was looking for a dog for his own son. Although not happy to leave Trixie behind, we knew that the arrangement was the best possible one for Trixie. She sent us a Christmas card every year until the inevitable happened. When we left Malaysia the family decided we would never again have a dog that we might have to leave behind. Naturally, on occupying the bank house at Farringdon Drive in Kingston we inherited the two dogs that came with the house. Not long after we arrived Ans waded in to a herd of cows in the street outside our house to rescue a small puppy being attacked by the cows. She nursed it back to health and then there were three.

After our beautiful house in KL the bank house in Kingston was a disappointment. It was old and dingy and there were steel bars everywhere with the bedrooms locked off from the rest of the house, something we had not needed in Kuala Lumpur. We did have a pool and we set out to make the best of things.

At the office, once again my handover was brief and I could not understand why my predecessor did not introduce me to Mayer Matalon, by far our most important customer. In Jamaica the bank was a public company and although the Canadian bank held a majority of the shares there were many local shareholders and Mr. Matalon was vice-chairman of the board, with Cedric Ritchie as chairman. Once my predecessor had left I telephoned to make an appointment and could not get past Mr. Matalon's secretary. After trying for an appointment for a few days, without success, I took a flask of coffee and a book and walked down Port Royal Street to Mr. Matalon's office.

'I am the Scotiabank manager and would like to see Mr. Matalon,' I said to his secretary.

'Oh, I'm sorry. You do not have an appointment and I'm afraid Mr. Matalon is very busy.'

'Well, you know I have tried to make an appointment but I'm sure he will have a few minutes sometime during the morning. I have my book here and I am very patient.'

I settled in for a long wait but after a few minutes I was ushered into the inner sanctum and warmly welcomed by Mr. Matalon. The secretary had not realised that there had been a change of management. About a week later I received a phone call from Mr. Matalon.

'I'd like to see you,' he said.

'Oh, good. I'll be right down,' I answered, knowing from the staff that the usual protocol was for me to go to his office anytime he needed to see me.

'No, no, I'll be right up,' he said, to my surprise.

'Fine, I'm free now.'

To the astonishment of the staff Mr. Matalon walked into the branch, to my knowledge for the first and only time he was ever there. It was a lovely gesture which I sincerely appreciated. He was a consummate businessman and we became good friends. Mayer Matalon was of enormous help to me in many ways, not only while I was in Jamaica, but for all the years I worked for Scotiabank and particularly when I became chairman of Scotiabank Jamaica with him still vice-chairman. I knew well that had he not approved I would not have been nominated for the position.

On the first Sunday the new general manager sent from Canada was on the island he dropped in at our house unannounced, to say that he had come out without any money. Could he borrow $10? Of course he could. He never mentioned it again and certainly never paid it back. Very strange because our house was not on the road to anywhere he might have been going. I guess he just wanted to have a look at me and my family. We soon fell out because approval for a very large loan had arrived in a telex from Toronto and I, naturally in my opinion, went ahead, advised the customer and advanced the funds. A couple of weeks later a letter arrived from Toronto imposing conditions on the loan that had not been spelled out in the telex. I asked the general manager to make it clear to Toronto that this was unacceptable. He demurred, saying that it would be better not to act on the telex in future. I was aghast. He was proposing to make customers wait two weeks more than was necessary. Along the way we had other differences because he seemed not to want to irritate anyone in Toronto while I felt that from time to time some irritation was desirable.

My deputy was a young Canadian on his first assignment out of Canada. He had arrived a few weeks before I did. His predecessor, the one who had told me he was considering accepting the offer of the position of manager, had told him that the house the bank rented for him was no longer available. He took him to a couple of very unacceptable options and then left him on his own. The young man, with a wife and child, arranged to rent a nice house and bought his own furniture. Apparently nobody told him the bank would provide furnished accommodation. Months later, in a meeting about an entirely different matter, the owner of the house the previous deputy had rented asked why the new man had refused to rent his house which, of course, he had not done, having been told it was not available. What a lousy trick to play on a colleague. Years after that, as head of International Banking I never explained to the trickster why I was not interested in his appeals for another international assignment.

One of the first meetings I had with a customer in Jamaica was with Oliver Clarke, then the editor of the *Daily Gleaner* newspaper, which had commenced publication as long before as 1834. In 1974 the paper was not popular with the Manley government and there was a concern about the threat to its ability to obtain the scarce foreign exchange needed to import the newsprint essential to daily publication. I mentioned to Oliver the paper's vulnerability as the result of having all its bank financing on an overdraft which could be called at any time. My thinking on this had not progressed further than pointing out the problem but Oliver was back in my office a couple of days later with a fully detailed plan for the newspaper to issue a bond that would provide much-needed long-term financing. My initial suggestion that the bank subscribe was ridiculed in Toronto. However, the bond was widely supported by the business community in Jamaica and hundreds of private individuals subscribed small amounts. The bank participated with a substantial contribution and I would like to think that it was my carefully-wrought written recommendation that did the trick. But probably Mayer Matalon had picked up the telephone and called the bank's chairman!

I had three great assistant managers, Rowbotham, Hastings and Crawford. They were full of tricks they played on each other and our regular daily fifteen-minute early morning meetings were never without a joke or two. I arranged for Wayne Powell, the accountant, to join the group and we set out to go through the last inspection report item by item, to make sure that everything that had been reported had been corrected. If not, we corrected it. This was something I had learned to do as long ago as Sunyani in the Gold Coast. It served me well then and did again in Jamaica as the team gained two successive excellent reports. On a scale of one to five we were awarded twos. When I complained to the inspectors that almost nothing was in the reports and they should have been graded at one, they replied that they never gave ones.

Crawford, who would do anything for anybody, if he remembered, went on to establish his own bank. Years later, on a visit to Jamaica, I received a small clock from him, a corporate give-away with his bank's logo, accompanied by a note thanking me because, he said, I had taught him all he knew. I replied very quickly to make sure that I made the point that he knew a great deal I never taught him. When his bank failed I was very glad I had made that clear.

Years after I had left Jamaica I would travel throughout the Caribbean and Latin America with the chairman and in Jamaica I would listen to him expound on the reason Scotiabank had established a branch there in 1889. It was trade; fish and lumber from Canada and sugar and rum on the return journey. I never corrected him, although in 1890 only 2.5% of Jamaican exports went to Canada and as late as 1925 only 0.3% of Canadian exports were to Jamaica and only 0.4% of its imports came from that island. I thought I knew a better story. In 1889 the bank was run from Halifax by a Scotsman named Thomas Fyshe who was married to Avis, the daughter of Anna Leonowens – yes, that Anna, she who had been governess to the children of King Mongkut of Siam in the early 1860s. Anna lived with Fyshe and her daughter in Halifax and I envisioned this dour bearded Scot sitting at the dinner table each evening opposite his adventurous world-travelled mother-in-law. I think he must have felt he should do something to assert his manhood. He took a trip to Jamaica and on his return sent a bank employee to establish a branch in Kingston. Of course, there was a good business reason. In the mid-nineteenth century British banks decided to refrain from involvement in foreign business, claiming that their funds should be available for use at home and until the eve of the Second World War legislation remained in place prohibiting American national banks from establishing foreign branches. So, according to an article by Neil C. Quigley published in Business History Review, Volume 63, Winter 1989, "the Canadian chartered banks pioneered both the amalgamation of international branch banking with domestic operations and the finance of international trade between the Caribbean and the United States…" The pioneering was led by the Bank of Nova Scotia.

Although, as usual, I was happy in my work I was aware that Ans disliked Jamaica. In fairness, she disliked and feared it. She feared it for the children and for all of us, I suppose. Daily I was downtown at work. She was uptown at home. The children were across town at school. And in between there were riots and disturbances. The factions of the politicians Michael Manley and Edward Seaga were at war. Violent war. No sooner were the kids out of school for the summer holidays than Ans had them on a plane to Austria, where the three of them went to stay in a small village hotel not too far from Klagenfurt. At a reception in Jamaica Ans had revealed her frustration and had said that she wished she could go and sit quietly on top of a mountain. The Dutch ambassador knew where to recommend for quietude and did so. I managed a week there once. Here is a little story from that time. My son Malcolm had become friends with the son of the inn at which he, Maggie and his mother were staying. I guess having learned German in Hong Kong came in useful. The boy, about the same age as Malcolm, attended a boarding school but came home at weekends. Malcolm had been buying innumerable packets of gum to collect the cards of the players in the forthcoming 1978 football world cup. He had a book full of them arranged team by team. On the weekday that he was to leave the inn to fly back to Jamaica his young friend cycled ten or twelve miles from his boarding school to bring Malcolm the one card he needed to complete his book. Malcolm assures me he still has that book.

When accepting the appointment in Jamaica I had advised the bank that two years was as long an assignment as I was able to contemplate. The children needed to get into a good high school in which they could settle down and work their way towards university. I said that my next assignment could be anywhere in a large city in North America or Europe, but it would need to be somewhere I could remain for about ten years. Nobody in the bank had raised any objection or even commented and nothing had been promised. Not long before the two years was up the general manager told me that Mr. Kent was visiting from the executive offices in Toronto and wanted to know if I would agree to extend my stay in Jamaica. I laughed. I had been tipped off a few days before that I was to be asked to extend my stay and I had been given good reason to expect that if I agreed I would be asked soon thereafter to replace the general manager and this notwithstanding that there was a deputy general manager in place. What a temptation! Scotiabank Jamaica was the biggest, most successful and most profitable bank in the country with twenty-five or more branches. What a chance to achieve the prospects I felt I had given up when I left Nigeria. I had a list of things I would do in the first week! I was sorely tempted to agree to stay and hardly slept the night I was given the tip. But in the bright light of a Jamaican early morning, a time of day in the tropics I love, I came to my senses. I realised that even if Ans agreed that we should stay it would not be what she really wanted. Also, it was time for us to be somewhere the kids could settle, walk to school like normal children, and in due course get into a decent university. And so, with a heavy heart, I said I would not extend my stay. My replacement was Jack Keith and within weeks of replacing me he was upstairs in the general manager's chair where he remained for several years. I never told Jack that he had my job.

We left Jamaica on 12 August 1978 and from Ans' cousin's house in New York after a short stay we drove to Canada in my new Cadillac. A couple of days later we hired a real estate agent, told her we wanted a house within walking distance of the two schools we had been advised were the best for the children. We bought the third house we viewed, and the real estate agent said she had never seen a decision made so quickly. The family was installed, and I headed back to Jamaica for a week to hand over my branch to Jack Keith.

Although Ans had not been happy in Jamaica, the children maintain it is the country they liked best. For my part I was sad to say goodbye to Jamaica, an island full of charm and charming people. I did not know then that I would become chairman of the bank there and make at least forty-five visits to the island before I retired from Scotiabank and even one last visit after I retired to chair my final annual general meeting.

Canada and the Caribbean

> I am not the same having seen the moon
> shine on the other side of the world.
>
> **Mary Anne Radmacher**

I was not thrilled to be back in the executive offices of the bank. The head office is in Halifax, Nova Scotia, where the bank originated, but there is no executive function there, with all senior executives housed in the splendid buildings on King Street West, Toronto. I was an assistant general manager, a promotion, I suppose, responsible in part for loan applications coming in from the Far East. So, from being responsible for loans and deposits, customers and staff, balancing the books and ensuring the bank windows were clean and the pens still chained to the counter, here I was looking only at a few loan applications each day. I was bored. However, one bright spot was that I finally met David Brierley, who had been the Toronto spokesman for my shipping loans and other applications I had submitted in my Far East days. He had emigrated from Trinidad with his wife and two boys years before. I think he was bored too.

One morning he told me, 'These reports I have to write giving the board of directors the details of loans drive me crazy. My boss insists on editing them.'

'Well, I suppose they have to be accurate.'

'Oh, certainly. But does the board really care if I use a full stop or a semi-colon?'

David and I were scheduled to go to Jersey in the Channel Islands to conduct a loan audit on the trust company there. However, before that happened I conducted a loan audit on the Caribbean regional office in Toronto and immediately recognised where I should be. Loan applications large and small, but mostly in between, came in thick and fast from the network of branches throughout most of the Caribbean. The assistant general manager in charge of credit had been moved to the domestic bank. I applied for the vacancy, perhaps to the surprise of some, leaving behind what was thought to be the glamorous Far East and opting for the Caribbean. Bob Taylor was the senior vice-president in charge of the region. He interviewed me and seemed a bit suspicious of me, but I was given the job.

Soon after I joined the Caribbean regional office I engineered a vacancy for a supervisor. I knew who I wanted to fill it. I named David Brierley and the move was approved. The very next day the approval was rescinded. His own department did not want to let him go. I held the job open for almost a year, doing much of the extra work myself and lobbying repeatedly. Eventually David joined me, starting a partnership that lasted for most of the next twenty years and included David joining me at Butterfield Bank in Bermuda after we both retired from Scotiabank. David was one of the very few who would tell me when I was wrong. That was valuable, even if occasionally I did not listen to him, as he will be quick to point out. He can relate some nice stories, not all to my credit. The trace of his Trinidadian lilt adds to his skills as a raconteur.

In December 1979 I was sent to sort out a problem with a hotel owner who had fallen behind with loan payments. If need be I was to take the keys. When I harangued the customer a little he was upset, telling me that he had built an extension to the hotel and that he had bought another hotel. The bank manager seemed to know nothing about either. So we went to have a look. Sure enough, there was the extension and there was the other hotel. When I got back to Toronto a curious crowd gathered in the office to find out if I had taken the keys. I explained that the customer had used his cash flow, which, memorably, he called his cash floor, and had borrowed elsewhere to finance his new ventures.

'Yes, but did you take the keys?'

'No. I authorised a further loan to consolidate all his debts and get him back on track.'

He was a valuable customer for many years, renowned for his malapropism, 'We will jump off that bridge when we come to it.'

The second trip to the Caribbean was in February 1980. A new manager, who had arrived in St. Lucia a week or two before, on his first posting out of Canada, had complained that he had to be brought home. His wife was terrified by strange bangs at night on the corrugated iron roof of the bank house. She was sure that people were trying to break in. I was able to solve the mystery and reassure them by pointing out the several laden coconut trees overhanging the roof. I became very familiar with the islands of the Caribbean and by the time I retired from Butterfield Bank had made 191 business trips to the region.

David Brierley and I worked hard to make sure that credit applications were handled quickly. We had both been branch managers and thought it important to reduce the time customers had to wait for an answer. We developed some expertise in financing hotels and resorts. Over the years we built up a very large portfolio. There wasn't much competition so we could dictate our own conservative terms. Frequently Americans would arrive in Toronto to seek financing and would leave in disgust when we told them they had to put up 40 or 50% of the amount needed to buy the hotel that was their target. They would tell us they could get 90% financing from their American banks. 'Go to it,' we would say. Two or three months later they would be back, ready to agree to our terms, having discovered that most banks did not like hotels, resorts, offshore locations or casinos or all four. Despite having to repossess and sell a hotel now and again and in the process always managing to reduce the amount owed to us, our losses over eighteen years were negligible. We did have some adventures though, including the time when a well-known management company walked out of a hotel without telling the staff or guests. David and I found ourselves in Toronto on a Friday afternoon in charge of a hotel in the Caribbean full of guests with no food in the place and no management. We worked out what to do and our local manager got it done.

In mid-1983 I was surprised to be appointed senior vice-president and general manager in charge of commercial lending in Canada. Later Bob Taylor told me that the bank's president had asked him to name the best lender in the bank. Bob had said that I was second best only to himself. If I was surprised I am sure the domestic bank people were even more so. No doubt each of the three senior vice-presidents who reported to me wondered why I rather than they had been selected for the top job. The most experienced of the three, Bill Penny, who had every right to be aggrieved by my appointment, was most helpful to me and cheerfully assisted me to settle into an unfamiliar routine. I disliked the structure of the department. Each senior vice-president had a team headed by a general manager and each looked after part of Canada. The process was laborious and slow, with loan applications passing through too many hands. By the time an application reached the person with the authority to approve or deny it was burdened by the comments of half a dozen people, mostly negative. Few loan applications, if any, are perfect and to prove that you are awake and on the ball it is not difficult to find and comment on something that could have been better. It was a wonder that anything was ever approved, and it was difficult to understand the enormous losses of the previous years. I ruled that all applications were to go to the person immediately below the person with the authority to approve it. That speeded things up and reduced the need for manpower, but the ruling was not popular and my successor reverted to the old system soon after I left, despite loan losses for several years having been reduced to next to nothing.

I spotted an advert in a newspaper depicting a small pig with wings about to take flight. In response to my letter the advertisers kindly provided me with the art work which I arranged to have made into a poster. Nicely framed it hung on the wall behind my chair in the conference room I used for the meetings at which I decided on loan applications. An occasional wave of my hand over my shoulder towards the poster made an economical way of indicating what I thought of the deal then being proposed.

I was bored and not very happy in the job. But Ans was happier than she had been for some time. She had become involved as a volunteer with an organisation running a tearoom in a local home for the elderly. Soon she was in charge and that developed into her becoming president of an organisation lobbying government to do more about supervising nursing homes, conditions in many of which were lamentable. She worked endlessly and tirelessly with the result that her organisation was successful in having new legislation passed, and Ans became an occasional interviewee on radio and television and somewhat notorious with the nursing home people.

Out of the blue I was headhunted for the position of CEO of a bank in the United Arab Emirates. I took a couple of days off in September 1984 and flew to Dubai to attend an interview, having first tried to learn all the cultural customs I should remember, such as not showing the soles of my shoes and rattling my cup in its saucer when I had had enough coffee. The sheik interviewing me seemed to think that I was handicapped by the fact that I had worked for large banks. His bank was small. That I had been alone without much support for a good deal of my years in Africa, Hong Kong and Malaysia did not seem to impress. The sheik gave the job to an American who had worked for a small private bank. The new CEO soon crashed the bank, by which time I was back in Toronto soldiering on and still a bit bored. However, although Ans had not mentioned any reservations about my attending the interview, I discovered on my return that she had been upset. She seemed to believe that rather than trying to improve the fortunes of the family I had ulterior motives. I returned from the Middle East after three days to find waiting for me a strange letter from a lawyer saying that my wife felt I was about to desert the family not long before the wedding of my daughter. As a secular humanist who does not believe there is any divine meaning to my life and that my job on earth is to provide for my family and be the best man I can be, despite all my many faults, it was more than disappointing to learn that after twenty years of marriage I had not managed to make my wife really know who and what I was and to understand that I would not have taken a job in the Middle East if she had objected. I responded to the lawyer by pointing out that I was paying the bill for this nonsense and heard no more from her until years later.

During the three years in the Canadian credit job I was involved in many interesting loans and differing situations. One involved a man who owned several apartment buildings. I became involved when the regional office recommended we foreclose and take the inevitable loss on the sale of the buildings, which provided security for the loan which was in arrears. I had doubts and so said to Reagh Turner, 'Reagh, please go and have a look at these apartments and let me know what you think.'

Reagh came back from his trip to the small town and reported, 'The apartments are in impeccable condition. The problem is the recent and ongoing loss of tenants. It may take a while to fill them again but once he does, if we can hang on until the economy picks up a bit, he will be back on track.'

I trusted Reagh's opinion, so we called the customer in and explained that if we were to refrain from selling him out he had to take no salary and cut expenses to the bone. We would take all the rental income as interest on the loan. At the end of the explanation and once he understood the implications he declared, 'I knew God would save me.'

The head of the regional office was incensed by the decision Reagh and I had made and to my astonishment declared that the customer 'deserved to be bankrupted' even though that would involve the bank in a certain loss. He objected to administering the loan on the terms we had decided. So, rather than argue, I asked Reagh to handle it for a couple of years. The interest we collected wasn't too bad, 7 or 8% per annum, and not a lot less than the appropriate rate. Eventually Reagh arranged for the customer to sell one building. That and an improvement in the rental market sorted out the problem and the loan was refinanced on normal terms. The bank avoided a loss except for a small amount of interest and we did not devastate a small businessman and his family. Of course, regulators now impose ridiculous rules, perhaps because they cannot trust bankers to be completely honest about the difficult situations in which they find themselves. Under current regulations we would not have been able to carry the loan without putting up large provisions making the proposition unpalatable for the bank.

International Banking

Those who enjoy responsibility usually get it;
those who merely like exercising authority usually lose it.

Malcolm Forbes

While attending a banking course at Queen's University, Kingston, Ontario I was summoned to a meeting in Toronto with the president of the bank. He advised me I had been appointed executive vice-president in charge of the International Banking division, replacing Bob Taylor and Kevin Rowe. Kevin was to go off to Hong Kong in charge of the Far East region so that solved that problem, kind of. I don't think he was ever convinced he was reporting to me. Bob Taylor was to continue to work with me for a year until he retired. That could be awkward. Bob had been my boss for five years in the Caribbean regional office. We agreed that for the next year I would stay in Toronto and Bob would do all the considerable travelling required to attend various board meetings of subsidiaries and to sort out problems in other places. In between he worked on the best retirement speech I ever heard. I am proud that we remained good friends. When he retired Bob tracked down Veasy Collier, the third in the book *Three Against the Wilderness* authored by Veasy's father Eric Collier. I had given Bob the book and he had enjoyed it as much as I, and so the two of us with my brother-in-law who, with his family, was visiting from Holland, made the journey to Williams Lake in British Columbia. We watched the annual rodeo on Saturday and on Sunday, with Veasy as guide, we travelled far into the bush. We had to negotiate a sometimes almost invisible trail and saw through at least half a dozen fallen trees blocking the track, which obviously had been unused for months, if not years. After several hours we arrived at the lone and now deserted cabin in which the "Three" had battled the wilderness. On the way back we diverted to a large lookout tower and gazed over 360 degrees of endless miles of uninterrupted forest. That was a journey not to be forgotten, particularly for my brother-in-law. There is nothing like that wilderness in Holland.

The assistant secretary of the bank, Louise Boyd, came to my office to offer me the choice of my coloured pencil. This was a tradition that dates from the earliest days of the bank. It sounds a little silly, but traditions are important and if you see a document marked in the colour used by the chairman and which is forbidden to all others you pay attention. I had been appointed on the same day as another executive vice-president. Two colours were available; a shade of green different from the green used by Peter Godsoe, and orange. Louise was giving me first choice and I chose the orange. Even though I said I would never use the silly things, of course eventually I was seduced by the long sharp orange pencils sitting on my desk in a pewter pot, fashioned as a giveaway gift for the opening of Kuala Lumpur branch years before. I started marking documents with my orange pencil, thereby acquiring the nick name of "Agent Orange". It would be comforting to think that the name came only from the colour of the pencil, but I suspect that some of my perceived personal characteristics played their part in associating me with the toxic chemical used by the Americans in Vietnam. I still have a T-shirt which was presented to me at a regional conference inscribed in large letters with "What part of no do you not understand?"

Within two or three weeks of my appointment the vice-chairman to whom I reported resigned unexpectedly. The chairman asked me if I would carry on without a vice-chairman. Did he think I was going to fall on my sword? Of course I would carry on. And carry on I did without a vice-chairman for the next eleven years, interrupted in 1989 by the appointment of a vice-chairman, a non-banker who lasted about one year. His claim to fame seemed to be that he maintained he could always fashion a compromise to settle every dispute. I once told him that sometimes one argument is right and the opposing one is wrong. Compromise is not always the correct solution.

When the original vice-chairman resigned I told the chairman that unless he wanted me to be running to him several times a day I would need to have larger limits of authority. He asked me to send him a memo. Feeling sure that, just on principle, he would reduce whatever limits I asked for, I submitted a memo suggesting limits larger than those of the now departed vice-chairman. The memo came back approved, with one small insignificant reduction. Limits differed for different things. So much for new loans, so much for renewing existing loans at an annual or other review, so much for lending to governments and for capital expenditures and so on. I did not take that memo with me when I left Scotiabank and I now forget the details but one limit for lending was $100 million and a neat comparison to my first lending limit in Africa of £100.

One of my first decisions was to close the Manila regional office, which was little more than an expensive post office. As the result of closing the Caribbean regional office based in Toronto, David Brierley became head of credit for all International. For eleven years I enjoyed authorising thousands of loans that exceeded David's substantial limit, most of them good and a few bad. And the worst, I hear you ask? David Brierley will tell you about the one I authorised despite his recommendation that I decline it. Everyone else, other than the silly branch manager who had submitted the proposal, also recommended decline. At the meeting at which the details of the loan were presented and my questions answered by one of David Brierley's staff, I said, 'Go back to the branch and have the manager confirm that he has personally investigated the facts he has presented.'

David, on whom I could always rely to have studied every file before it was presented, said, 'Even if he has investigated, this is a load of rubbish and should be declined.'

'Well, we do have to assume the people in the field have some credibility. We cannot always be totally negative. Please go back to him.'

In due course the loan was presented again, together with the manager's assurances that he had fully investigated the facts. Again, David recommended it be declined. Nevertheless, I approved it and noted on the file David's recommendation that it be declined.

Of course, it was a bad loan. It turned out that the verification performed by the manager had not involved third party confirmation of the facts. He had done no more than ask the applicant to repeat the claims he had already made. The whole thing was an unmitigated disaster. Unfortunately, the circumstances were unique and I cannot tell the full story for fear of identifying the customer, but after David had spent months chasing assets all over the country in question the saga ended with him buying for the bank at auction, for next to nothing, a useless article in the very unlikely event it turned out to have the value claimed by the borrower. Probably it is still in bank custody somewhere.

One of my best decisions was to call for repayment of a loan that had rolled over every three months for several years at a £20 million level and had recently been increased to £30 million. As they say, a rolling loan gathers no moss. Despite the vehement protests of the branch manager I insisted, indeed eventually instructed, that he ask for repayment at the next rollover date. The large international company paid up. It filed for bankruptcy a few weeks later with a long list of international banks as its creditors. I do not recall the matter ever being mentioned by my chairman and my bonus later in the year certainly did not reflect the value of my decision. I am sure that, if asked, the chairman would have said I was paid to make such decisions.

I took home most weeknights from two or three to half a dozen loan applications, which I would study after dinner and would deal with at my ten o'clock credit meeting next morning. Although the meeting was called a credit committee and various people would present the applications and make recommendations, and their initials were recorded on the decision together with mine, the authority to approve or decline was mine and mine alone. I have known of other banks where two or three people were permitted to pool their individual limit and so together approve loans larger than any one of them could have approved alone. In my view this had the effect of making no one person responsible. I believe a single person who knows he or she is responsible, although willing to hear the views of others, makes for better credit decisions. If I was travelling the applications for loans greater than David Brierley's substantial limits would wait for my return, unless David decided to telephone me wherever I happened to be. David and I made an excellent team and our lending record, measured by losses or lack of them, was second to none over the years we worked together at Scotiabank and later at Butterfield Bank, despite being regarded by some as rather aggressive lenders.

Of course, my job entailed a great deal more than credit. I was responsible for the people and the branches in more than forty countries and I travelled a great deal, often offering silent blessings to Bernard D. Saddow, who invented the wheeled suitcase in 1970. After Bob Taylor retired my travel schedule was extraordinary. There was rarely a month I was not on a visit somewhere and often to several countries on one trip. For example, in October 1996, at the request of my chairman, I had a look at the branches of a French bank that were for sale. In eight days I visited Guadeloupe, Martinique, St. Barthélemy, St. Maarten, St. Martin and Guyane. I declined the opportunity to buy the branches, and I did not take the time to visit Devil's Island and assume I will never have another chance to do so. I now regret that in all my travels I took little time off to see the sights. However, I did visit the South Atlantic island of St. Helena after the British Foreign Office asked Scotiabank to advise on the opening of a bank on the remote island. In January 1995 I took a weekend off between official visits to Athens and Cairo. On a Friday afternoon I flew to Amman in Jordan. On Saturday I rented a car and drove to the Dead Sea, where I dipped my toes into the water, which is nine times saltier than the Atlantic Ocean; then I drove south down the Desert Highway past Wadi Rum and all the way to Aqaba, Jordan's only sea port. I was disappointed to find it looked nothing like the film set in *Lawrence of Arabia*. It seemed to me more like an enormous lorry park with hundreds of trucks waiting to carry goods into Iraq, probably breaking the sanctions of the day. Now Aqaba is being developed into a tourist resort. After a quick look round, I drove north to Petra, where I took an uncomfortable camel ride through the narrow gorge to view the famous rock-carved city. Returning to Amman the next day, because all the street signs were in Arabic, I hired a taxi to lead me back to my hotel. I was on duty in Cairo on Monday morning.

After completing the business of the day in Cairo branch I told the manager, Brian Cunningham, that since we had an hour or so to spare I would like to see Khan el Khalili, the huge market. I forget why Brian rather than the driver drove the bank car, but he parked in an unusual place and assured me it would be fine. When we returned after a quick stroll round the fascinating bazaar the car was gone. A nearby policeman apologised profusely.

'Effendi, I am so sorry. Oh, Effendi, Effendi.'

He then grabbed a young man who happened to be passing and instructed him to take us to where the car had been towed. When the young man protested the policeman slapped him. I then intervened and said we would take a taxi. The journey passed the University of Cairo, where a demonstration was taking place. Students blocked the road and were banging on the roof of the taxi. I think Brian was worried in case I was upset but I have had my car roof banged by a more threatening crowd. The students were not aggressive, and we soon arrived at the sad parking lot where the shiny bank car stood among dust-covered wrecks that looked as if they had been there since the time of King Farouk. An elderly man sat in a wooden shack. Papers were shuffled and shuffled again and after ten minutes seemingly we were no closer to gaining possession of the car. Then it dawned on me. I told Brian I would take a walk, and left. As soon as there were no witnesses the car was released, no doubt for a small personal consideration.

In the market I had bought a fez and thinking of this reminds me of an incident years later in Morocco. By chance I was following a group of Japanese tourists being led by a Moroccan guide with a cap and flag. There were discussions about buying a fez and the guide recommended the red ones on display beside a small number of green ones.

'But want gleen,' said a middle-aged Japanese man.

'No, you buy red,' said the guide.

'But rike gleen,' and a green fez was purchased.

Ten minutes later the proud wearer of the green fez was pestering the guide, 'Why evelybody raughing?'

'Because a green fez is worn by a boy who has just been circumcised.'

It was during the Moroccan visit I fulfilled an ambition. It would now be called an item on my bucket list, even though I do not have one. In Casablanca I took a taxi to Rick's Café. As I alighted the doorman asked, 'Are you coming for dinner, sir?'

'No, I am coming to say hello to Rick.'

'Oh, good. She is at the bar.'

At the bar sat the American lady who brought to the real world the fictional gin joint depicted in the film *Casablanca*. I had a drink, listened to the piano player while watching the dinner guests, shook Rick's hand and left. Mission accomplished.

I felt that one of the most important parts of my job was to put the right people in the right places and to hire young people who would become the international bankers of the future. I was dissatisfied with the candidates being produced by the human resources department and annoyed when they turned down a very suitable young Canadian whose family I had known in Jamaica and whom I had recommended. They did not have the courtesy to let me know and I did not learn of the decline until weeks later when I thought to enquire. The lad went on to become a chartered accountant. Convinced that the people in human resources did not know what to look for I decided to advertise and recruit my own trainees. I was assured that I would never find any acceptable applicants as the result of a newspaper advertisement. The first time I tried I ended up having to review over one hundred applications. I interviewed a dozen or more and hired four or five. I sent them to work in the domestic bank for six months at a very basic clerical level with costs paid by International. It all took a good deal of my time because trainees had to write to me every month to let me know what they were doing, and I would reply, helpfully I hope. If I was told that a trainee had been put to work to complete last year's filing I yanked him out of the branch without delay. After six months I brought them into the International division, mostly to the credit department. When I considered them ready, off they went on an international posting. I went through this procedure each year for several years. My aim was to hire people with the kind of diverse background and experience that I thought would help make them good international bankers. Secretly I hoped to hire a future chairman of the bank and I nearly made it. One man I hired became very senior but retired soon after the appointment of a new chairman. It had looked as if he might have been in the running then or would be next time round. I have no idea what caused his retirement, but I do know that many newly-appointed chief executives dislike having an obvious replacement ready and waiting in the wings.

Many years after I retired I decided, on a whim, to take my boat, an MJM 34Z, single-handed from Sint Maarten to St. Kitts. I docked at Port Zante. I had authorised the funding some years before for the construction of the first stage. Although it was not the purpose of my visit I resolved to call on the manager of the Scotiabank branch at Basseterre. I had hired him, which was not one of my better decisions. At the branch I gave my card to the secretary who disappeared into the manager's office. Seconds later the excessively excitable manager came rushing out shouting, 'I knew you would come. I knew you would not forget.'

'How could I forget?' I asked, wondering what it was I should have remembered.

'I knew it. I knew you would come. Ten years ago today you hired me.' Of such things are legends born.

Occasionally I would receive a letter from a young man asking if I would give him half an hour of my time to provide guidance with his career. Now I didn't fall off the back of a turnip truck. I knew the smart aleck thought he had discovered a great way to get through the door and to impress me so that I would hire him. I always made time and never once did I hire anyone who came to me by that route, only because I never found anyone worth hiring. One case was amusing, if a little annoying. I was giving the advice he had requested to a young Indian lad. I asked about his education, his age and if he had travelled. He mentioned several countries in which he had lived. Because of his age the travel, clearly, had been with his parents. I asked if his father was military or diplomatic and asked him, jokingly, about his politics, because he had attended the London School of Economics, an alma mater of several renowned politicians, some very left-leaning and controversial. I do not remember the answers but a few days later the bank received a complaint from the Canadian Human Rights Commission. I had no right to ask a potential employee about his age or his father's occupation. I responded that the lad had not been a potential employee but a young man who had written to me asking for advice. I provided a copy of his letter and explained that it had not been possible to give him useful advice without knowing something about him. I heard no more about the matter.

I would be remiss if I did not relate the most remarkable incident in my Scotiabank career; an incident that could have changed my life if it had ended badly for the other participant. A group of the most senior Scotiabank people were attending a weekend working conference at a downtown Toronto hotel. The other participant, let me call him A, was a man with whom I rarely spoke because his responsibilities were in a different area of the bank from mine. We had exchanged few words over the years and never anything but pleasantries. After a long day of meetings, I walked into the private dining room set aside for us by the hotel. I was carrying the dinner I had selected from the buffet and looked for a place to sit. The choice was among nine or ten round tables each with places for six or eight. Several tables were full and a few had varying numbers of people already seated. I noticed A seated at a table with two or three others but walked past to the next table, at which there were two vacant places. I took one and a few minutes later the chairman took the other next to me. I enjoyed a glass of wine with my dinner, said goodnight and went to my room. I had done no more than take off my jacket when I remembered I had left on a windowsill in the dining room the notes I had prepared for the presentation I was to give the following morning. As I re-entered the dining room A approached and to my great surprise grabbed a handful of my shirt at my left breast and said that he wanted to speak to me outside. He did not appear to be drunk and I was astonished. Not wanting a scene in the dining room, I walked out to the corridor, with A still holding a handful of my shirt. We walked what must have been twenty-five or more paces with me still in A's clutches and him saying nothing more in response to my irritated questioning than he wanted to speak to me. We came to the end of the corridor where we stopped. A turned to face me, still holding my shirt. I told him enough was enough, placed my hands on his chest and moved him away from me, not roughly but with firm pressure. Without warning he moved a step closer and threw a weak punch to my head which, with a dip, I almost avoided. However, he knocked off my spectacles. Old instincts returned unbidden and without thought I hit him with a straight right and a left hook to the face. He landed on his back at least ten feet away, shouting for the police to be called because he had been assaulted. His blood was everywhere but with great good fortune he had not hit his head or I could have ended up in jail. Several colleagues had followed us at a distance. I am not sure if they had seen me being grabbed in the dining room or if they were headed to the rest room, outside which A and I had stopped. Several took care of him and one, who later became chairman of the bank, suggested I join him. Together we spent a couple of hours with the then chairman and the group surrounding him, me with my bloodstained shirt sleeve rolled up. The fracas was not mentioned and I doubt the chairman knew about it at the time. I am sure he was briefed later. I never did find out what had motivated A but have always assumed that it had irritated him that neither I nor the chairman had taken a seat at his table.

All weekend I thought about what I should do on Monday morning. I considered offering the chairman my resignation but thought that might make it too easy for him to accept. As an alternative I thought of giving an assurance that such a thing would never happen again. But I realised I could not honestly give such an assurance. I had not thought about it or consciously decided to throw punches. It had been an instinctive throwback to my teens and the boxing ring and would almost certainly happen again if anyone threw a punch at me. In the end I did nothing, and the chairman said nothing; except at the next quarterly conference when the bank results were discussed with a hundred or so of the bank's more senior people. As usual nobody had sat in the front two rows facing the platform on which the chairman and I and two or three others were sitting. The chairman jokingly said that nobody wanted to get too close to me and then hastily added 'or himself'. And that was that.

When I was close to age sixty-three and my normal retirement age approached, I decided that I certainly did not want to retire. However, I felt that the modest increase in my pension I would earn by continuing to work at Scotiabank would not be close to what I could earn working elsewhere. I signified my intention to retire and did so, but by agreement continued at my desk at Scotiabank still in charge of the International Division. I enjoyed drawing a salary and a pension and I looked back on the successes and failures of the last eleven years. I could give you a list of the branches I caused to be opened, the banks the purchase of which I negotiated, the countries in which we established new operations, the bank houses I bought or refurbished in the belief that our managers worked better when their family was happy and well housed, the countless loans I authorised. I could tell you of the very large and profitable hotel and resort loan portfolio David Brierley and I built up. But I realise that none of it matters very much. What we did was easily undone by successors in furtherance of the latest "great idea". Nothing brought this home more clearly that the recent announcement by Scotiabank of the sale of much of its Caribbean franchise that I and so many others worked so hard, over so many years, to build into the most complete Caribbean banking network. A network profitable, low risk and easily managed, now to be sold for what appears to be a very low multiple of annual net profit. No doubt somebody can provide what sounds like a good reason. Since the successes don't mean much, it makes it easier to feel that the failures are equally unimportant. That absolves me from giving you a list. However, I will mention that I had inherited operations in Greece and Cairo. I recommended to Peter Godsoe, by then chairman, that either we should close these isolated branches or we should begin to expand operations to create a viable presence in the region. He wanted to expand and expressed his interest in a branch in Israel. So I negotiated the purchase of the branches of Barclays Bank in Rhodes, Corfu and Thessaloniki, investigated a purchase in Cyprus, which I declined, and reopened our long-closed branch in Beirut, a city which, at the time, was enjoying a period of stability. I posited that the Lebanese Central Bank would allow a couple of foreign banks to open to prove that normality had returned but that the locals would then argue against more foreign competition. Beirut was closed soon after I retired and within a year of opening. It was not a success, only partly because David Brierley was no longer heading the international credit department. His successor apparently would not approve any loans. I did not get around to Israel and I failed to get much done in China and the Far East although I did manage to obtain approval for a second branch in India. The Greek operations were sold after I retired. There were problems with management, but I have always believed that if you close a branch rather than sort out problems, eventually you will end up with no branches. However, given what happened to the economy in Greece the decision may have been serendipitous.

One of the best things I ever did, on the suggestion of Bill Clarke, was to create a charitable trust in Jamaica which, by the time I retired, had capital contributed by Scotiabank Jamaica of the equivalent of about Can$7 million and a legal structure that permitted the spending for charitable purposes only the income earned on the capital. The first donation was four dialysis machines for a new clinic in Montego Bay. After I retired I was told that my successors tried to unwind the trust and bring the capital into profit. Fortunately the legal structure of the trust prevented this. Talk about greed! It seems typical of the industry and many of the people in it these days.

In Toronto I was delighted to be introduced to Mohammed Yunis, the founder of the Grameen Bank, the originator of microlending. Long after I met him, he received the Nobel Peace Prize for his work. I was fascinated by the concept of microlending and sent Chester Hinkson to Bangladesh to gain first-hand knowledge of the process by which people who have no access to bank credit can borrow money. Curry for breakfast, curry for lunch and curry for dinner, said Chester when he came back to Toronto. With help from Susan Gibson and Chester, who is originally from St. Lucia, we established a microcredit bank in Guyana which resulted in Scotiabank receiving the 1994 Canadian Award for Private Sector Contribution to International Development. In researching the project I had asked a butcher in Guyana what difference it would make to his business if he had a small amount of cash. He explained, 'Right now, I have no cash and to get an animal to butcher I have to take a cow on credit from the farmer. Once I have sold the meat I pay the farmer. If I had cash I would not take the skinny old cow the farmer gives me. I would choose the nice fat cow I want. The cash price would be a lot better than the credit price for the skinny cow and I could make a decent profit.'

The butcher was one of the first customers and Scotia Enterprise was successful for several years until I retired, after which my successors sold the operation to a local microcredit bank. On the establishment of Scotia Enterprise Cheddi Jagan had made pointed remarks about a foreign company being the first on the scene and several local microcredit institutions had followed our lead.

On a visit to Costa Rica I arranged financing for the construction of the infrastructure for one of the first treetop canopy tours, which earned me considerable scorn in Toronto. The loan was repaid in quick time and the financing was featured in an annual World Bank report.

I was retired, drawing a pension and still at my desk, and I am guessing that I annoyed my colleagues, more than usual, that is. At least one of them must have figured I was holding up promotions. No doubt headhunters were told I was available and I began to receive calls. Negotiations to become CEO of a bank in Kuwait were well advanced when, purely by chance in October 1997, over a lunch tray in my office, I saw an advert announcing that the Bank of N.T. Butterfield and Son was looking for a chief executive officer. Kuwait or Bermuda, what a choice. My résumé had been updated for the London head-hunter for Kuwait. By that evening a fresh copy was on its way by FedEx to a headhunter also in London. The following week I flew to Bermuda and attended the first interview. Two more interviews in Bermuda followed a week or two apart. The Butterfield chairman visited me in Toronto and had a walk round Scotiabank's International division, with him incognito of course. I took him to lunch at a restaurant, figuring it would be improper to use the Scotiabank dining room at my disposal. By the end of November 1997 I knew I had the job in Bermuda and asked my chairman to let me go immediately, claiming Butterfield Bank needed me more than Scotiabank. He agreed on condition that I would go to Jamaica in February 1998 to chair the annual general meeting of Scotiabank Jamaica, which I duly did.

In the 2002 film *About Schmidt* Jack Nicolson plays a recently retired official of an insurance company who visits his old office only to see his files, the sum of his career, being boxed up ready to be dumped in the garbage. After chairing the general meeting of Scotiabank Jamaica and while on my way back to Bermuda I called at the executive office in Toronto to hand in my notes and Jamaican briefing books. In my beautiful wood-panelled former office I was surprised to see the files I had compiled carefully over the previous dozen years and more being boxed up to be sent to storage. Each slim file, on a few pages, contained useful information about a branch or country, often the names of the manager's wife and children, some details of the most important customers and a variety of facts about the management and directors of subsidiaries, the calculation of their bonuses, the central bank, our buildings and so on. Each file was handy to take with me to read on the plane before a visit and to update on the way back, but apparently was too much trouble for my successor to read or to transfer to a laptop, even though his responsibilities did not extend to the credit authorising part of my job, which had been assigned elsewhere. So, when I saw the film *About Schmidt* I knew exactly how Schmidt felt.

Bermuda

You can go to heaven if you want.
I'd rather stay in Bermuda.

Mark Twain

I arrived in Bermuda to take over as president and chief executive officer of the Bank of N.T. Butterfield and Son Limited on the afternoon of Sunday 14th December 1997, having left Scotiabank on Friday 12th. On landing in Bermuda I took a taxi to the apartment I had purchased a couple of weeks before in the joint names of myself and my wife. I had persuaded Dr. King, the chairman, to increase my salary by the amount the bank was prepared to pay as a rent allowance – but the increase not to be included in any bonus calculations, he ruled rather shrewdly. By the time I retired the apartment had almost been paid for. On the evening of the day I arrived Dr. King picked me up at the apartment and we attended a black-tie dinner at City Hall "Commemorating the 100th Anniversary of the elevation of Hamilton to the status of City". I was seated next to the Catholic bishop and so was on parade for the bank on day one. Next morning in the bank I sat at my desk thinking *Is it not passing brave to be a king and ride in triumph through Persepolis.* However, the desk was bare and the office empty. There was not a scrap of paper that might tell me a little about the bank. Perhaps there was to be no triumph. My predecessor, who had lasted about three months at the bank and had never moved out of the hotel at which he stayed, had left me nothing in the way of information. He had closed the books as at 30th June 1997, declared the bank in good condition, recommended an increase in the dividend, which the board approved, and departed, leaving behind a very large hotel bill. As I interviewed the senior officers who had survived his purge I found many of them wary of me and unwilling to say much that would help me understand the bank, its workings and the problems I might face. Although I understood the shock of having to deal with three different CEOs within a few months I was not greatly impressed by most of them. Fortunately, Peter Rodger, senior vice-president and group legal adviser as well as secretary to the board, and Graham Brooks, executive vice-president, group asset management, went out of their way to be helpful. I came to rely on them while I attempted to assess the capabilities of the others. Of the twelve senior officers pictured in the June 1997 annual report only four, including Graham and Peter, were listed in the June 2002 interim report.

Although Ans came to Bermuda for a few days during my first Christmas there and seemed to like the island she never expressed any desire to join me in Bermuda. I do not think she appreciated that I saw my new job as the pinnacle of a long career or how much I relished the challenge and the opportunity I felt it provided for improving the fortunes of the family. Although she said she understood my plan to relinquish my Canadian residency, seemingly her lawyer, whom I had asked her to consult, convinced her I was not to be trusted. Our relationship deteriorated even further and eventually we were legally separated. I am forced to presume I put too much effort into my career and too little into my marriage.

At the bank I started to find out about my new responsibilities. I first needed to assure myself of the quality of the assets and then to understand the liabilities, threats and opportunities. Loans totalled about $1.2 billion (at the time of writing the Bermuda dollar is pegged to the US dollar on a one to one ratio). I still have the certificate I received from the senior vice-president, credit risk management, assuring me we held adequate provisions for all doubtful loans. Nevertheless, I wanted more comfort and was delighted when David Brierley agreed to join me from Scotiabank and assume responsibility for reviewing all the loans. I knew that he would reveal any weaknesses in the portfolio my predecessor might have overlooked. David was soon in charge of lending in Bermuda, up to a generous lending limit. A detailed examination of investments totalling about $900 million and comprised mostly of short-duration investment-grade marketable securities suggested that we had no problems there, although I would need to keep a close eye on the department and its people and review the guidelines used for investments. Deposits with other banks of over $2 billion seemed to me to be concentrated with too few banks and I set about writing some detailed guidelines which were simple and quick to implement. Reviewing and recommending limits for deposits with banks and exposure in the form of deposits and loans to different countries and reporting annually on the process to the Scotiabank board had long been part of my responsibilities. I now needed to become comfortable with the trust side of the business. A new man had arrived to run the trust company not long before I had been hired and so I hoped he would be quick to point out any weaknesses, if he spotted them. Eventually I hired Ian McCulloch, a very experienced retired trust man I knew, and one by one he reviewed the trusts for which we were the trustees. Not on the balance sheet and mentioned only briefly in the 1997 annual report were the Butterfield Funds, in which nearly $2 billion was invested. All seemed well in that department and I was delighted when in 1998 the funds won two prestigious awards from Standard & Poor's Micropal Offshore Territories Survey, including a first place out of 103 groups surveyed. Also not on the balance sheet were assets and properties held in trust, agency or in a fiduciary capacity totalling over $15 billion. Now I was beginning to relax. My predecessor had said the bank was in good shape and it seemed that the most urgent thing for me to do was to put some written policies in place since I could find none. I had to come up with a detailed strategic plan as well as thinking about how and when to replace some of the senior people. Relaxation did not last long.

In the second week of my tenure I was asked to sign approval of the sale of a foreign subsidiary my predecessor had decided to get rid of. I certainly agreed with his decision to sell the business to the management of the subsidiary but was confused about the need for me to sign a guarantee to the bank that henceforth was to provide the money needed to fund the loans made by the subsidiary.

'Who has been providing the funding until now?' I asked.

'We have, directly and through our guarantees.'

'Well, it certainly makes sense for us to get rid of the exposure to the loans made by the subsidiary, over which we have little control, but why on earth would we retain the exposure by issuing guarantees?'

'Well, they cannot get funding without our guarantee.'

'Let me see if I understand this. Although the subsidiary is profitable, we are uncomfortable with our exposure to the market in which it makes loans. So we have decided to sell. But you are suggesting we give up the profit the subsidiary makes but retain all the risk through our guarantees. Why on earth would we do that?'

There was no sensible answer although the senior officer making the proposal tried to find one and pointed out that before my arrival we had sold another subsidiary under similar terms.

We did not sell for a couple of years until we could do so without providing a guarantee. Of course, for cancelling the sale I was not popular with the management of the subsidiary but at least the incident suggested to me how far I could rely on the person who had been given the task of selling. He was soon gone. Incidentally, the subsidiary that had been sold before my arrival proved to be a major problem. We had guaranteed the loans it had made. These had been taken by the buyer and we now had no control over them. Since it was easier for the buyer to call on our guarantee than to try to work out of a difficult situation we paid up on many calls.

Our Cayman subsidiary had fared well over the years, mainly providing banking services to locals. I knew the island well from my Scotiabank days and was happy with what I found there. Butterfield had merged with a small bank in Cayman in 1989 and under Nick Duggan, a leader in the banking industry on the island, it had grown into a very significant operation. Duggan had fallen out with my predecessor and Conor O'Dea had taken over as CEO before my arrival. We were delighted to appoint Duggan to the board of directors. After it had been acquired the bank continued to grow until it became the largest and most significant bank of the many operating in Cayman. That was the inspiration for my attempt to broaden Butterfield's Caribbean footprint by establishing a small office in Barbados. My successor followed up on the plan by buying a very small bank there. Some years later, after my successor was gone, I was asked by the then CEO of Butterfield what he should do with the Barbados operation. I told him it posed little risk, enjoyed good margins and was easily managed. With a small but growing captive insurance industry on the island it was a good fit for Butterfield and was a twenty-year project to grow it into a substantial operation along the lines of the growth in Cayman. The vision was not shared and the Barbados bank was soon sold to a Trinidad-based bank.

In February of 1998 I visited Guernsey to see our small operation which provided banking, treasury, trust, investment management, third party fund administration and custody services. I found little to concern me other than the fact that it did not make significant profits. To have the risk of a subsidiary so far from home producing so little was a worry but over the years, assisted by several acquisitions, including ANZ Bank Guernsey Limited and the local operations of Canadian Imperial Bank of Commerce, the business grew and was augmented by further acquisitions after my retirement.

Our Hong Kong operation was very small and our manager there complained that I had not visited him. Graham Brooks told him that when he made some money I might come. We had only two significant customers in Hong Kong, both major banks, one of which could not give us any more business because of our small size and the other was almost permanently in danger of being sold. At last in 2002 Graham Brooks made a marvellous deal to sell 90% of the business for about seventeen times the net profit for the previous year.

I also visited London, where my predecessor had been obliged to give up our branch licence but had retained a very small subsidiary, said to offer corporate finance and institutional stockbroking. I was not impressed, to say the least, and we soon sold the company for a small profit over book value.

The next few months until June 1998, the end of the financial year, involved long hours for me and for some of the changing senior team. Having poked my nose into everything and having announced to some of the team that I intended to take a large write-off at the end of the year I was told, 'We can't do that. We announced last year that we had cleaned the credit book and the bank was on track to achieve dramatically improved performance.'

'Well,' I said, 'I am certainly not going to put my name to a balance sheet that is not accurate and since there are significant bad loans on the books, among other problems, a write-off and large provisions are essential.'

When I told the chairman what I intended to do he was disappointed but made no attempt to deter me from the course I had set. Indeed, throughout my tenure the chairman, a medical doctor, never interfered with the banking decisions I made but did prod me from time to time with helpful suggestions. I used to joke that we had agreed that if he did not interfere with my bank I would not prescribe for his patients. Of course, we had never discussed any such thing.

I will never forget the look on our faces when Graham Brooks and I saw the first draft of the 1998 annual report. With only a day or two until the deadline for printing we had no alternative but to sit down together and rewrite it. The report was a shadow of the ones produced in later years but at least it was clear and unvarnished. It announced record core earnings up over 18% from the year before but diminished to a net profit of $2.4 million by a variety of charges, including a provision of $26.1 million in respect of the doubtful loans I had been assured we did not have but which David Brierley had soon brought to light; $4 million for long-unreconciled items on the books that had not been properly balanced for years; $2.4 million for the write-off of goodwill and an unused computer system; and finally a $29.9 million provision for future medical benefits.

Immediately after the announcement of the results the CEO of the other significant bank in town telephoned to say he could no longer honour or give customers credit for our cheques.

'Ha ha, don't pull my leg. Things are bad enough.'

It turned out that he was serious. I had to assemble a group of my colleagues to march down the road to explain our published balance sheet to a senior group at the competition and to explain that what we had written off was the year's profit. We were still better capitalised than they were.

The chairman was concerned about the hours I was working and knew that I was a scuba diver but had not dived in Bermuda waters. So he invited the late Teddy Tucker MBE to have lunch with us in the bank, which was reputed to have in Chris Malpas the best chef and corporate dining rooms in Bermuda and in which I had ruled that alcohol could not be served to staff at lunchtime. Mr. Tucker was world-famous for his expertise on all things related to the Sargasso Sea and for having discovered over one hundred shipwrecks. I was delighted to meet this man and hear a little about some of his fascinating adventures. On parting he said, 'Next time Peter comes down I'll give you a call.'

I did not know at the time that the Peter he referred to was his great friend and companion on many expeditions, Peter Benchley, the author of *The Deep* and *Jaws*. *The Deep* had been filmed in Bermuda in 1977 and Teddy Tucker was included in the cast. I regret that the call to join Peter and Teddy on a dive never came.

The great preoccupation in 1999 was, of course, the threat of all the computer systems in the world going crazy at one second past midnight on 1st January 2000. When computer storage space was at a premium many programmers, not believing their programmes would last for more than a few years, had used only two numbers to represent a four-digit year, so that the 00s of 2000 would be no different to the computer than the 00s of 1900. Imagine what that would do for interest calculations. Although some maintained the extent of the problem was exaggerated there were many reports suggesting that unless fixes were implemented there would be chaos. I could not afford to be complacent. Butterfield Bank had a myriad of computer programmes cobbled together and I worried about them even without the threat of the Millennium Bug. I appointed a small team to concentrate on examining every programme and to find and fix every potential problem. When the leader of the team, Ed Benevides, came to me towards the end of 1999 and said everything was now in order he suggested that I throw a party for his people. I pointed out that while he and his staff had been diverted from their normal duties others had been covering for them. We would have a party for everybody if and when we proved that we did not have a problem. At midnight on 31st December 1999 I was standing at a Butterfield Bank ATM in the bank lobby. I still have a receipt for a withdrawal of $200. It is dated 01/01/00 and timed 00:00. To my great relief everything worked. I arrived home at 3am to find my friends and neighbours waiting for me to go with them for the first swim of the year.

In February we held the party I had promised Ed Benevides, but it was a party for all the staff and their spouses and we spared no expense. I termed it a grand celebration of the bank. It was after that party that I saw for the first time some response from the staff to my oft-repeated remark that a successful and profitable bank can do more for its staff than a bank that is struggling. I began to see a reduction in the error rate and the efficiency in many departments began to improve. As a team we produced fourteen successive quarters with record earnings. Indeed, for several years after my retirement the bank continued to produce great results and I like to believe that these were based on the foundations my team had put in place.

Over the years David Brierley and I had many laughs which provided some relief from our concerns. One involved a loan to a factory in a Gulf state, booked in London long before our arrival. It was a bad loan the instant it had been approved in Bermuda and David took a trip to the Gulf in an attempt to collect the substantial amount owing. Not making any headway with the foreign national factory owner David managed, somehow, to have his passport seized and impounded. A few weeks later the owner of the passport contacted us to say that, after all the years during which we had been chasing him, he really now did want to sit down to discuss things with us. Would we please release his passport so that he could travel to Bermuda? Ha ha! David eventually collected a large part of what was outstanding in our books, allowing us to reverse to profit a large part of the provision we had made.

After David's retirement and my own in 2002, in 2008 a loss of $151.8 million was recorded in the investment portfolio, of which $25 million was for Icelandic bank paper and $119.2 million for US mortgage-backed paper. Other losses of over $60 million were recorded. Further substantial losses in 2009 brought the bank very close to failure, from which it was rescued at great cost to the shareholders.

I am now going to write something for which I am sure I will be accused of being wise after the event. The difference between an investment banker and a lending banker is that an investment banker before buying an asset asks to be advised of the rating. Ah, triple A, let us buy $119 million of these. A lending banker, just like David Brierley and me, asks, if I lend this money or buy this paper, what can I do if I don't get paid? Oh, I see, I will own a small share in each one of 5,000 home mortgages scattered all over the United States. How am I to find these homes and how do I foreclose on a small share of a mortgage? I think I'll pass on this. I hear the objections loud and clear. How can I criticise Butterfield for mistakes that were duplicated and far exceeded at many large and important banks. The mistakes were made in the investment departments. In large banks the investment people and the lenders pass each other in the corridors. It is rare for them to work together. In a small bank the CEO has the time and opportunity to be closely involved with the lending and the investment departments; which is why when recruiting my successor I repeatedly asked the candidates if they were truly hands on managers. All said they were, but I have yet to discover how to test the truth of such answers. Years later a former director of the bank told me that the process for hiring my replacement was the most rigorous he had ever seen but we ended up hiring the wrong man.

Coming up to the end of my first year at Butterfield Bank, during which I felt that we had begun to put the bank on track for success, I nevertheless felt uneasy. The management was composed of locals who had never worked anywhere else and of expatriates, except David Brierley and me, who, mid-career, had left a major bank in some other country. Why had they left? Could it be that they had not been doing very well? Although I tried to keep my finger on every pulse and to make or be a part of every significant decision, I feared that a hitherto modestly successful banking career could end in a disaster which I had failed to anticipate and prevent. I decided to resign while the going was good. As I was considering when and where to tell the chairman, he walked into my office and invited me to a dinner to celebrate the first anniversary of assuming my position. I was so startled and embarrassed by the coincidence of his invitation coming precisely at that moment that I stammered a request for a rain check. I am sure that made him wonder but, ever polite, he did not question me. In the next few days, as I mulled over the probable damage to the bank likely to be caused by yet another early departure of its CEO, I reversed my decision and decided that it was right that I should soldier on. It was a couple of years before the chairman invited me to dinner again.

A remarkable event occurred early in December 2000. I had approved a loan to finance the sale of a major Bermuda business to a black Bermudian businessman. Other than the fact that it was a white-owned business being sold to a black man the deal was very ordinary and similar, if much smaller, to many I had approved in my Scotiabank days. The *Mid-Ocean News* reported it as a loan of over $12 million and said an unnamed source had suggested the approval for the loan had been influenced by the Bermuda government. On 4th December the minister of finance categorically denied any involvement. On the 5th December the bank's vice-president and I announced that we had structured the sale of the business and were pictured with the buyer and seller signing the relevant papers. I stated that the transaction had been authorised on its merits and that there had been no contact with government. On 8th December things became very nasty.

> "The Bank of N.T. Butterfield & Son boardroom could be 'waist-deep' in blood when outraged directors confront chairman Dr. James King and chief executive officer Calum Johnston at the next board meeting as to why they were kept in the dark over the multi-million dollar BGA sale," said the *Mid-Ocean News*, which went on to say, "Now, some members of the board are reportedly irate, since a loan of this magnitude affects the depositors and shareholders and the directors' fiduciary responsibility."

The chairman was overseas and, when contacted by an angry director, had to remind him that the making of loans was the responsibility of management and that directors were not told about loans about to be made other than, in accordance with a policy I introduced, loans of more than 25% of the bank's capital. Indeed, when I assumed office I insisted that the details of all significant loans made would be advised to the board at the next meeting after approval and annually thereafter. This allowed the board to fulfil its correct role of supervising management, with directors absenting themselves from the room when loans with which they were in any way connected were discussed. For the board meeting after the sensational articles I had a bucket and mop placed prominently in the boardroom to deal with the blood. They were not required. The chairman refused to permit David Brierley to present the report on the so-called controversial loan and the board passed and published a resolution unanimously declaring the board's full confidence in the chief executive officer and the management team of the bank. The offending newspaper failed to comment that apparently there were at least a few directors who were unaware of the policies of the bank or their duties as directors.

At a board meeting early in the fourth year of my five-year contract the subject of succession planning was raised by a director, although it was not on the agenda. I had probably been remiss in not bringing to the board a succession plan, which would have said that in my absence the management team could be expected to carry on for a maximum of six months until I recovered or was replaced. The board had never asked for a succession plan. Indeed the board had never asked for anything that I can remember other than, soon after my appointment, a strategic plan and comments on the plan submitted by my predecessor. When asked I was already preparing my plan. All the reports placed before the board over the years were from a schedule I created based on my belief that the board should have a succinct report on everything that could pose a risk to or an opportunity for the bank. Board members should have the chance to question and dig more deeply into anything they chose and should be encouraged to do so.

When Director Butt asked if I would step aside if the right replacement was found I was tempted to tell the board that while they might find a younger person they were unlikely to find one more suited to be CEO of their bank than the one they already had. However, for some years an old friend in the Caribbean who owned hotels and casinos had been asking me to work for him. He wanted me to assist in the transition of management from himself to his son. So, although I thought the board was being foolish in not seeking to extend my contract on a year to year basis, I agreed without hesitation that I would step aside provided my contract was honoured in full.

Within ten minutes of the end of the board meeting two senior staff members were in my office. It was too soon for me to go, they said. They wanted to approach the chairman to protest, but I refused to allow this. I had been unwise enough to have been very outspoken about the atrocious performance of previous management. I could not help being outraged by some of the things I had uncovered; carelessness, incompetence and more, the like of which I had never seen on such a scale anywhere in my career. It far surpassed Kuala Lumpur. I presumed that my tirades had irritated more than a few in an island where someone you might mention is known as a relation or a friend or as a friend of a friend. When Mr. Butt first asked his question, I remembered that it had been said that several directors had wanted 'blood on the boardroom floor' and even if their ire had been misguided I was not entirely sure that this was not the first salvo in a "get rid of Johnston" campaign. So, I told my colleagues that I believed the chairman was smart enough to know what he wanted. In any case I had worked in banks for over fifty years and would be leaving Butterfield in the best shape it had ever been in, perhaps with the exception of the boardroom.

Despite a letter from a fund manager with a significant shareholding addressed to every director, except me, urging them to let me continue for as long as I was able, the search for a replacement went ahead. After a rigorous process to find and select my replacement I handed over to the successful candidate a year after the matter had been raised at the board meeting. I prepared to leave the beautiful but troubled island of Bermuda, where I had found a lot of black people too ready to blame every shortcoming on the very many injustices of the past and too many white people, who had benefited from great injustices perpetrated by their ancestors, unwilling to make more than token efforts to begin to level the playing field. Could I have done more? Of course I could but I am content to allow the words of Renee Webb, a former Bermuda MP and minister to sum up my legacy. In an article published in the *Bermuda Sun* in the week of 16th January 2006 Ms. Webb said, "There definitely has been a shift in the economic climate that had historically limited blacks' access to money." She said "the shift had begun 'in a real way' under Calum Johnson (sic), the former Bank of Butterfield CEO, who opened things up for black entrepreneurs. Prior to his appointment the old boys network in place at both banks had restricted black access to capital."

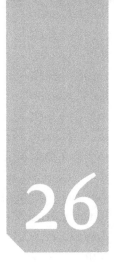

SintMaarten
and Fort Augustus

By mid-2002 I was at my desk in Sint Maarten trying to learn about the hotel business. I knew something about financing hotels but not a great deal about running them. I am not sure I learned very much and am quite sure that I contributed little. I was a fish out of water. The son I was supposed to be helping turned out to be smarter than the father who said he needed help. I soon handed over the presidency to him.

In addition to the hotels and casinos, the company was building a development consisting of villas and condominium apartments called Aqua Marina. I bought Villa Margarita, with its large garden and a dock on the lagoon, and soon purchased an MJM 36Z motor launch which I named *Thistle*. Motor launches are known to real sailors as "stink pots" but I reasoned that the joy of a boat in the Caribbean is getting to interesting islands and I decided that I would get there more easily with a proper engine. *Thistle* was built in Boston.

I sailed (read motored) her to Newport, Rhode Island from where I had her shipped to Tortola. I picked her up there and took her single-handed to Sint Maarten, encountering ten to twelve-foot waves on the way. These forced me to increase power to rise to the crest and to power back to slip over and avoid shooting off the top of every wave. It was all very tiring. When out of sight of land and battling the elements with not a bird or boat in sight I again wondered what I had let myself in for. I was relieved when, after ten hours, the lights of Anguilla and neighbouring Sint Maarten were sighted in the distance with *Thistle* pointed, as planned, exactly for the middle of the two islands. Over the years I and friends enjoyed many great day trips on *Thistle* and from time to time I took her to various islands for several days at a time. These longer trips were always single-handed; I was willing to drown myself but not anyone else. The best trip of all was a single-handed trip from Sint Maarten all the way to Grenada to celebrate New Year 2013 with my good friends Elie and Leslie Bendaly. On the way there and back I called at many islands, some of which I had known from my Scotiabank days.

It was in Sint Maarten that one of the happier events of my life occurred. Brenda, the long-time widow of my best friend in Ghana in the 1950s, came back into my life. She became a frequent visitor who preferred Sint Maarten to Bermuda. She particularly enjoyed day trips on *Thistle* to Pinel Island, where we would anchor and swim ashore for lunch. Brenda, a beautiful, generous soul, brought so much kindness and joy with her that it changed my house into a home. But it was still *my* house and I resolved to sell and build a new solar-powered villa in Sint Maarten with Brenda's input so that it would be *our* house and home. Tragically, Brenda died in Sint Maarten on 12th May 2015. I sold Villa Margarita, *Thistle* and the dinghy *Partick* in August 2015 and retired to Hidden Cove in Bermuda. But I was unsettled by the loss of Brenda and was discovering I did not like Bermuda very much. I had a look at Panama and at St. Lucia for an alternative but decided neither was for me.

On a trip to Scotland to attend a family function in Glasgow my German grandnephews, Angus and Malcolm, then aged nine and seven, expressed a wish to hunt for Nessie in Loch Ness. A group of us went north and hunted but Angus was the only one to claim to have seen Nessie. He had to be persuaded that the small speck on his camera was not worth taking to show and tell at school. Apparently, the flask of whisky I took with me was too small to be effective. I saw nothing in the water. But I saw Fort Augustus again. I had spent several weeks there when I was twelve and had stopped there many times when visiting Scotland from overseas. They say you must go away to appreciate what you left behind. I guess I am a slow learner. I had been away for sixty-five years but realised that Fort Augustus appeared to be exactly what I wanted; a small friendly community in a beautiful village in which I could walk to everything I needed, surrounded by wonderful countryside. The Caledonian Canal runs through the middle of the village and I decided I could sit by the locks and scoff at the antics of the summer boaters. A couple of weeks after the trip I returned to Fort Augustus from Bermuda and bought a house in the village.

When I am asked what I used to do for a living I have no option but to say I was a banker, although I was once told that 'a banker owns a bank, you were a bank clerk'. When asked, I feel the need to explain that I was not the kind of greedy banker frequently in the news over the last few years. In Bermuda I was reported as having said, 'Bank of Butterfield believes that one of the main functions of a community bank is to marshal the savings of the community and to mobilise them in support of the legitimate aspirations of members of the community.' It would be stretching things a little too far to claim that during my career I always kept in mind what I had been told at age seventeen in the Clydesdale Bank – that if I became a banker I would be a cross between a doctor and a minister of religion. Nevertheless, I believe that, like

David Brierley and many others who worked with me, I made my decisions based on what was best for the customer within the confines of what was an acceptable risk for the bank. I hope some will say that on occasion I stretched "acceptable" farther than most would have done. So now I am happy in Fort Augustus by the banks of the Caledonian Canal, no longer a foreigner; no longer having to submit the same personal information annually to a bureaucratic government department while begging to be allowed to remain for one more year; no longer having to justify my presence in somebody else's country. I am where I belong.

> The secret of a good old age is simply an
> honourable pact with solitude.
> **Gabriel Garcia Márquez**